AMERICAN JESUS

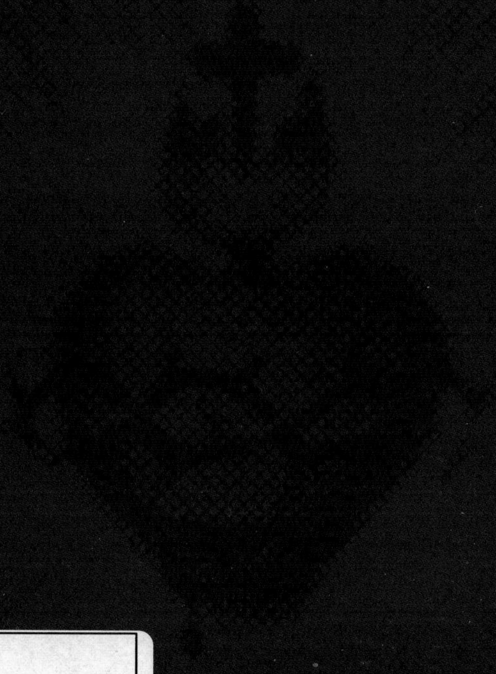

Book One: Chosen

MARK MILLAR
STORY

PETER GROSS
ART

JEANNE McGEE
COLOR

CORY PETIT
LETTERING

DREW GILL
PRODUCTION & DESIGN

IMAGE COMICS, INC.

www.imagecomics.com

Robert Kirkman - Chief Operating Officer
Erik Larsen - Chief Financial Officer
Todd McFarlane - President
Marc Silvestri - Chief Executive Officer
Jim Valentino - Vice-President
ericstephenson - Publisher
Joe Keatinge - PR & Marketing Coord.

Branwyn Bigglestone - Accounts Manager
Tyler Shainline - Administrative Assistant
Traci Hui - Traffic Manager
Allen Hui - Production Manager
Drew Gill - Production Artist
Jonathan Chan - Production Artist
Monica Howard - Production Artist

ISBN: 978-1-60706-006-2

INTRODUCTION
by Simon Pegg

Everyone loves an origin story. Whatever subsequent scrapes a superhero leaps, crawls or broods into, the beginnings of their tale are always the most enduring. Even those poor lost souls who aren't fans of the comic book know something of Superman's spaceship, or Spider-Man's bite, or Batman's mom and dad. It's the same with that other of the most famous hero legends, Christianity. We may not read all the Bible on a regular basis, say our prayers before bedtime, or pay weekly visits to our local parish church, but we know the story of Advent. Even if the further adventures of J.C. get sketchy for the less faithful as the big man grows older, stables, wise men, and little donkeys are burned with unassailable clarity into our collective memories. Mistletoe, presents, and figgy pudding aren't the only reasons Christmas is more interesting than Easter.

With this collection, Mark Millar invents the re-origin of a figure close to all our hearts and posits it in a small American town. Posing the question "What would it be like now, in a contemporary society, if a deity made a comeback?"

Jodie Christianson is an ordinary boy, fond of underachieving, high scores, and stroke mags. As far as he knows, the biggest thing on the horizon for him is pubic hair. Most young people feel an odd sense of detatchment from the world, the feeling that they are somehow different from everybody else. For Jodie, this vague suspicion is confirmed by an eighteen-wheel truck and a series of occurrences that convince even the town's most faithless that this boy is destined for greatness in the Biblical sense. Mark Millar's engrossing narrative, coupled with Peter Gross's beautifully affecting artwork, creates a story which is at once funny, intelligent, and ultimately disturbing. Jodie's journey is a brilliantly everyday story about one boy and his destiny. Forget the "Good Book," sit back, and enjoy a REALLY good one.

*Actor / writer / director Simon Pegg is best known for his work on **Shaun Of The Dead**, **Hot Fuzz** and **Star Trek**. In his spare time he writes introductions for comic-book collections.*

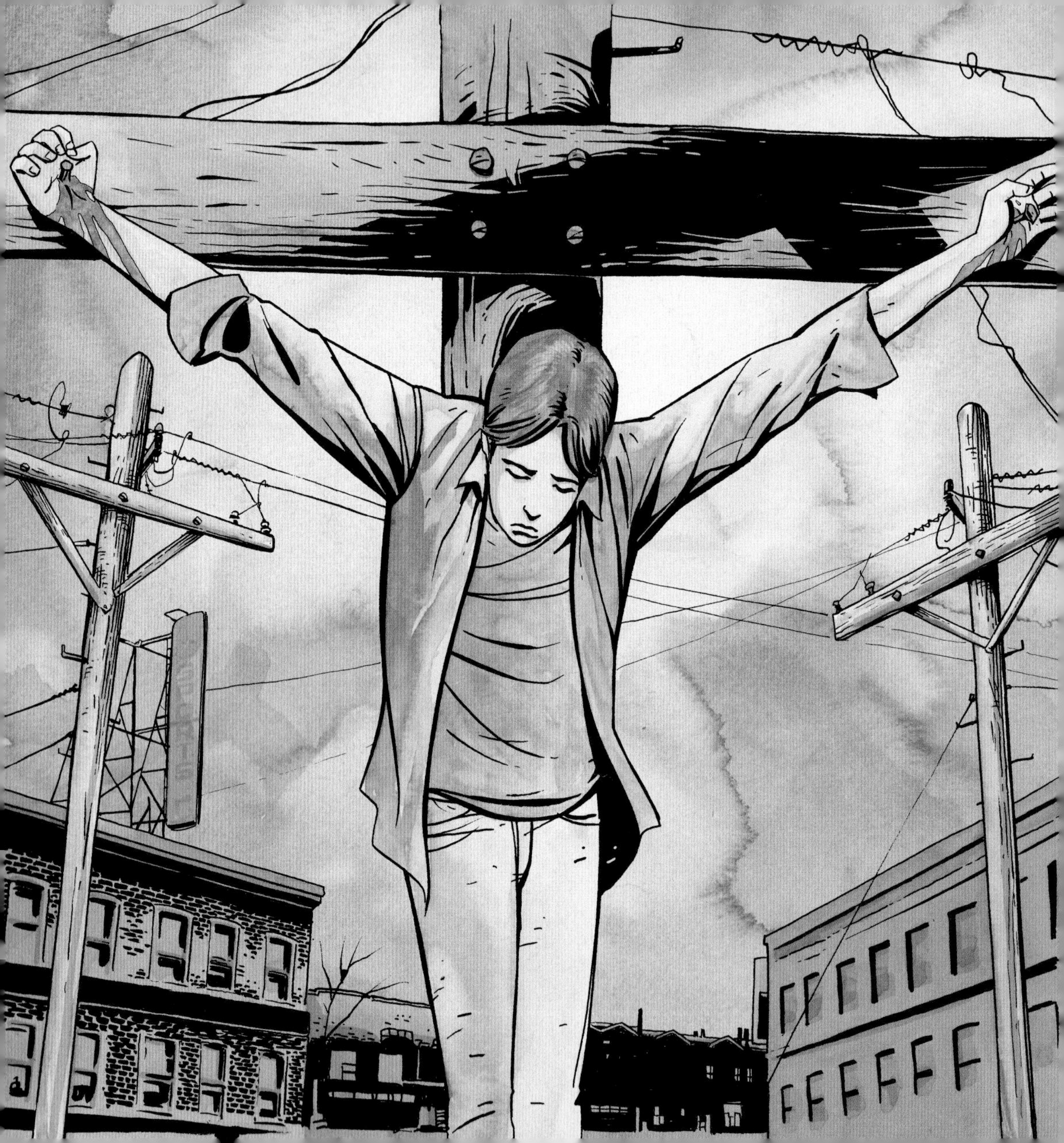

CHAPTER 1

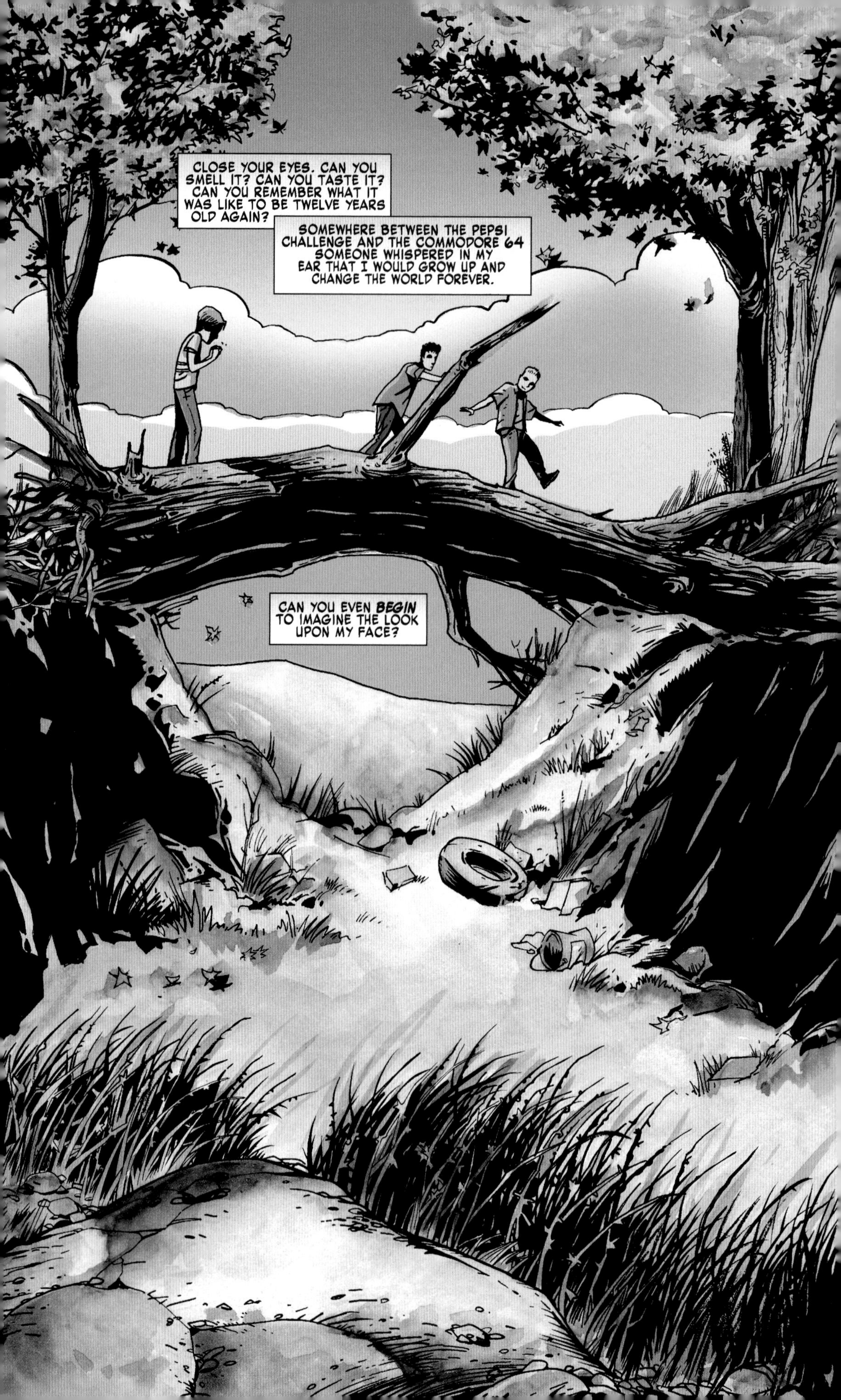
CLOSE YOUR EYES. CAN YOU SMELL IT? CAN YOU TASTE IT? CAN YOU REMEMBER WHAT IT WAS LIKE TO BE TWELVE YEARS OLD AGAIN?
SOMEWHERE BETWEEN THE PEPSI CHALLENGE AND THE COMMODORE 64 SOMEONE WHISPERED IN MY EAR THAT I WOULD GROW UP AND CHANGE THE WORLD FOREVER.
CAN YOU EVEN BEGIN TO IMAGINE THE LOOK UPON MY FACE?

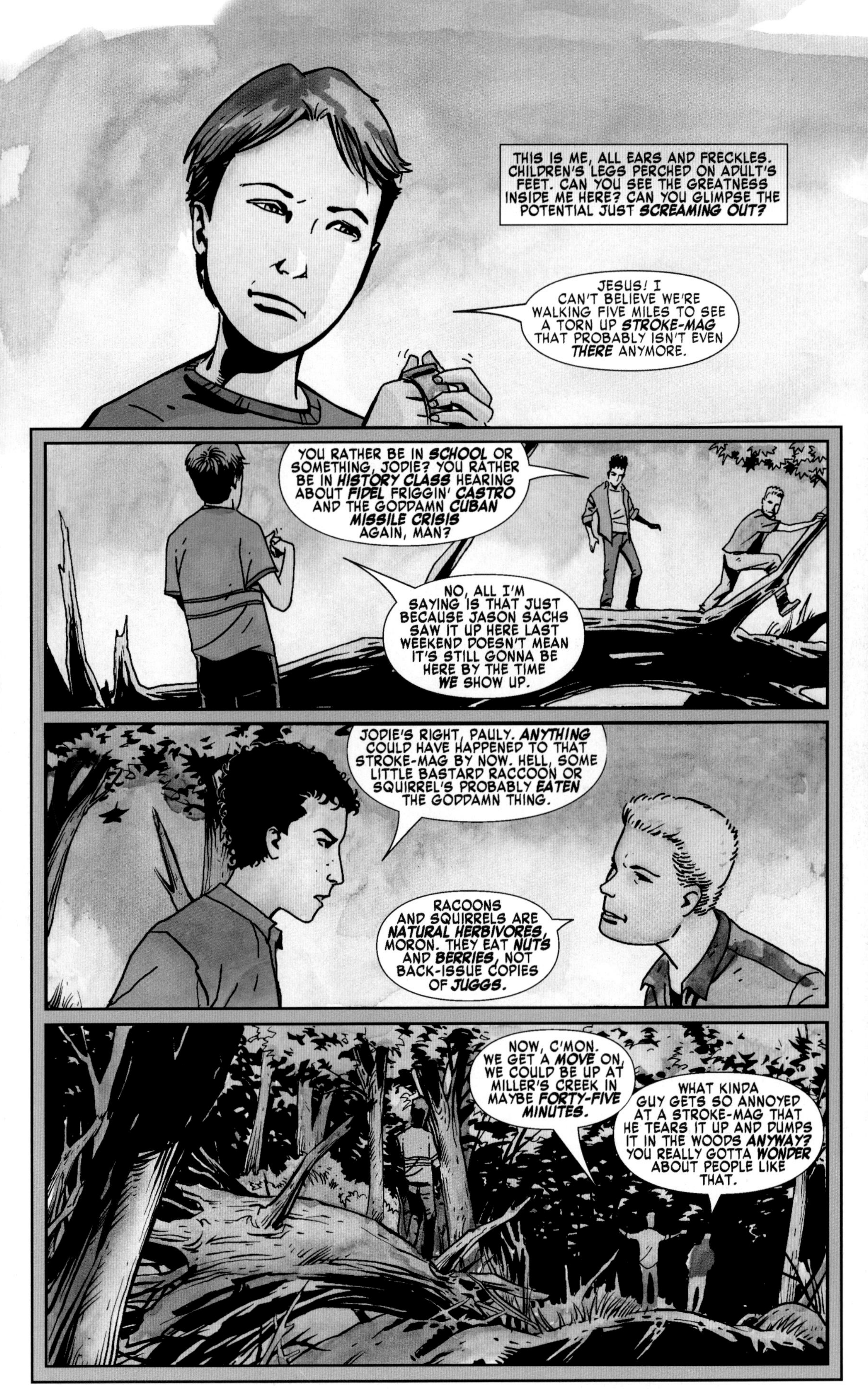

THIS IS ME, ALL EARS AND FRECKLES. CHILDREN'S LEGS PERCHED ON ADULT'S FEET. CAN YOU SEE THE GREATNESS INSIDE ME HERE? CAN YOU GLIMPSE THE POTENTIAL JUST SCREAMING OUT?
JESUS! I CAN'T BELIEVE WE'RE WALKING FIVE MILES TO SEE A TORN UP STROKE-MAG THAT PROBABLY ISN'T EVEN THERE ANYMORE.
YOU RATHER BE IN SCHOOL OR SOMETHING, JODIE? YOU RATHER BE IN HISTORY CLASS HEARING ABOUT FIDEL FRIGGIN' CASTRO AND THE GODDAMN CUBAN MISSILE CRISIS AGAIN, MAN?
NO, ALL I'M SAYING IS THAT JUST BECAUSE JASON SACHS SAW IT UP HERE LAST WEEKEND DOESN'T MEAN IT'S STILL GONNA BE HERE BY THE TIME WE SHOW UP.
JODIE'S RIGHT, PAULY. ANYTHING COULD HAVE HAPPENED TO THAT STROKE-MAG BY NOW. HELL, SOME LITTLE BASTARD RACCOON OR SQUIRREL'S PROBABLY EATEN THE GODDAMN THING.
RACOONS AND SQUIRRELS ARE NATURAL HERBIVORES, MORON. THEY EAT NUTS AND BERRIES, NOT BACK-ISSUE COPIES OF JUGGS.
NOW, C'MON. WE GET A MOVE ON, WE COULD BE UP AT MILLER'S CREEK IN MAYBE FORTY-FIVE MINUTES.
WHAT KINDA GUY GETS SO ANNOYED AT A STROKE-MAG THAT HE TEARS IT UP AND DUMPS IT IN THE WOODS ANYWAY? YOU REALLY GOTTA WONDER ABOUT PEOPLE LIKE THAT.

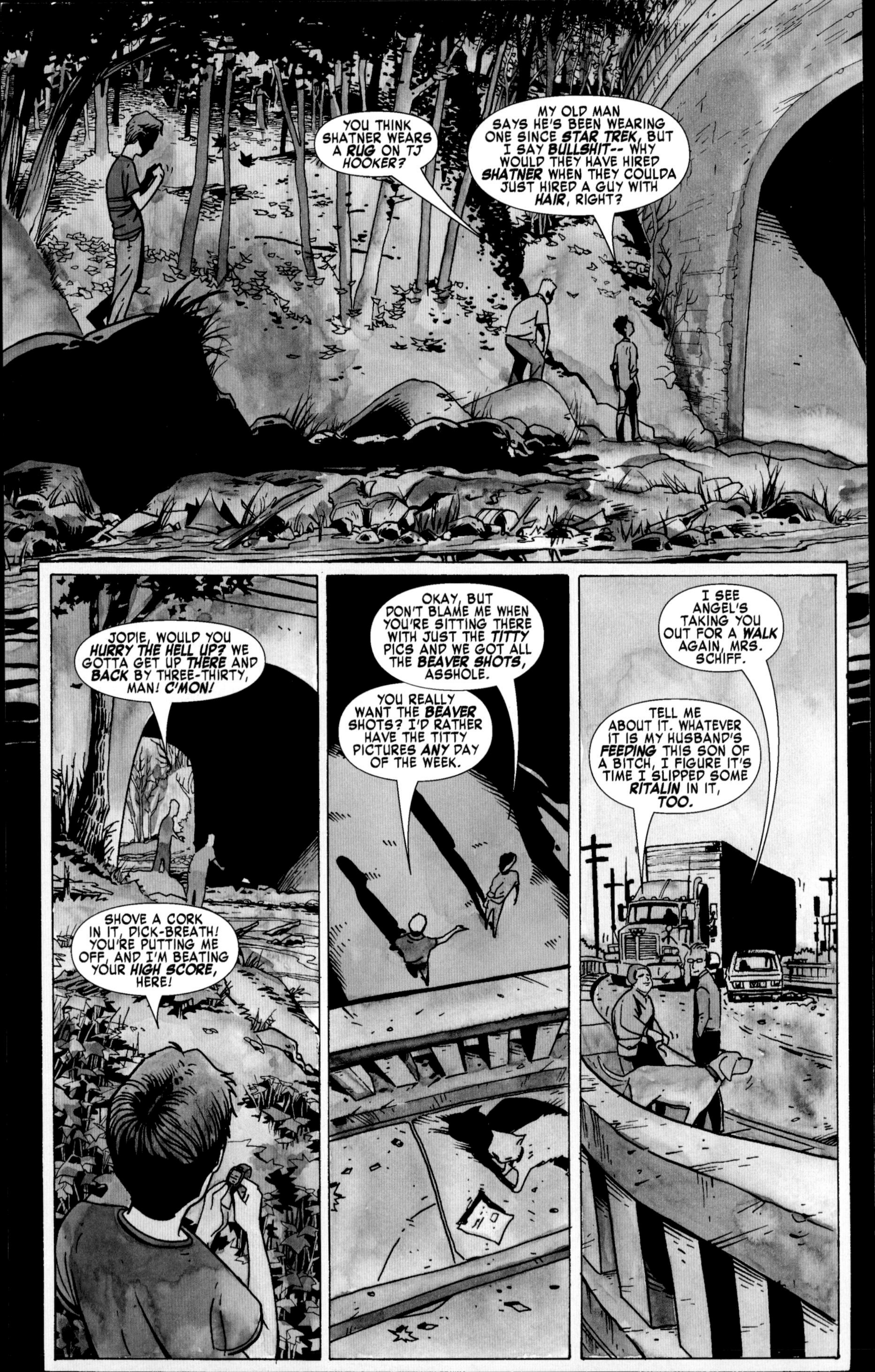
YOU THINK SHATNER WEARS A RUG ON TJ HOOKER?
MY OLD MAN SAYS HE'S BEEN WEARING ONE SINCE STAR TREK, BUT I SAY BULLSHIT-- WHY WOULD THEY HAVE HIRED SHATNER WHEN THEY COULDA JUST HIRED A GUY WITH HAIR, RIGHT?
JODIE, WOULD YOU HURRY THE HELL UP? WE GOTTA GET UP THERE AND BACK BY THREE-THIRTY, MAN! C'MON!
SHOVE A CORK IN IT, DICK-BREATH! YOU'RE PUTTING ME OFF, AND I'M BEATING YOUR HIGH SCORE, HERE!
OKAY, BUT DON'T BLAME ME WHEN YOU'RE SITTING THERE WITH JUST THE TITTY PICS AND WE GOT ALL THE BEAVER SHOTS, ASSHOLE.
YOU REALLY WANT THE BEAVER SHOTS? I'D RATHER HAVE THE TITTY PICTURES ANY DAY OF THE WEEK.
I SEE ANGEL'S TAKING YOU OUT FOR A WALK AGAIN, MRS. SCHIFF.
TELL ME ABOUT IT. WHATEVER IT IS MY HUSBAND'S FEEDING THIS SON OF A BITCH, I FIGURE IT'S TIME I SLIPPED SOME RITALIN IN IT, TOO.

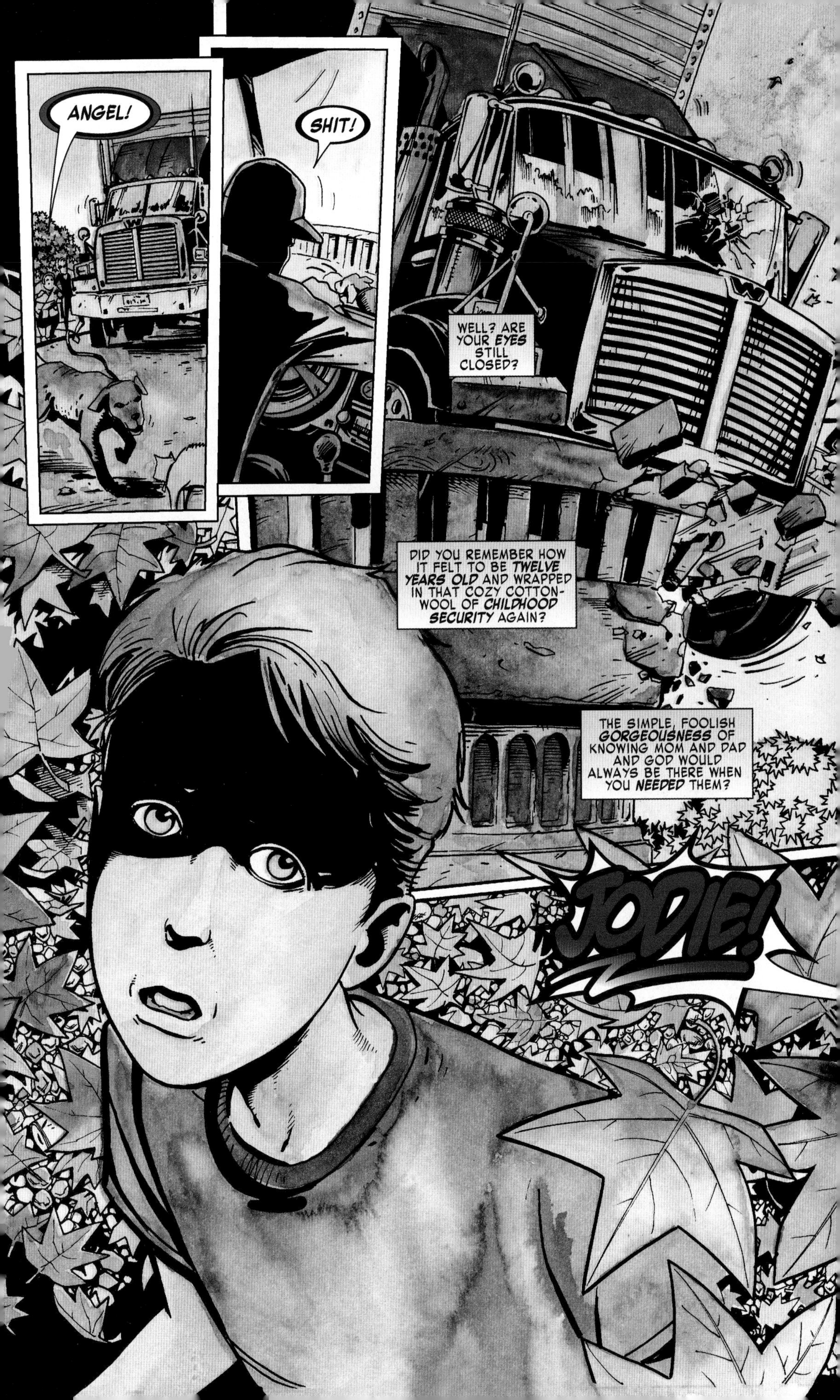
ANGEL!
SHIT!
WELL? ARE YOUR *EYES* STILL CLOSED?
DID YOU REMEMBER HOW IT FELT TO BE *TWELVE YEARS OLD* AND WRAPPED IN THAT COZY COTTON-WOOL OF *CHILDHOOD SECURITY* AGAIN?
THE SIMPLE, FOOLISH *GORGEOUSNESS* OF KNOWING MOM AND DAD AND GOD WOULD ALWAYS BE THERE WHEN YOU *NEEDED* THEM?
JODIE!

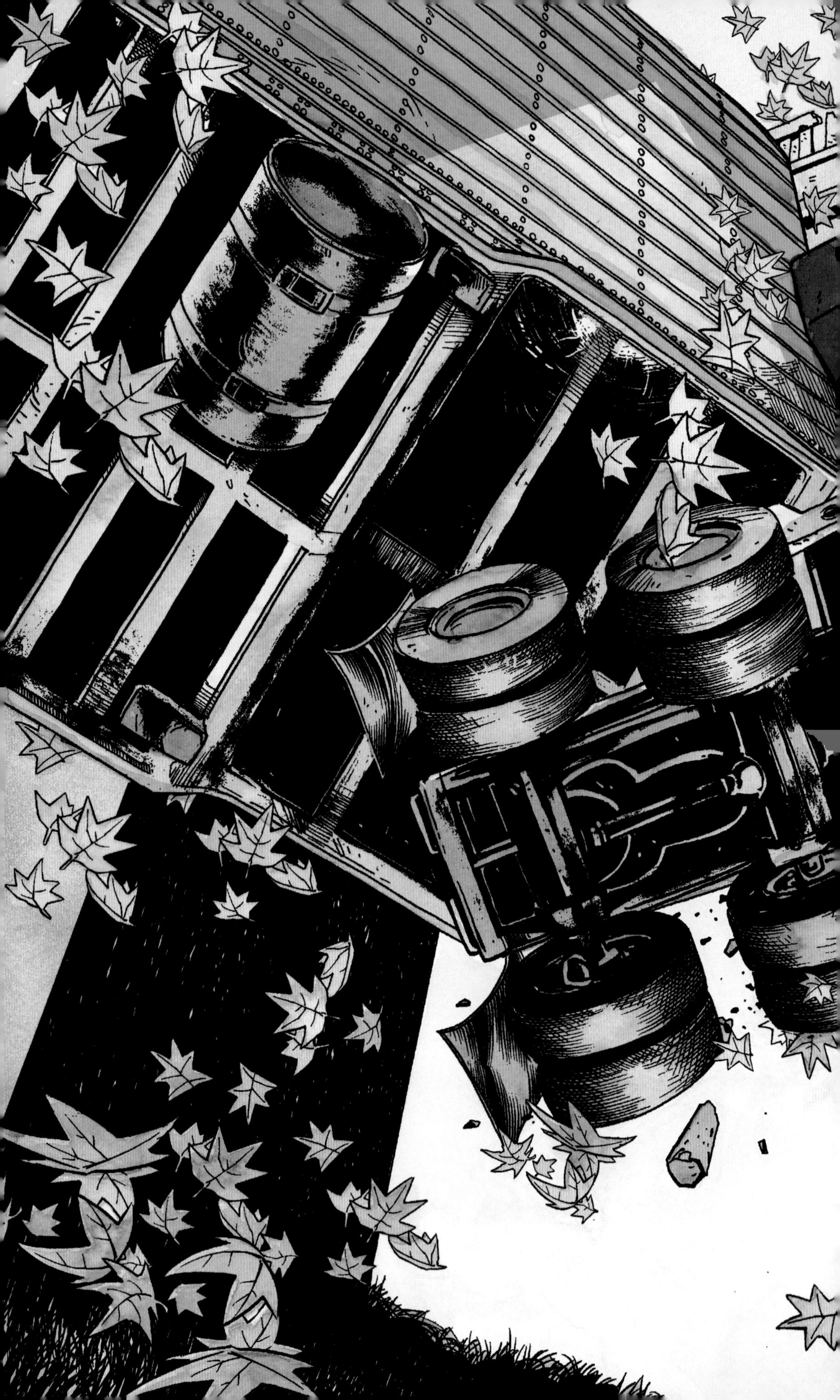

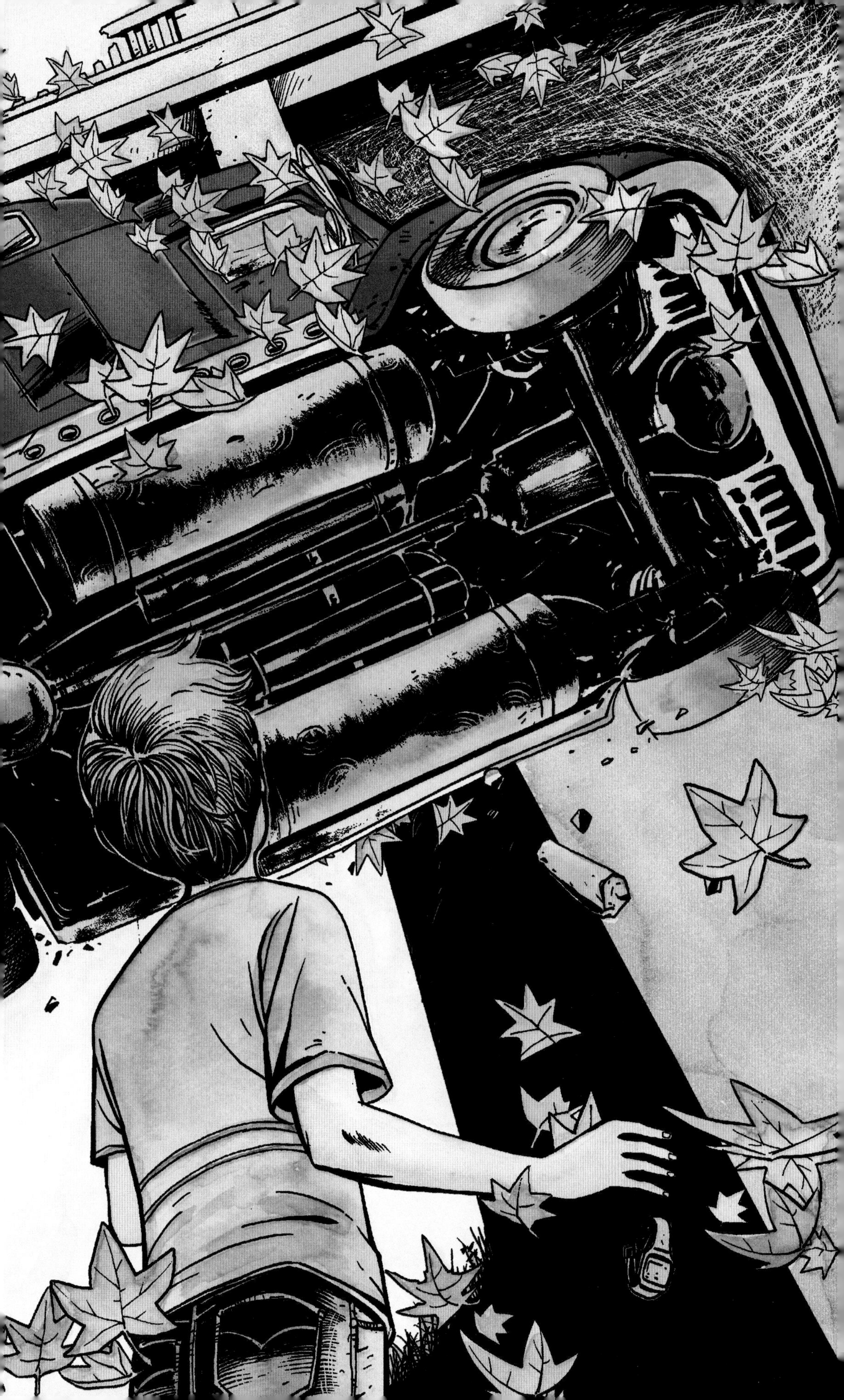

DOGS WORK IN MYSTERIOUS WAYS.

UH, MISTER AND MRS. CHRISTIANSON?

MY NAME IS TOM O'HIGGINS. *FATHER* TOM O'HIGGINS AND I'M THE, UH, NEW *CHAPLAIN* AFFILIATED WITH THE HOSPITAL SINCE FATHER MCGHEE WAS RELOCATED.

I HOPE YOU DON'T MIND ME INTRUPING LIKE THIS, BUT I JUST HEARD ABOUT YOUR SON AND WANTED TO SEE HOW YOU WERE HOLDING UP.

I KNOW THAT NEITHER OF YOU ARE *CATHOLIC*, BUT I WANTED YOU TO KNOW THAT THE HOSPITAL CHAPEL'S JUST DOWNSTAIRS, IF, Y'KNOW, YOU NEED ANYONE TO *TALK* TO, OR ANYTHING.

THANK YOU, FATHER. THAT'S REALLY VERY KIND OF YOU.

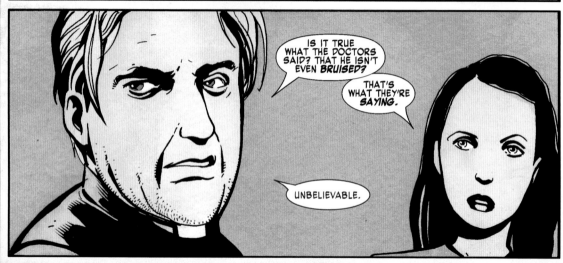

IS IT TRUE WHAT THE DOCTORS SAID? THAT HE ISN'T EVEN *BRUISED?*

THAT'S WHAT THEY'RE *SAYING.*

UNBELIEVABLE.

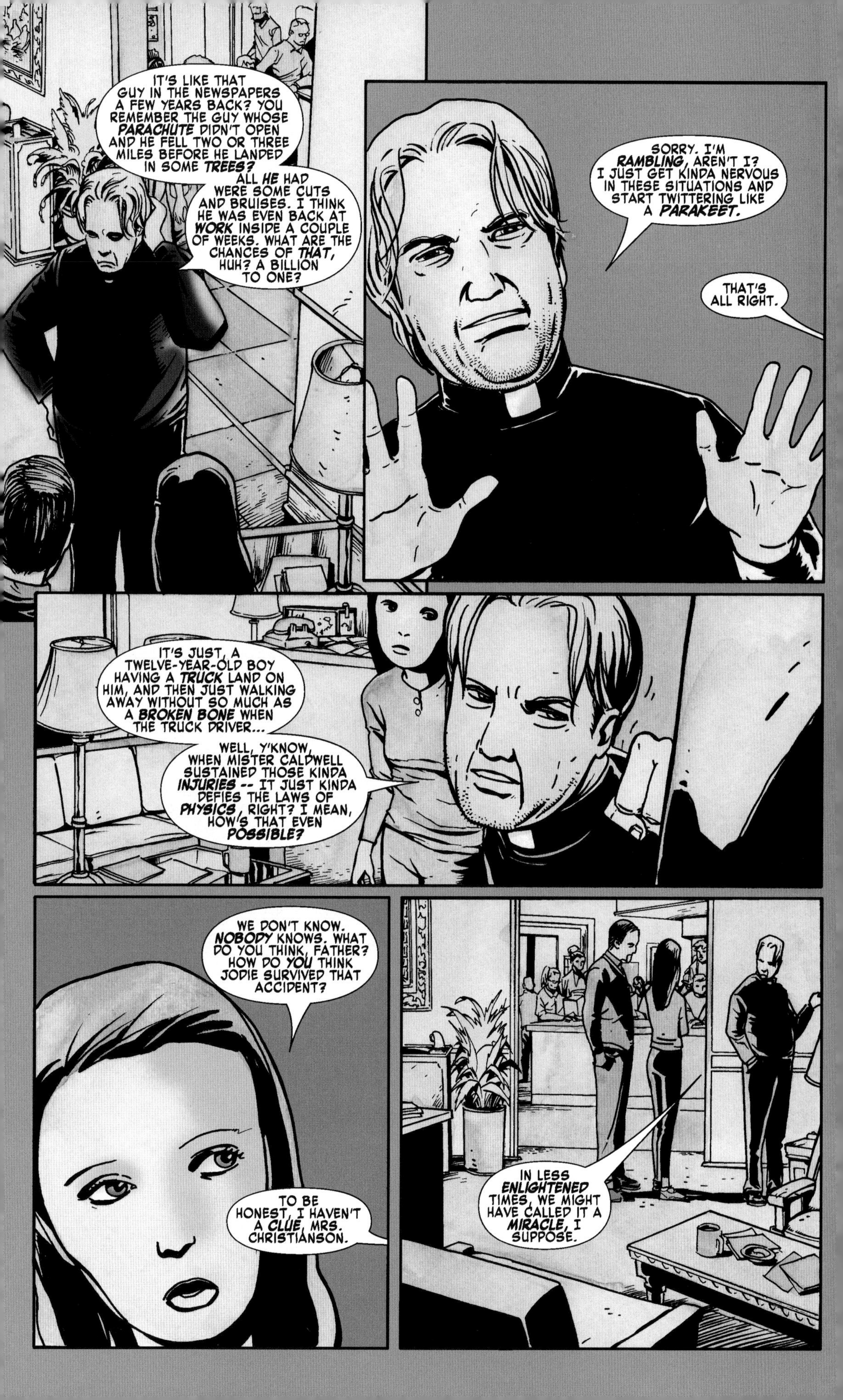
IT'S LIKE THAT GUY IN THE NEWSPAPERS A FEW YEARS BACK? YOU REMEMBER THE GUY WHOSE PARACHUTE DIDN'T OPEN AND HE FELL TWO OR THREE MILES BEFORE HE LANDED IN SOME TREES?
ALL HE HAD WERE SOME CUTS AND BRUISES. I THINK HE WAS EVEN BACK AT WORK INSIDE A COUPLE OF WEEKS. WHAT ARE THE CHANCES OF THAT, HUH? A BILLION TO ONE?
SORRY. I'M RAMBLING, AREN'T I? I JUST GET KINDA NERVOUS IN THESE SITUATIONS AND START TWITTERING LIKE A PARAKEET.
THAT'S ALL RIGHT.
IT'S JUST, A TWELVE-YEAR-OLD BOY HAVING A TRUCK LAND ON HIM, AND THEN JUST WALKING AWAY WITHOUT SO MUCH AS A BROKEN BONE WHEN THE TRUCK DRIVER...
WELL, Y'KNOW, WHEN MISTER CALDWELL SUSTAINED THOSE KINDA INJURIES -- IT JUST KINDA DEFIES THE LAWS OF PHYSICS, RIGHT? I MEAN, HOW'S THAT EVEN POSSIBLE?
WE DON'T KNOW. NOBODY KNOWS. WHAT DO YOU THINK, FATHER? HOW DO YOU THINK JODIE SURVIVED THAT ACCIDENT?
TO BE HONEST, I HAVEN'T A CLUE, MRS. CHRISTIANSON.
IN LESS ENLIGHTENED TIMES, WE MIGHT HAVE CALLED IT A MIRACLE, I SUPPOSE.

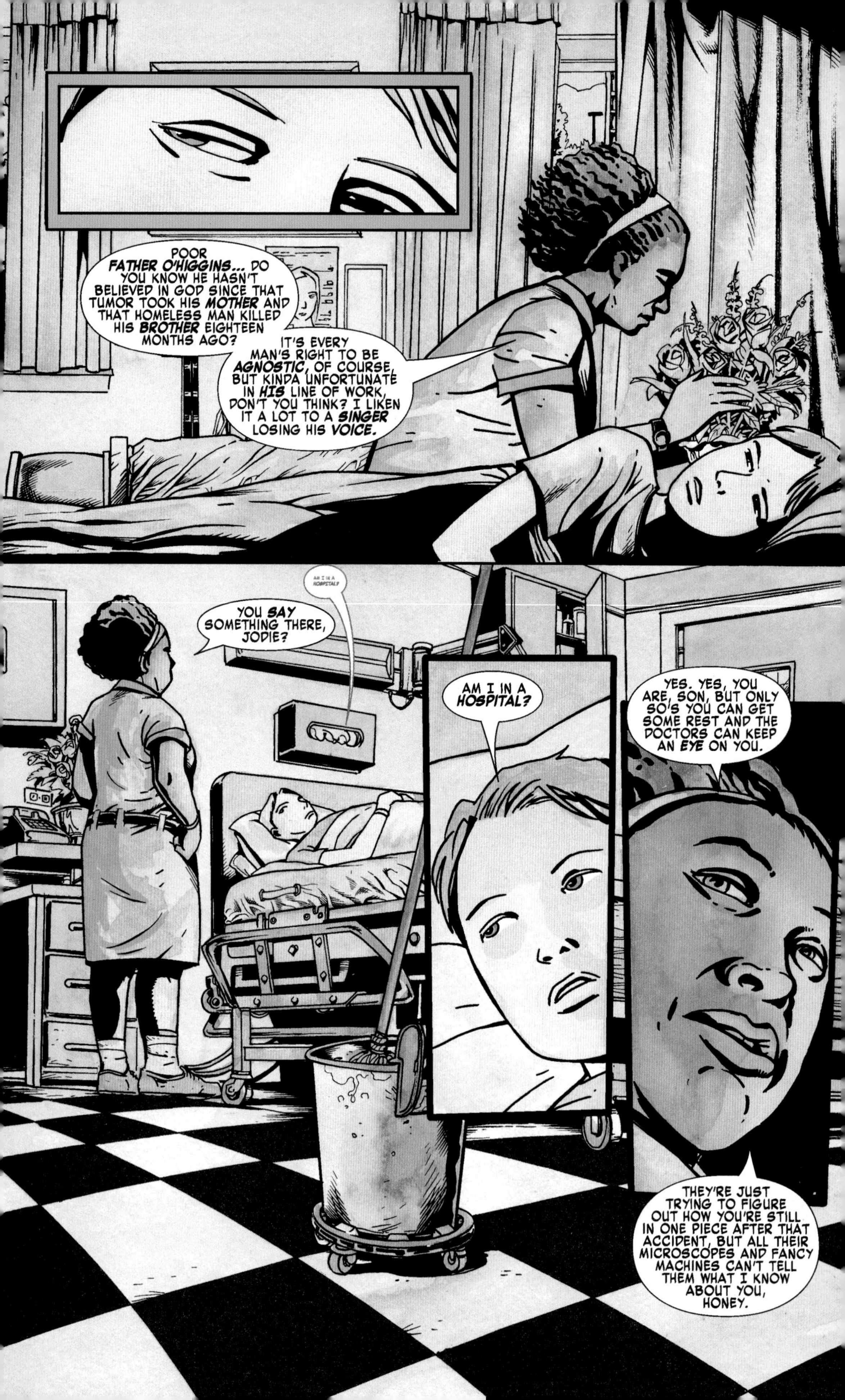
POOR FATHER O'HIGGINS... DO YOU KNOW HE HASN'T BELIEVED IN GOD SINCE THAT TUMOR TOOK HIS MOTHER AND THAT HOMELESS MAN KILLED HIS BROTHER EIGHTEEN MONTHS AGO?
IT'S EVERY MAN'S RIGHT TO BE AGNOSTIC, OF COURSE, BUT KINDA UNFORTUNATE IN HIS LINE OF WORK, DON'T YOU THINK? I LIKEN IT A LOT TO A SINGER LOSING HIS VOICE.
AM I IN A HOSPITAL?
YOU SAY SOMETHING THERE, JODIE?
AM I IN A HOSPITAL?
YES. YES, YOU ARE, SON, BUT ONLY SO'S YOU CAN GET SOME REST AND THE DOCTORS CAN KEEP AN EYE ON YOU.
THEY'RE JUST TRYING TO FIGURE OUT HOW YOU'RE STILL IN ONE PIECE AFTER THAT ACCIDENT, BUT ALL THEIR MICROSCOPES AND FANCY MACHINES CAN'T TELL THEM WHAT I KNOW ABOUT YOU, HONEY.

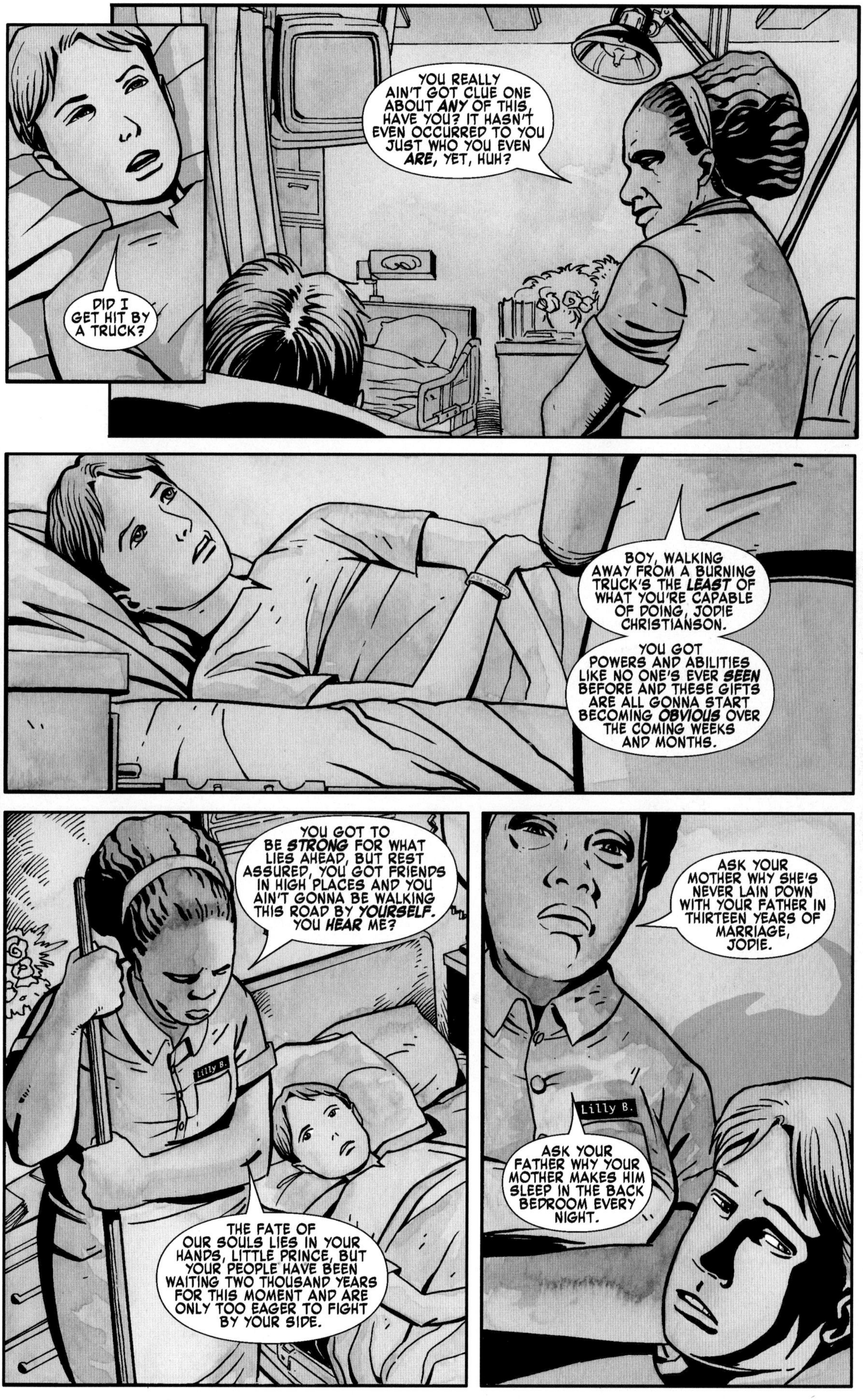
DID I GET HIT BY A TRUCK?
YOU REALLY AIN'T GOT CLUE ONE ABOUT ANY OF THIS, HAVE YOU? IT HASN'T EVEN OCCURRED TO YOU JUST WHO YOU EVEN ARE, YET, HUH?
BOY, WALKING AWAY FROM A BURNING TRUCK'S THE LEAST OF WHAT YOU'RE CAPABLE OF DOING, JODIE CHRISTIANSON.
YOU GOT POWERS AND ABILITIES LIKE NO ONE'S EVER SEEN BEFORE AND THESE GIFTS ARE ALL GONNA START BECOMING OBVIOUS OVER THE COMING WEEKS AND MONTHS.
YOU GOT TO BE STRONG FOR WHAT LIES AHEAD, BUT REST ASSURED, YOU GOT FRIENDS IN HIGH PLACES AND YOU AIN'T GONNA BE WALKING THIS ROAD BY YOURSELF. YOU HEAR ME?
Lilly B.
THE FATE OF OUR SOULS LIES IN YOUR HANDS, LITTLE PRINCE, BUT YOUR PEOPLE HAVE BEEN WAITING TWO THOUSAND YEARS FOR THIS MOMENT AND ARE ONLY TOO EAGER TO FIGHT BY YOUR SIDE.
ASK YOUR MOTHER WHY SHE'S NEVER LAIN DOWN WITH YOUR FATHER IN THIRTEEN YEARS OF MARRIAGE, JODIE.
Lilly B.
ASK YOUR FATHER WHY YOUR MOTHER MAKES HIM SLEEP IN THE BACK BEDROOM EVERY NIGHT.

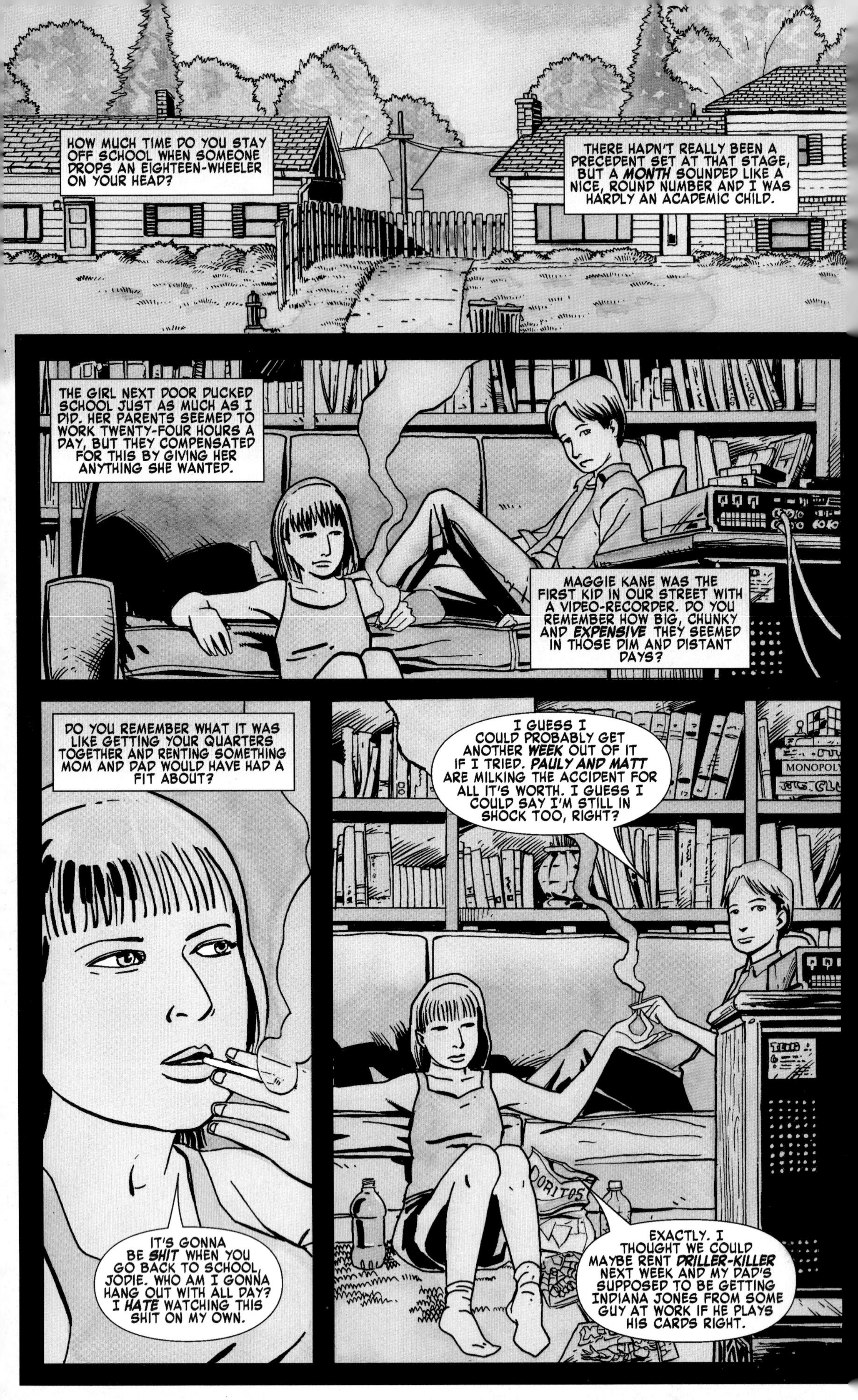
HOW MUCH TIME DO YOU STAY OFF SCHOOL WHEN SOMEONE DROPS AN EIGHTEEN-WHEELER ON YOUR HEAD?
THERE HADN'T REALLY BEEN A PRECEDENT SET AT THAT STAGE, BUT A MONTH SOUNDED LIKE A NICE, ROUND NUMBER AND I WAS HARDLY AN ACADEMIC CHILD.
THE GIRL NEXT DOOR DUCKED SCHOOL JUST AS MUCH AS I DID. HER PARENTS SEEMED TO WORK TWENTY-FOUR HOURS A DAY, BUT THEY COMPENSATED FOR THIS BY GIVING HER ANYTHING SHE WANTED.
MAGGIE KANE WAS THE FIRST KID IN OUR STREET WITH A VIDEO-RECORDER. DO YOU REMEMBER HOW BIG, CHUNKY AND EXPENSIVE THEY SEEMED IN THOSE DIM AND DISTANT DAYS?
DO YOU REMEMBER WHAT IT WAS LIKE GETTING YOUR QUARTERS TOGETHER AND RENTING SOMETHING MOM AND DAD WOULD HAVE HAD A FIT ABOUT?
IT'S GONNA BE SHIT WHEN YOU GO BACK TO SCHOOL, JODIE. WHO AM I GONNA HANG OUT WITH ALL DAY? I HATE WATCHING THIS SHIT ON MY OWN.
I GUESS I COULD PROBABLY GET ANOTHER WEEK OUT OF IT IF I TRIED. PAULY AND MATT ARE MILKING THE ACCIDENT FOR ALL IT'S WORTH. I GUESS I COULD SAY I'M STILL IN SHOCK TOO, RIGHT?
MONOPOLY
DORITOS
EXACTLY. I THOUGHT WE COULD MAYBE RENT DRILLER-KILLER NEXT WEEK AND MY DAD'S SUPPOSED TO BE GETTING INDIANA JONES FROM SOME GUY AT WORK IF HE PLAYS HIS CARDS RIGHT.

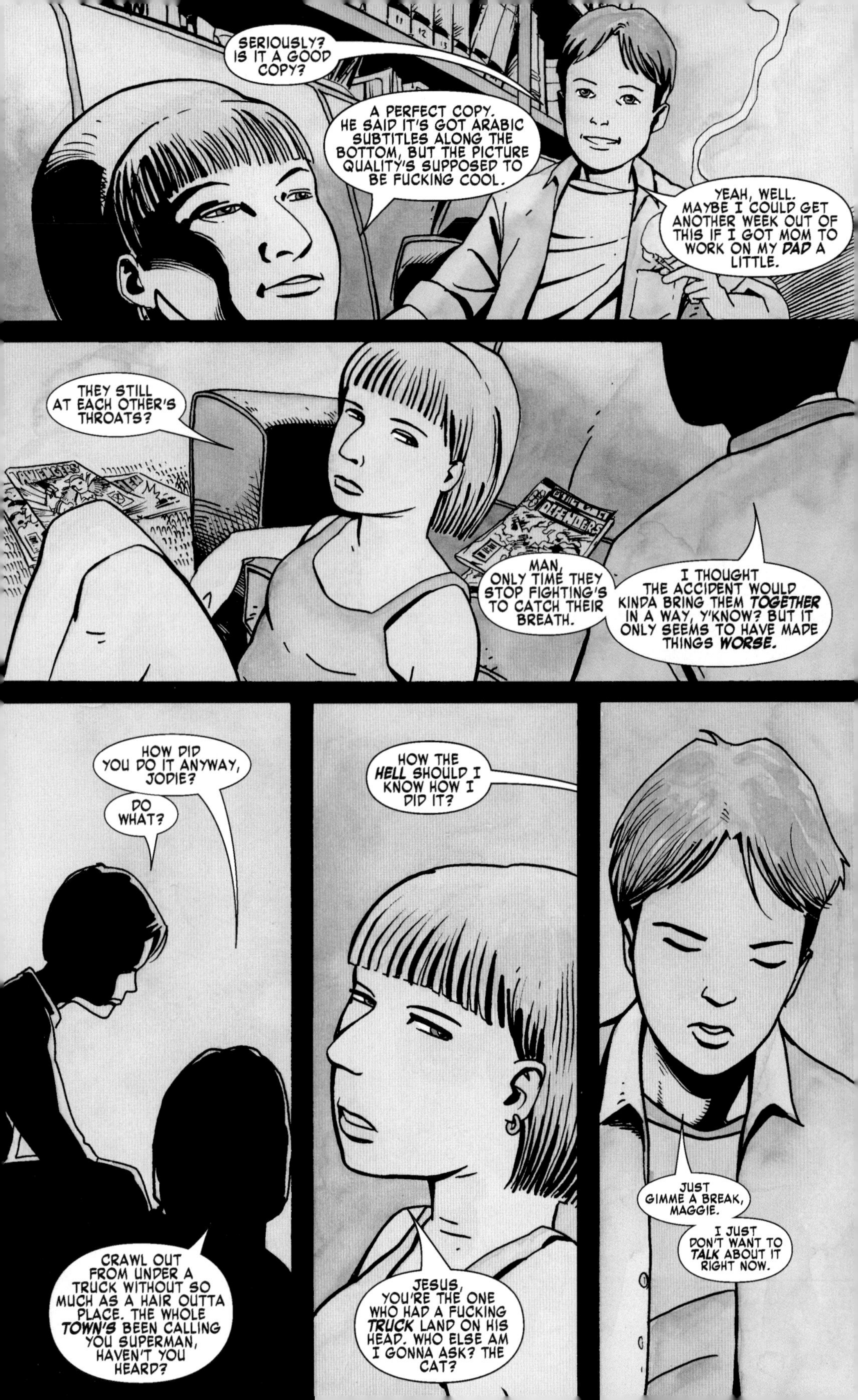
SERIOUSLY? IS IT A GOOD COPY?
A PERFECT COPY. HE SAID IT'S GOT ARABIC SUBTITLES ALONG THE BOTTOM, BUT THE PICTURE QUALITY'S SUPPOSED TO BE FUCKING COOL.
YEAH, WELL. MAYBE I COULD GET ANOTHER WEEK OUT OF THIS IF I GOT MOM TO WORK ON MY DAD A LITTLE.
THEY STILL AT EACH OTHER'S THROATS?
MAN, ONLY TIME THEY STOP FIGHTING'S TO CATCH THEIR BREATH.
I THOUGHT THE ACCIDENT WOULD KINDA BRING THEM TOGETHER IN A WAY, Y'KNOW? BUT IT ONLY SEEMS TO HAVE MADE THINGS WORSE.
HOW DID YOU DO IT ANYWAY, JODIE?
DO WHAT?
CRAWL OUT FROM UNDER A TRUCK WITHOUT SO MUCH AS A HAIR OUTTA PLACE. THE WHOLE TOWN'S BEEN CALLING YOU SUPERMAN, HAVEN'T YOU HEARD?
HOW THE HELL SHOULD I KNOW HOW I DID IT?
JESUS, YOU'RE THE ONE WHO HAD A FUCKING TRUCK LAND ON HIS HEAD. WHO ELSE AM I GONNA ASK? THE CAT?
JUST GIMME A BREAK, MAGGIE.
I JUST DON'T WANT TO TALK ABOUT IT RIGHT NOW.

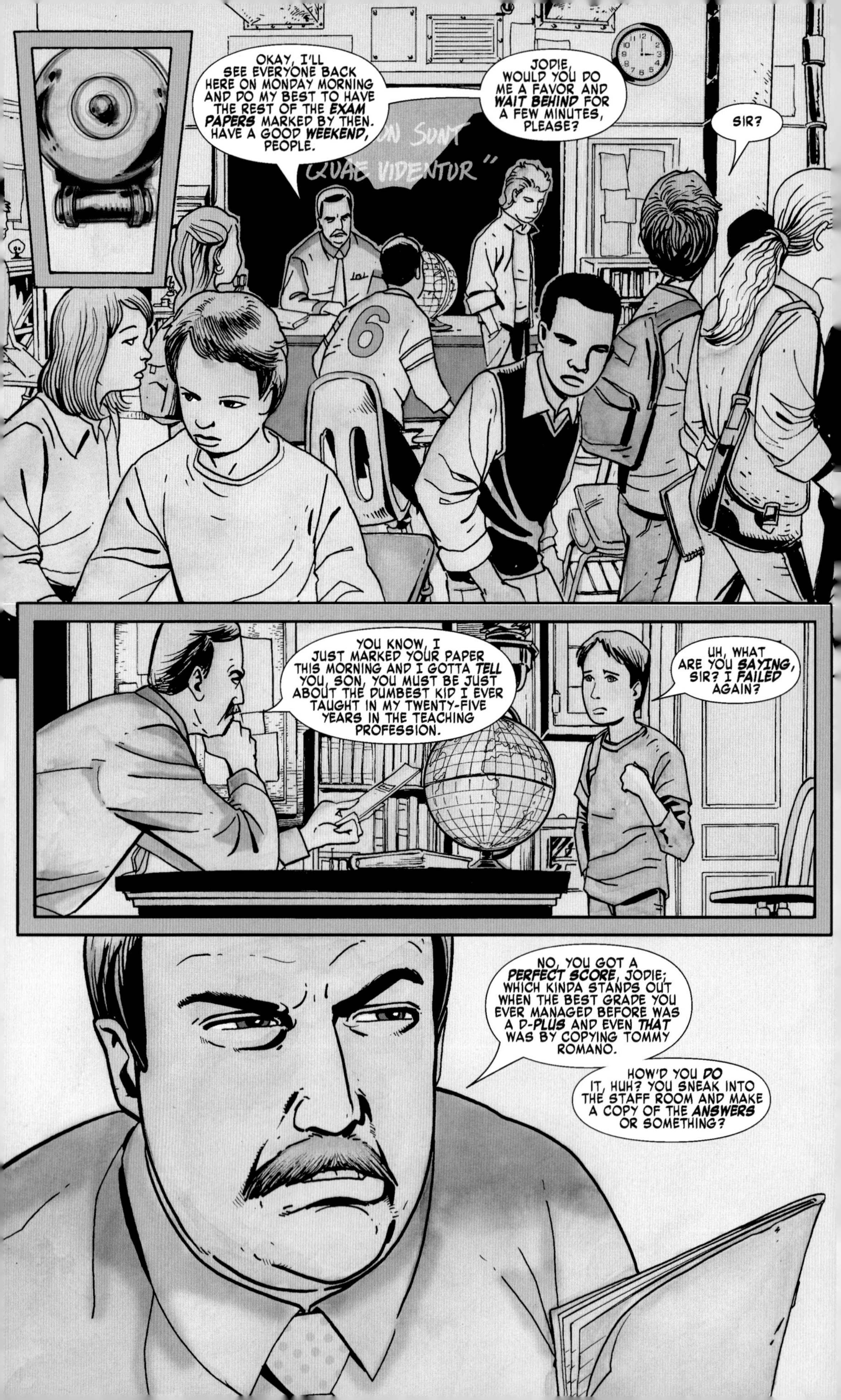

OKAY, I'LL SEE EVERYONE BACK HERE ON MONDAY MORNING AND DO MY BEST TO HAVE THE REST OF THE EXAM PAPERS MARKED BY THEN. HAVE A GOOD WEEKEND, PEOPLE.
JODIE, WOULD YOU DO ME A FAVOR AND WAIT BEHIND FOR A FEW MINUTES, PLEASE?
SIR?
YOU KNOW, I JUST MARKED YOUR PAPER THIS MORNING AND I GOTTA TELL YOU, SON, YOU MUST BE JUST ABOUT THE DUMBEST KID I EVER TAUGHT IN MY TWENTY-FIVE YEARS IN THE TEACHING PROFESSION.
UH, WHAT ARE YOU SAYING, SIR? I FAILED AGAIN?
NO, YOU GOT A PERFECT SCORE, JODIE; WHICH KINDA STANDS OUT WHEN THE BEST GRADE YOU EVER MANAGED BEFORE WAS A D-PLUS AND EVEN THAT WAS BY COPYING TOMMY ROMANO.
HOW'D YOU DO IT, HUH? YOU SNEAK INTO THE STAFF ROOM AND MAKE A COPY OF THE ANSWERS OR SOMETHING?

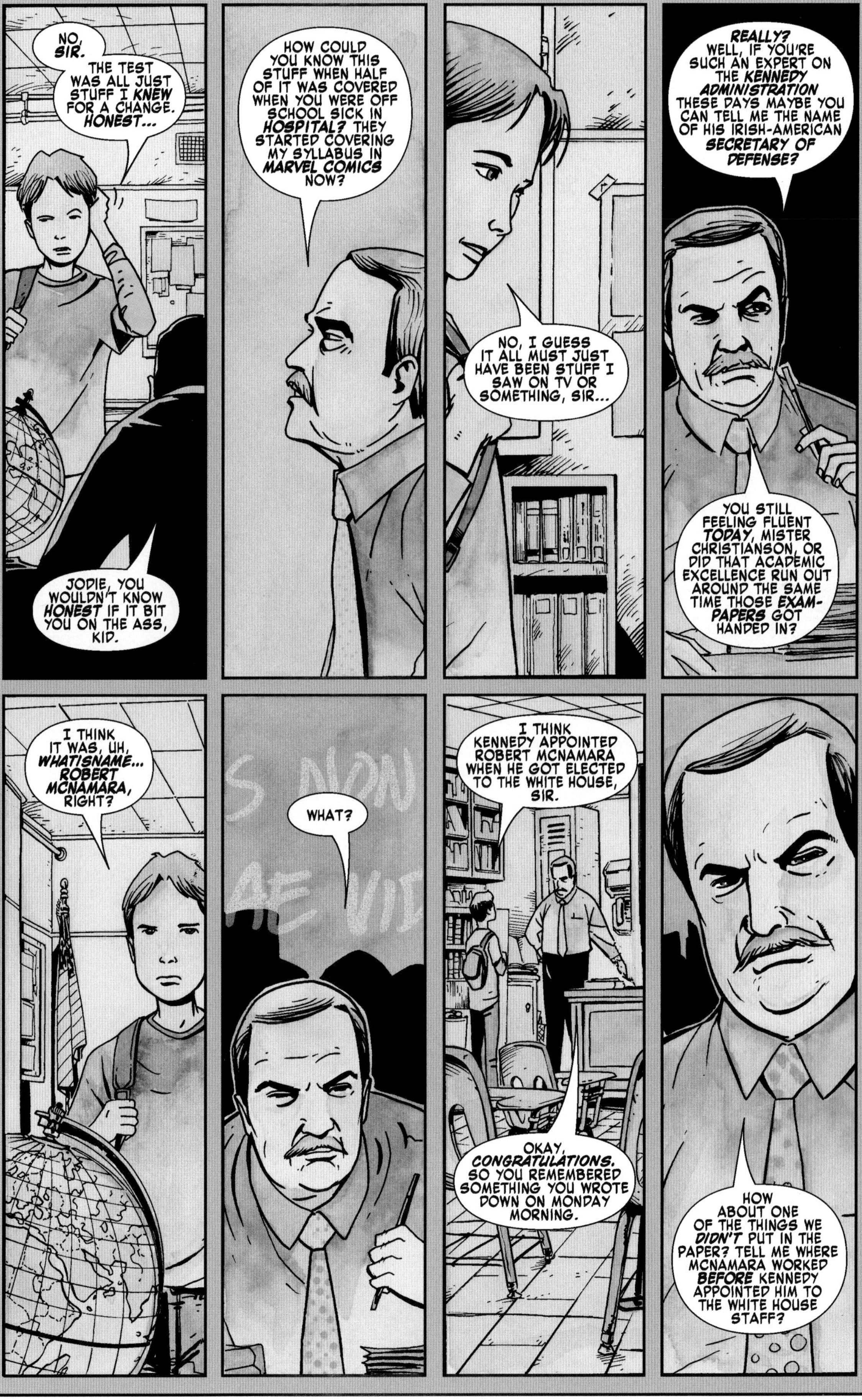
NO, SIR. THE TEST WAS ALL JUST STUFF I KNEW FOR A CHANGE. HONEST...
JODIE, YOU WOULDN'T KNOW HONEST IF IT BIT YOU ON THE ASS, KID.
HOW COULD YOU KNOW THIS STUFF WHEN HALF OF IT WAS COVERED WHEN YOU WERE OFF SCHOOL SICK IN HOSPITAL? THEY STARTED COVERING MY SYLLABUS IN MARVEL COMICS NOW?
NO, I GUESS IT ALL MUST JUST HAVE BEEN STUFF I SAW ON TV OR SOMETHING, SIR...
REALLY? WELL, IF YOU'RE SUCH AN EXPERT ON THE KENNEDY ADMINISTRATION THESE DAYS MAYBE YOU CAN TELL ME THE NAME OF HIS IRISH-AMERICAN SECRETARY OF DEFENSE?
YOU STILL FEELING FLUENT TODAY, MISTER CHRISTIANSON, OR DID THAT ACADEMIC EXCELLENCE RUN OUT AROUND THE SAME TIME THOSE EXAM-PAPERS GOT HANDED IN?
I THINK IT WAS, UH, WHATISNAME... ROBERT MCNAMARA, RIGHT?
WHAT?
I THINK KENNEDY APPOINTED ROBERT MCNAMARA WHEN HE GOT ELECTED TO THE WHITE HOUSE, SIR.
OKAY, CONGRATULATIONS. SO YOU REMEMBERED SOMETHING YOU WROTE DOWN ON MONDAY MORNING.
HOW ABOUT ONE OF THE THINGS WE DIDN'T PUT IN THE PAPER? TELL ME WHERE MCNAMARA WORKED BEFORE KENNEDY APPOINTED HIM TO THE WHITE HOUSE STAFF?

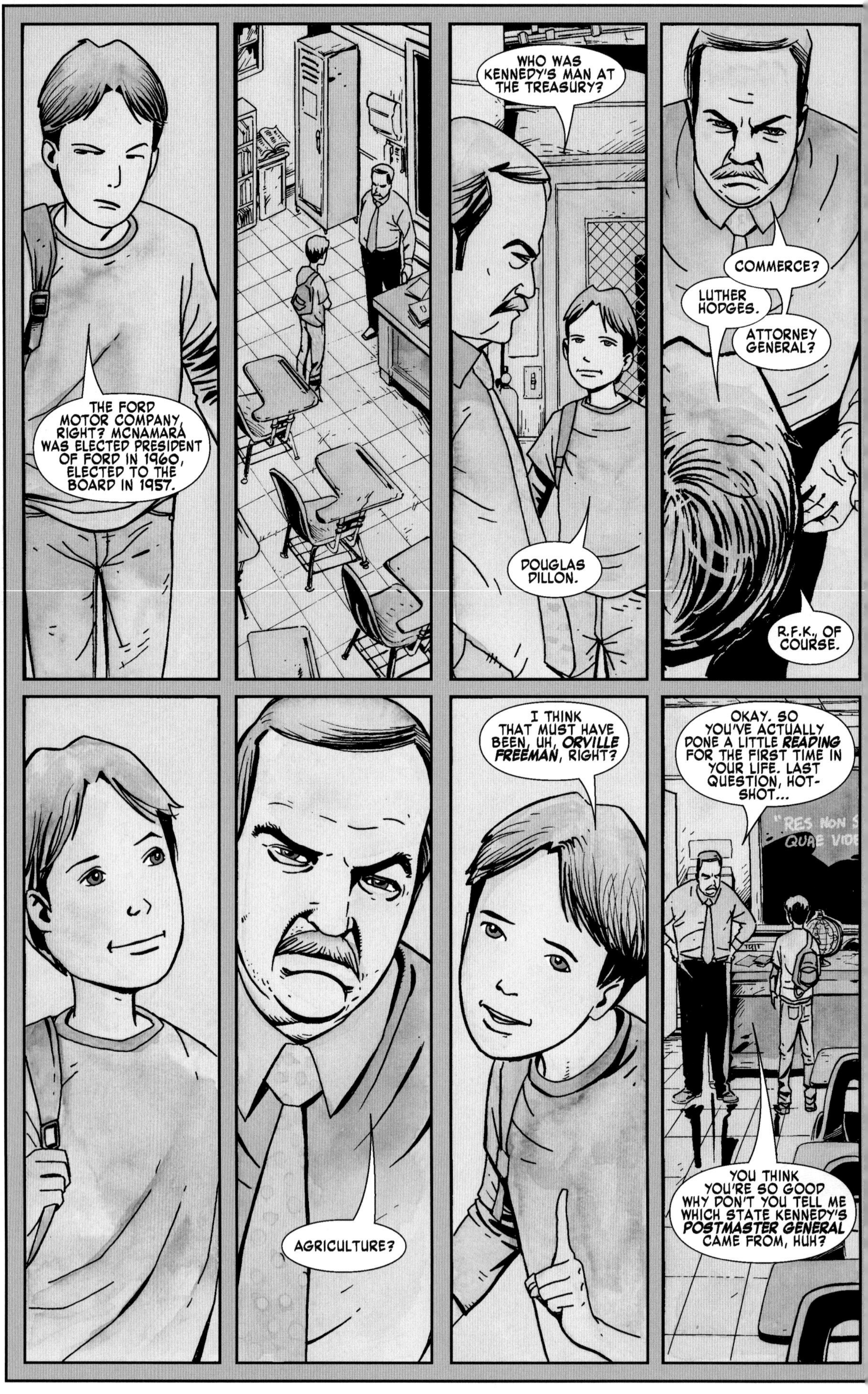
THE FORD MOTOR COMPANY, RIGHT? MCNAMARA WAS ELECTED PRESIDENT OF FORD IN 1960, ELECTED TO THE BOARD IN 1957.
WHO WAS KENNEDY'S MAN AT THE TREASURY?
DOUGLAS DILLON.
COMMERCE?
LUTHER HODGES.
ATTORNEY GENERAL?
R.F.K., OF COURSE.
AGRICULTURE?
I THINK THAT MUST HAVE BEEN, UH, *ORVILLE FREEMAN*, RIGHT?
OKAY. SO YOU'VE ACTUALLY DONE A LITTLE *READING* FOR THE FIRST TIME IN YOUR LIFE. LAST QUESTION, HOT-SHOT...
YOU THINK YOU'RE SO GOOD WHY DON'T YOU TELL ME WHICH STATE KENNEDY'S *POSTMASTER GENERAL* CAME FROM, HUH?

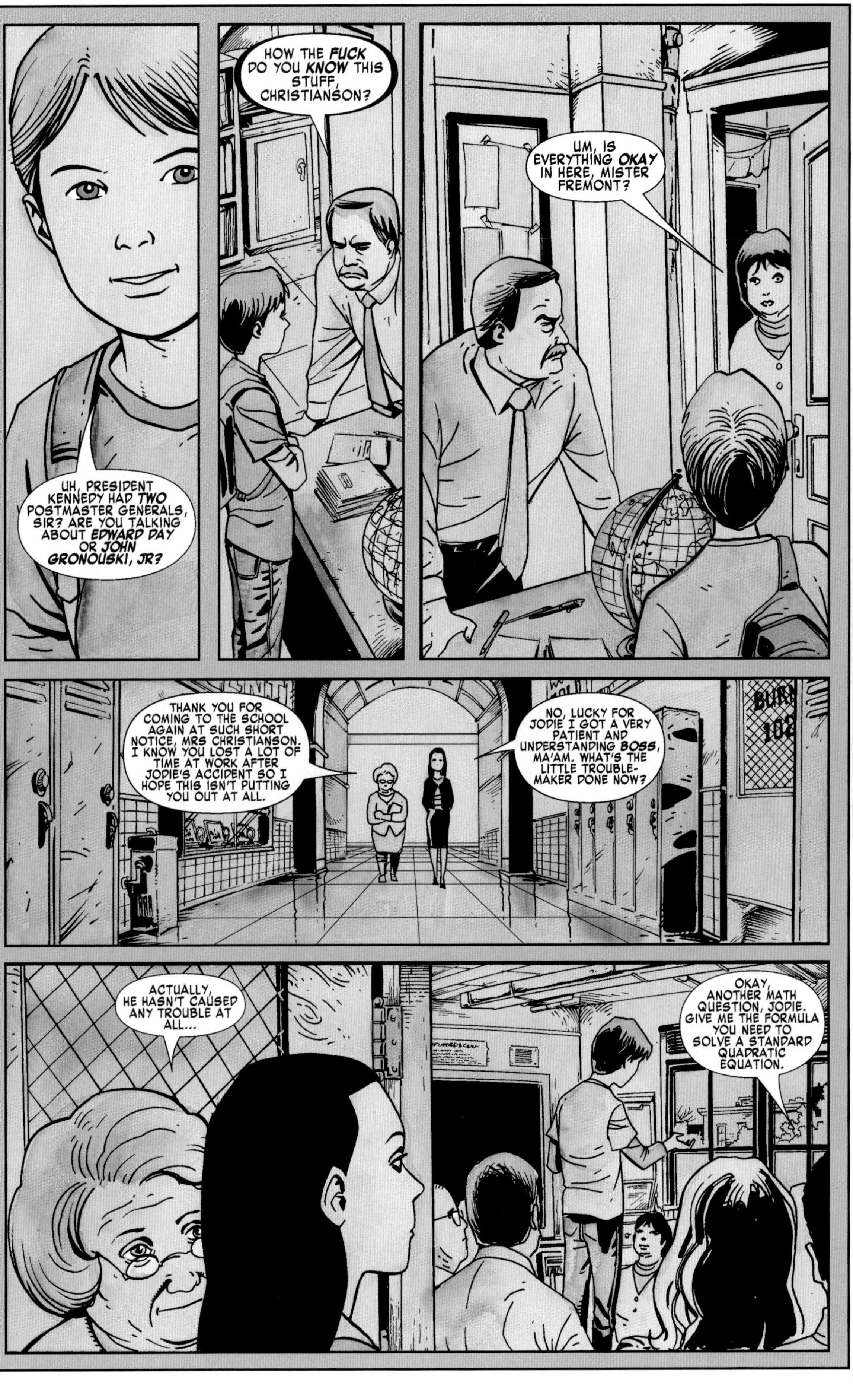
UH, PRESIDENT KENNEDY HAD TWO POSTMASTER GENERALS, SIR? ARE YOU TALKING ABOUT EDWARD DAY OR JOHN GRONOUSKI, JR?
HOW THE FUCK DO YOU KNOW THIS STUFF, CHRISTIANSON?
UM, IS EVERYTHING OKAY IN HERE, MISTER FREMONT?
THANK YOU FOR COMING TO THE SCHOOL AGAIN AT SUCH SHORT NOTICE, MRS CHRISTIANSON. I KNOW YOU LOST A LOT OF TIME AT WORK AFTER JODIE'S ACCIDENT SO I HOPE THIS ISN'T PUTTING YOU OUT AT ALL.
NO, LUCKY FOR JODIE I GOT A VERY PATIENT AND UNDERSTANDING BOSS, MA'AM. WHAT'S THE LITTLE TROUBLE-MAKER DONE NOW?
ACTUALLY, HE HASN'T CAUSED ANY TROUBLE AT ALL...
OKAY, ANOTHER MATH QUESTION, JODIE. GIVE ME THE FORMULA YOU NEED TO SOLVE A STANDARD QUADRATIC EQUATION.

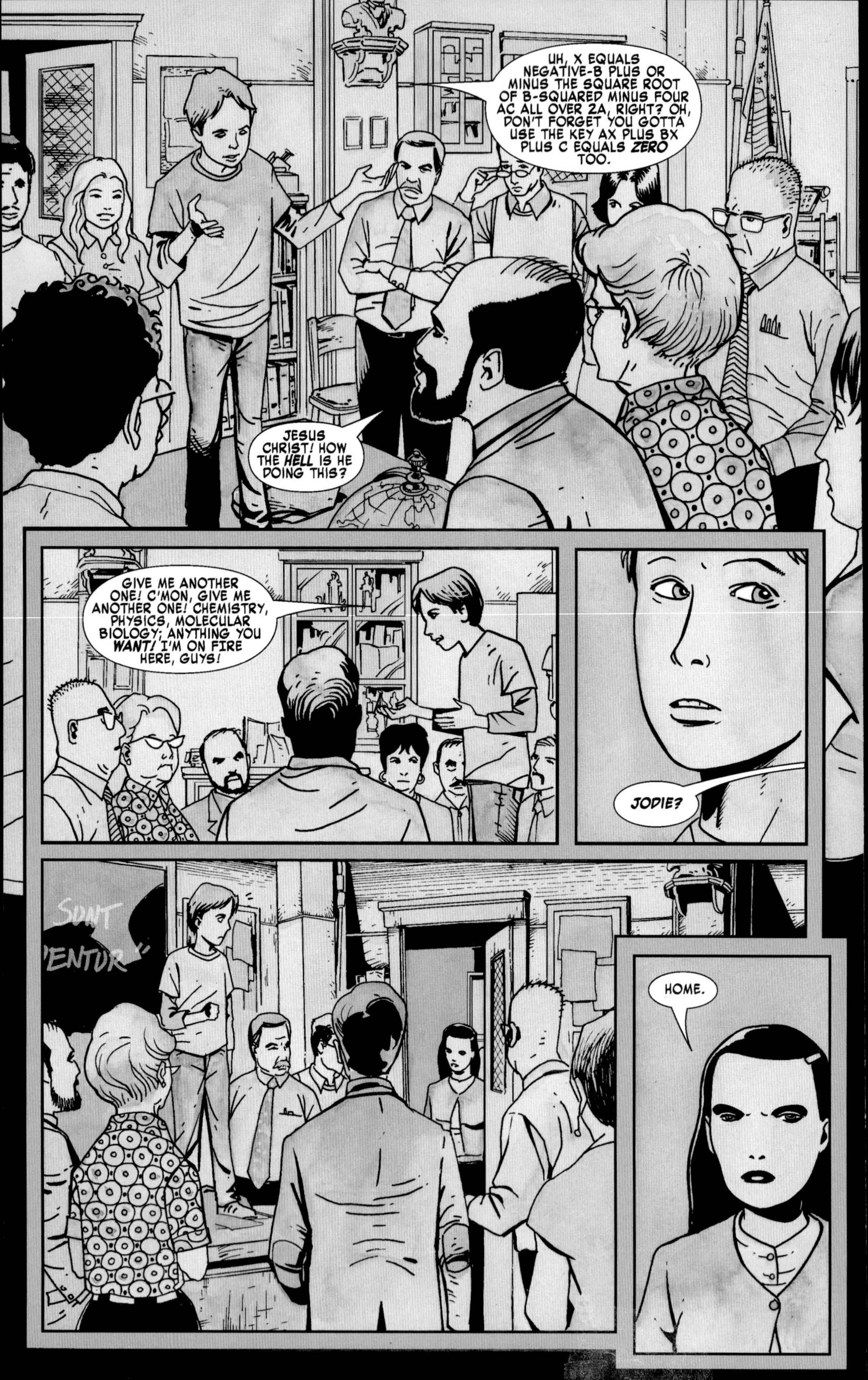
UH, X EQUALS NEGATIVE-B PLUS OR MINUS THE SQUARE ROOT OF B-SQUARED MINUS FOUR AC ALL OVER 2A, RIGHT? OH, DON'T FORGET YOU GOTTA USE THE KEY AX PLUS BX PLUS C EQUALS ***ZERO*** TOO.
JESUS CHRIST! HOW THE ***HELL*** IS HE DOING THIS?
GIVE ME ANOTHER ONE! C'MON, GIVE ME ANOTHER ONE! CHEMISTRY, PHYSICS, MOLECULAR BIOLOGY; ANYTHING YOU ***WANT!*** I'M ON FIRE HERE, GUYS!
JODIE?
HOME.

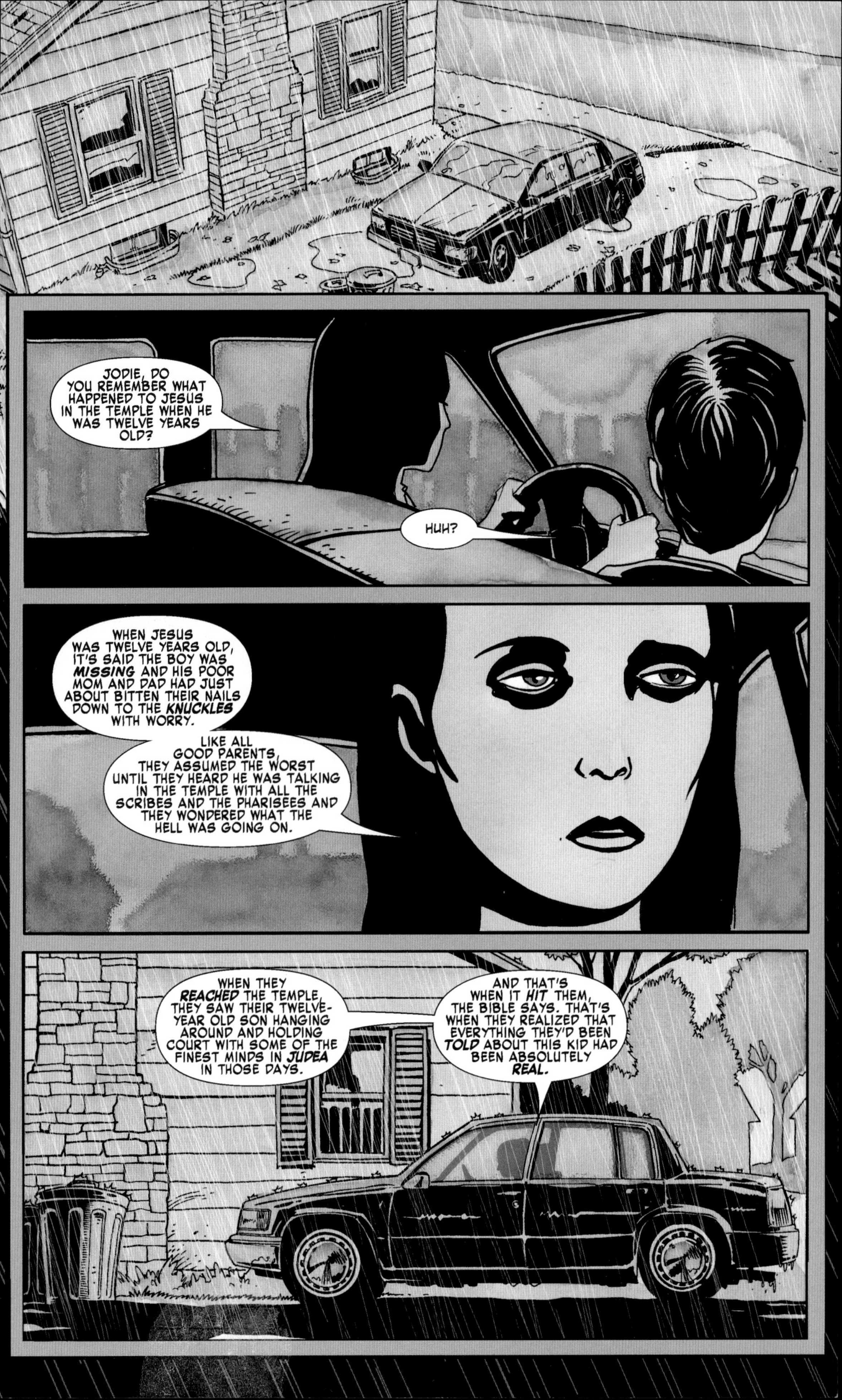

JODIE, DO YOU REMEMBER WHAT HAPPENED TO JESUS IN THE TEMPLE WHEN HE WAS TWELVE YEARS OLD?
HUH?
WHEN JESUS WAS TWELVE YEARS OLD, IT'S SAID THE BOY WAS *MISSING* AND HIS POOR MOM AND DAD HAD JUST ABOUT BITTEN THEIR NAILS DOWN TO THE *KNUCKLES* WITH WORRY.
LIKE ALL GOOD PARENTS, THEY ASSUMED THE WORST UNTIL THEY HEARD HE WAS TALKING IN THE TEMPLE WITH ALL THE SCRIBES AND THE PHARISEES AND THEY WONDERED WHAT THE HELL WAS GOING ON.
WHEN THEY *REACHED* THE TEMPLE, THEY SAW THEIR TWELVE-YEAR OLD SON HANGING AROUND AND HOLDING COURT WITH SOME OF THE FINEST MINDS IN *JUDEA* IN THOSE DAYS.
AND THAT'S WHEN IT *HIT* THEM, THE BIBLE SAYS. THAT'S WHEN THEY REALIZED THAT EVERYTHING THEY'D BEEN *TOLD* ABOUT THIS KID HAD BEEN ABSOLUTELY *REAL.*

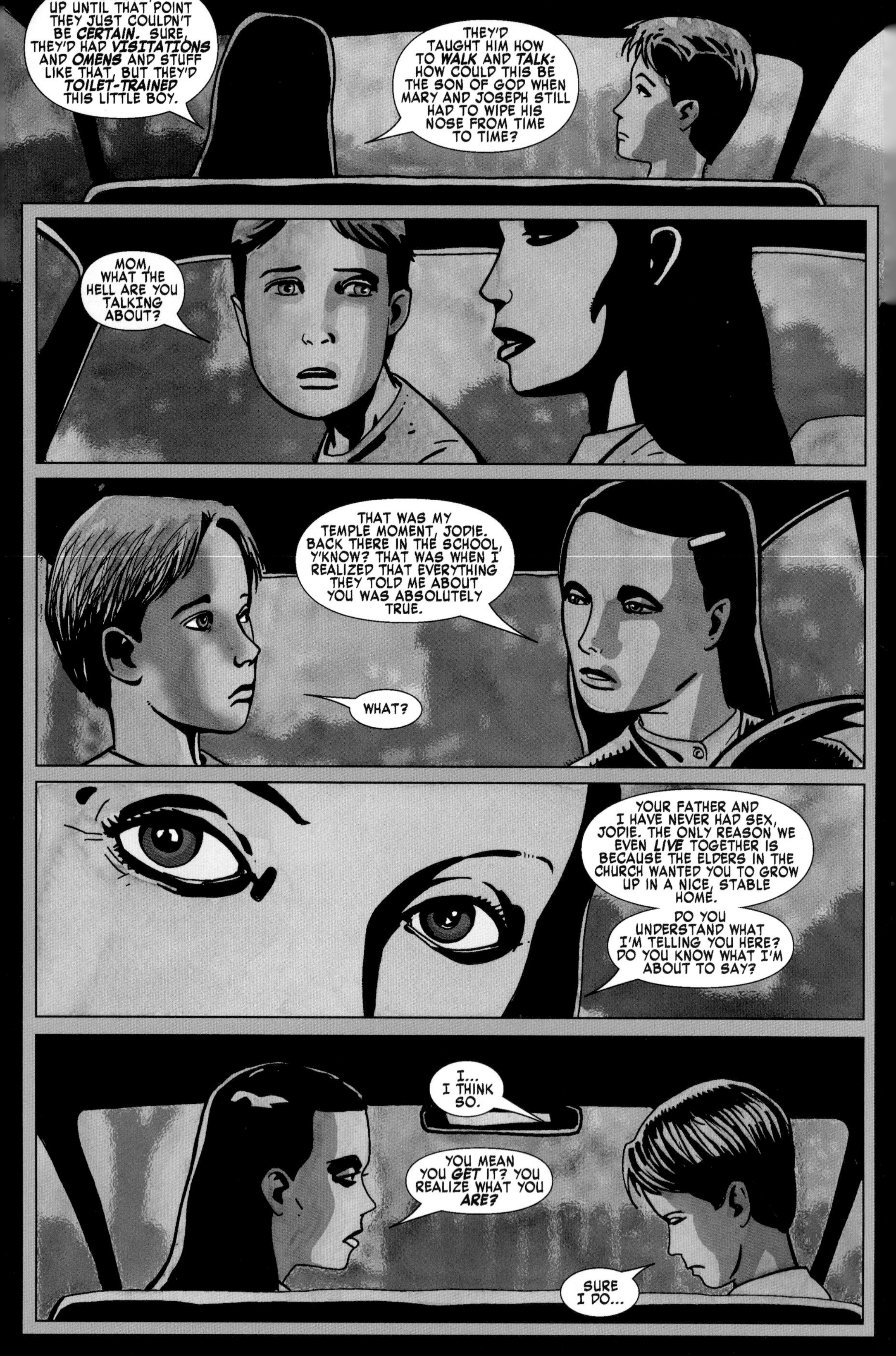
YOU SEE, UP UNTIL THAT POINT THEY JUST COULDN'T BE CERTAIN. SURE, THEY'D HAD VISITATIONS AND OMENS AND STUFF LIKE THAT, BUT THEY'D TOILET-TRAINED THIS LITTLE BOY.
THEY'D TAUGHT HIM HOW TO WALK AND TALK: HOW COULD THIS BE THE SON OF GOD WHEN MARY AND JOSEPH STILL HAD TO WIPE HIS NOSE FROM TIME TO TIME?
MOM, WHAT THE HELL ARE YOU TALKING ABOUT?
THAT WAS MY TEMPLE MOMENT, JODIE. BACK THERE IN THE SCHOOL, Y'KNOW? THAT WAS WHEN I REALIZED THAT EVERYTHING THEY TOLD ME ABOUT YOU WAS ABSOLUTELY TRUE.
WHAT?
YOUR FATHER AND I HAVE NEVER HAD SEX, JODIE. THE ONLY REASON WE EVEN LIVE TOGETHER IS BECAUSE THE ELDERS IN THE CHURCH WANTED YOU TO GROW UP IN A NICE, STABLE HOME.
DO YOU UNDERSTAND WHAT I'M TELLING YOU HERE? DO YOU KNOW WHAT I'M ABOUT TO SAY?
I... I THINK SO.
YOU MEAN YOU GET IT? YOU REALIZE WHAT YOU ARE?
SURE I DO...

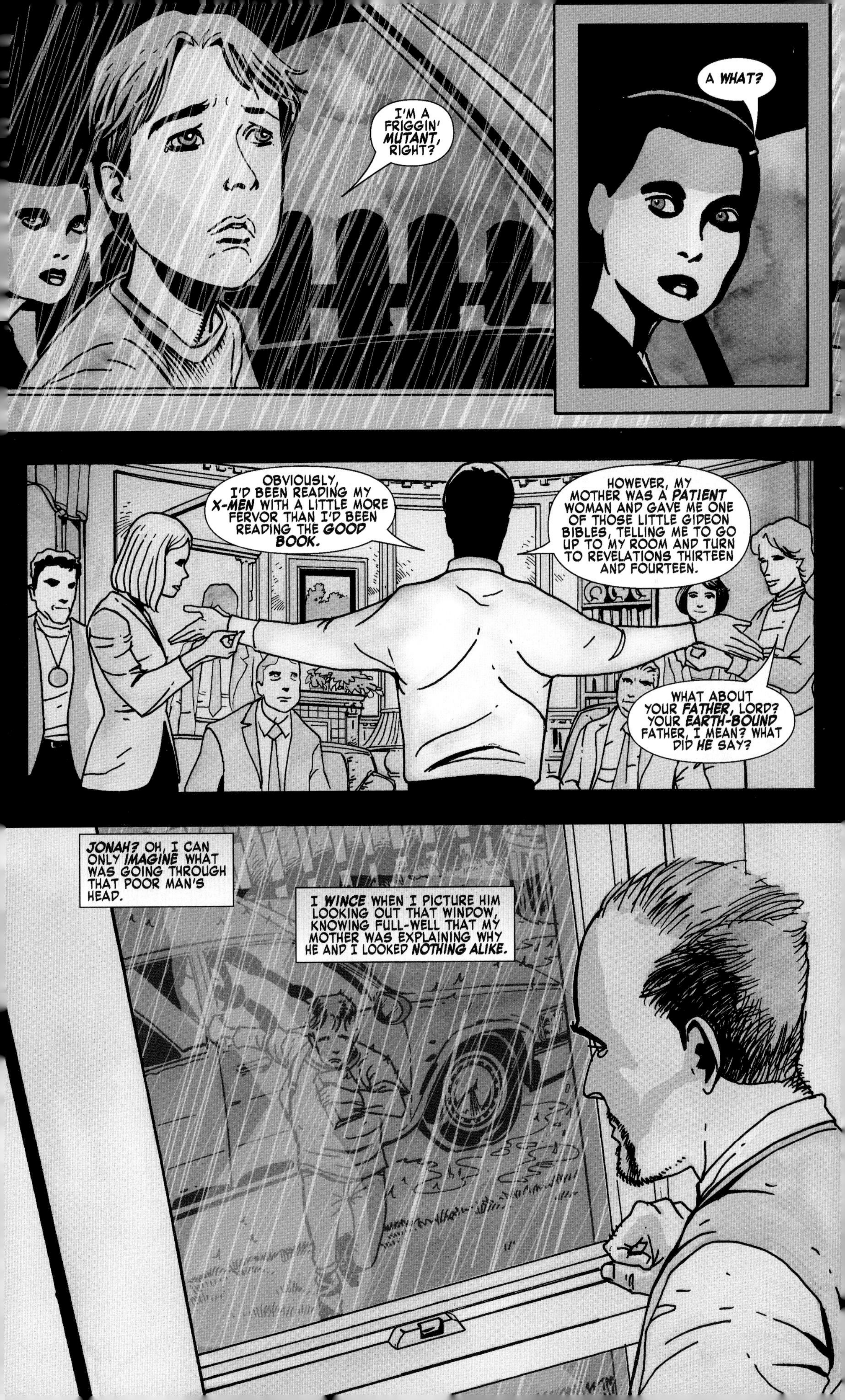
I'M A FRIGGIN' MUTANT, RIGHT?
A WHAT?
OBVIOUSLY, I'D BEEN READING MY X-MEN WITH A LITTLE MORE FERVOR THAN I'D BEEN READING THE GOOD BOOK.
HOWEVER, MY MOTHER WAS A PATIENT WOMAN AND GAVE ME ONE OF THOSE LITTLE GIDEON BIBLES, TELLING ME TO GO UP TO MY ROOM AND TURN TO REVELATIONS THIRTEEN AND FOURTEEN.
WHAT ABOUT YOUR FATHER, LORD? YOUR EARTH-BOUND FATHER, I MEAN? WHAT DID HE SAY?
JONAH? OH, I CAN ONLY IMAGINE WHAT WAS GOING THROUGH THAT POOR MAN'S HEAD.
I WINCE WHEN I PICTURE HIM LOOKING OUT THAT WINDOW, KNOWING FULL-WELL THAT MY MOTHER WAS EXPLAINING WHY HE AND I LOOKED NOTHING ALIKE.

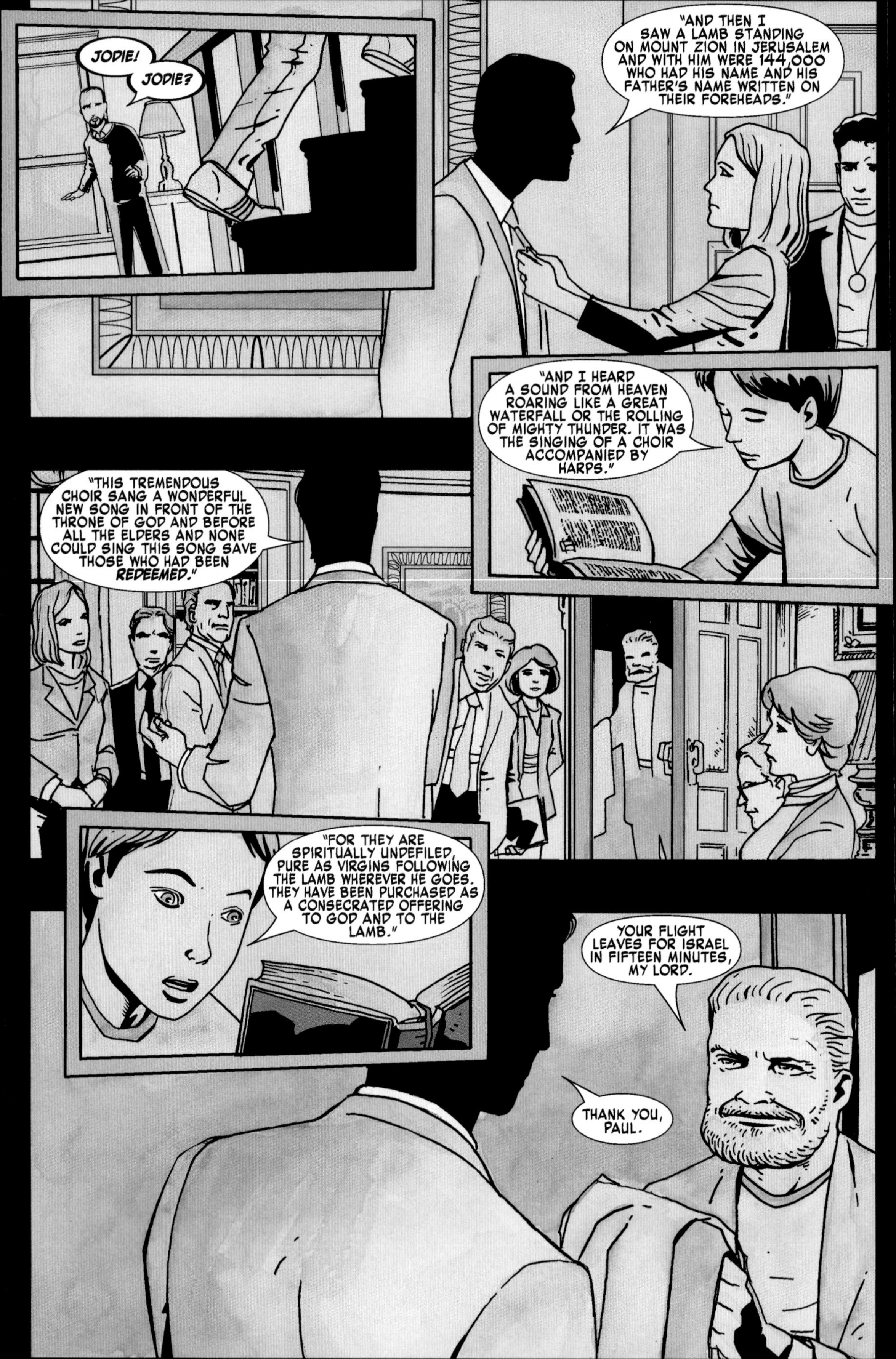
JODIE!
JODIE?
"AND THEN I SAW A LAMB STANDING ON MOUNT ZION IN JERUSALEM AND WITH HIM WERE 144,000 WHO HAD HIS NAME AND HIS FATHER'S NAME WRITTEN ON THEIR FOREHEADS."
"AND I HEARD A SOUND FROM HEAVEN ROARING LIKE A GREAT WATERFALL OR THE ROLLING OF MIGHTY THUNDER. IT WAS THE SINGING OF A CHOIR ACCOMPANIED BY HARPS."
"THIS TREMENDOUS CHOIR SANG A WONDERFUL NEW SONG IN FRONT OF THE THRONE OF GOD AND BEFORE ALL THE ELDERS AND NONE COULD SING THIS SONG SAVE THOSE WHO HAD BEEN *REDEEMED*."
"FOR THEY ARE SPIRITUALLY UNDEFILED, PURE AS VIRGINS FOLLOWING THE LAMB WHEREVER HE GOES. THEY HAVE BEEN PURCHASED AS A CONSECRATED OFFERING TO GOD AND TO THE LAMB."
YOUR FLIGHT LEAVES FOR ISRAEL IN FIFTEEN MINUTES, MY LORD.
THANK YOU, PAUL.

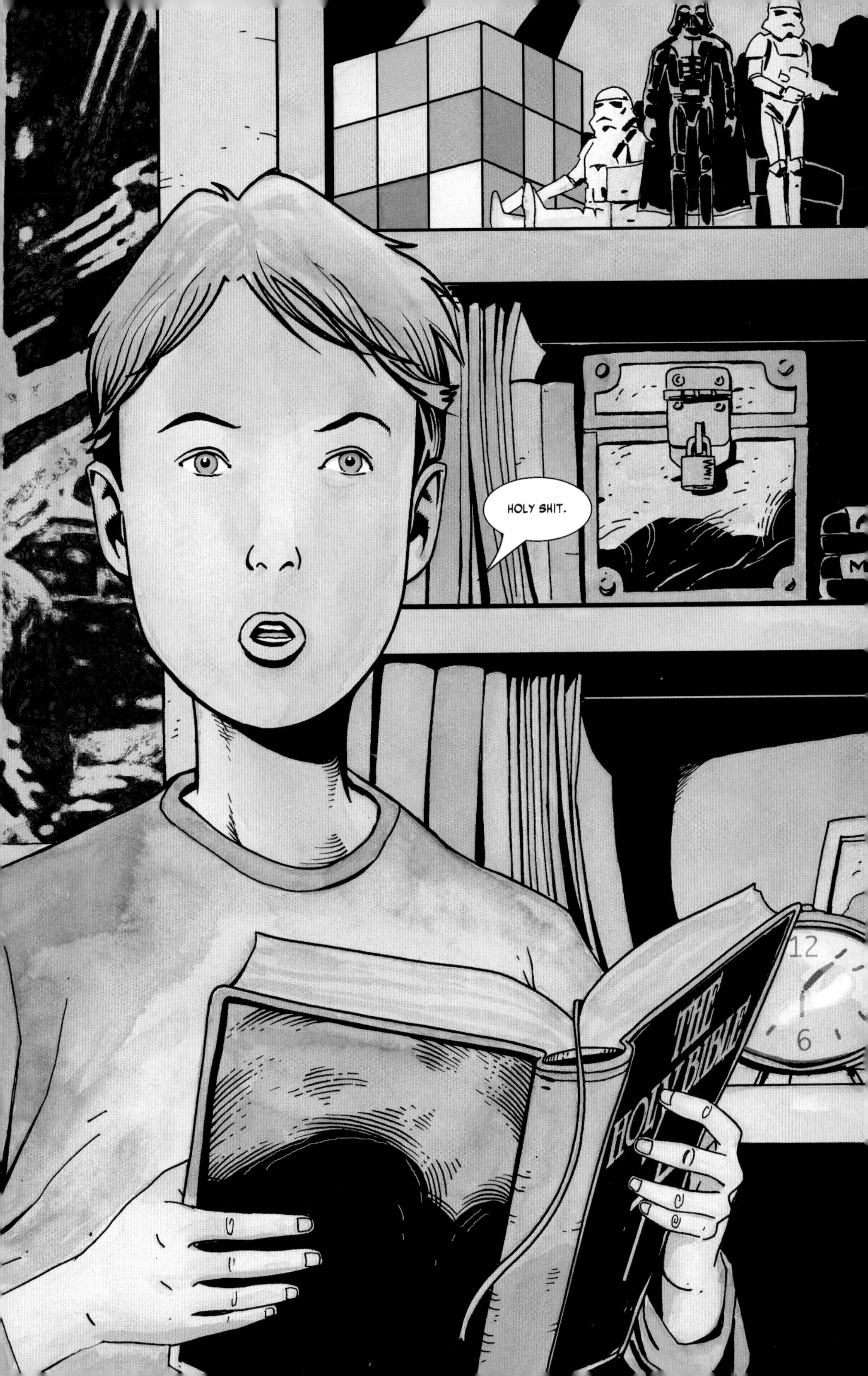
HOLY SHIT.
THE HOLY BIBLE

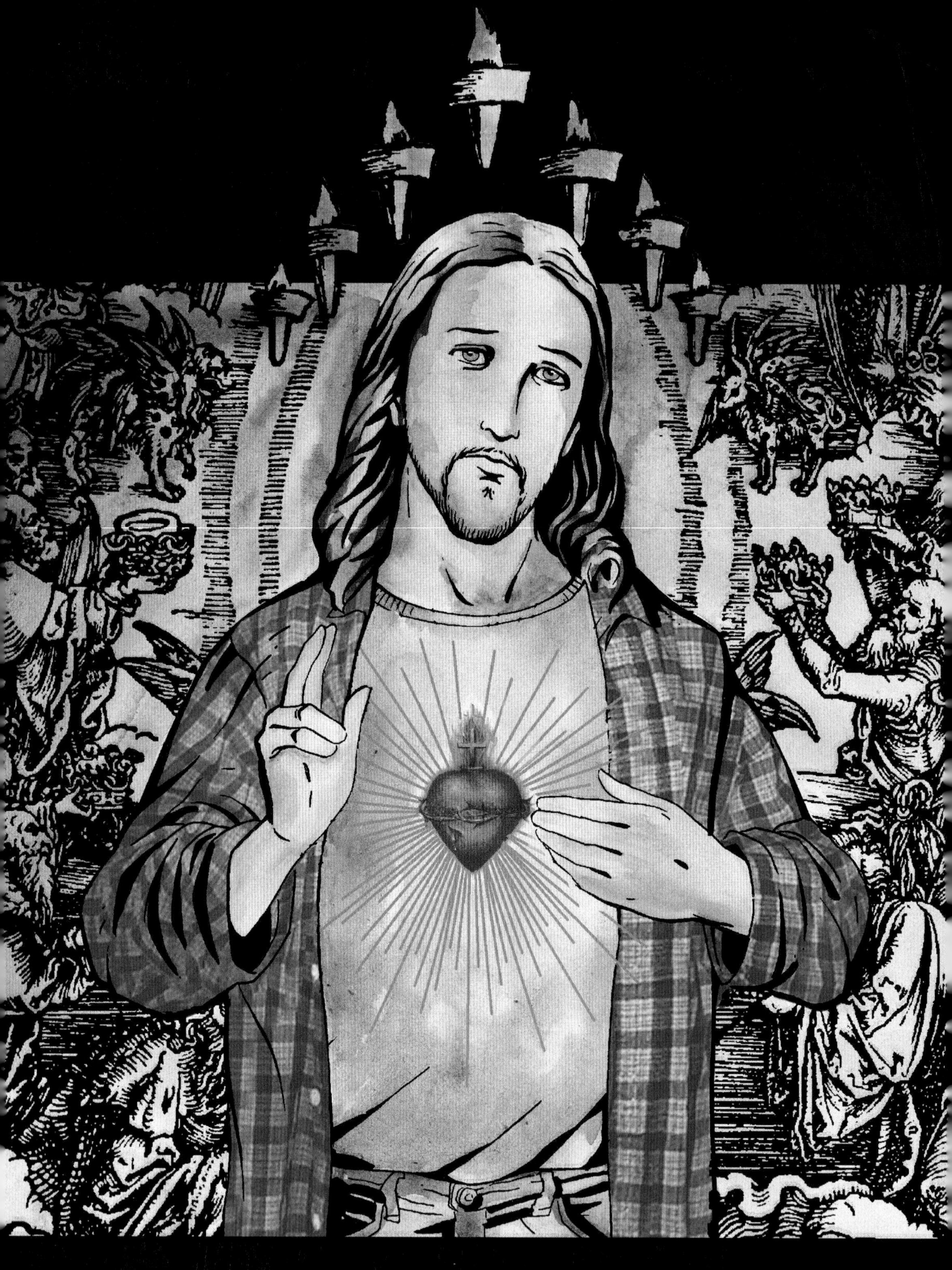

CHAPTER 2

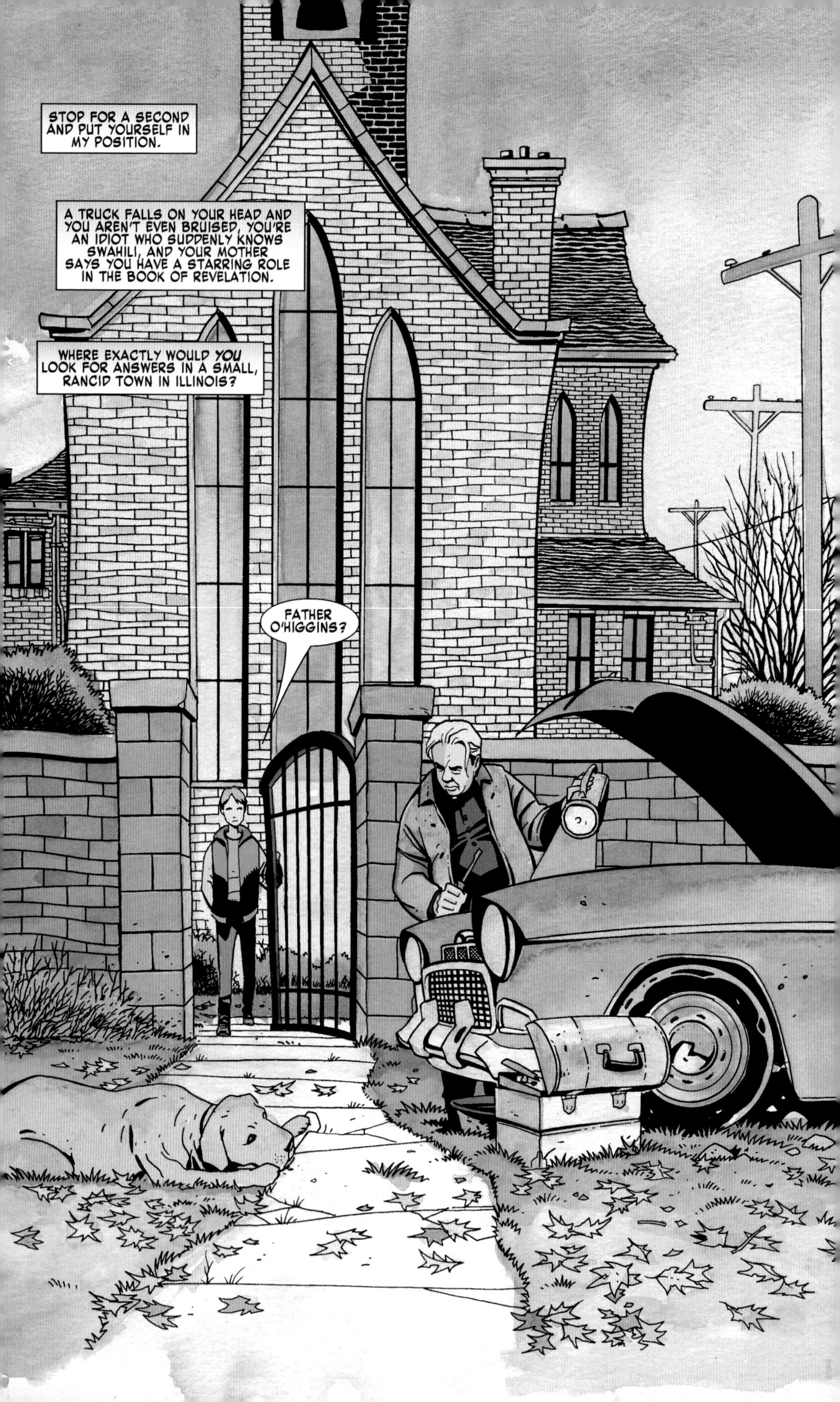

STOP FOR A SECOND AND PUT YOURSELF IN MY POSITION.
A TRUCK FALLS ON YOUR HEAD AND YOU AREN'T EVEN BRUISED, YOU'RE AN IDIOT WHO SUDDENLY KNOWS SWAHILI, AND YOUR MOTHER SAYS YOU HAVE A STARRING ROLE IN THE BOOK OF REVELATION.
WHERE EXACTLY WOULD *YOU* LOOK FOR ANSWERS IN A SMALL, RANCID TOWN IN ILLINOIS?
FATHER O'HIGGINS?

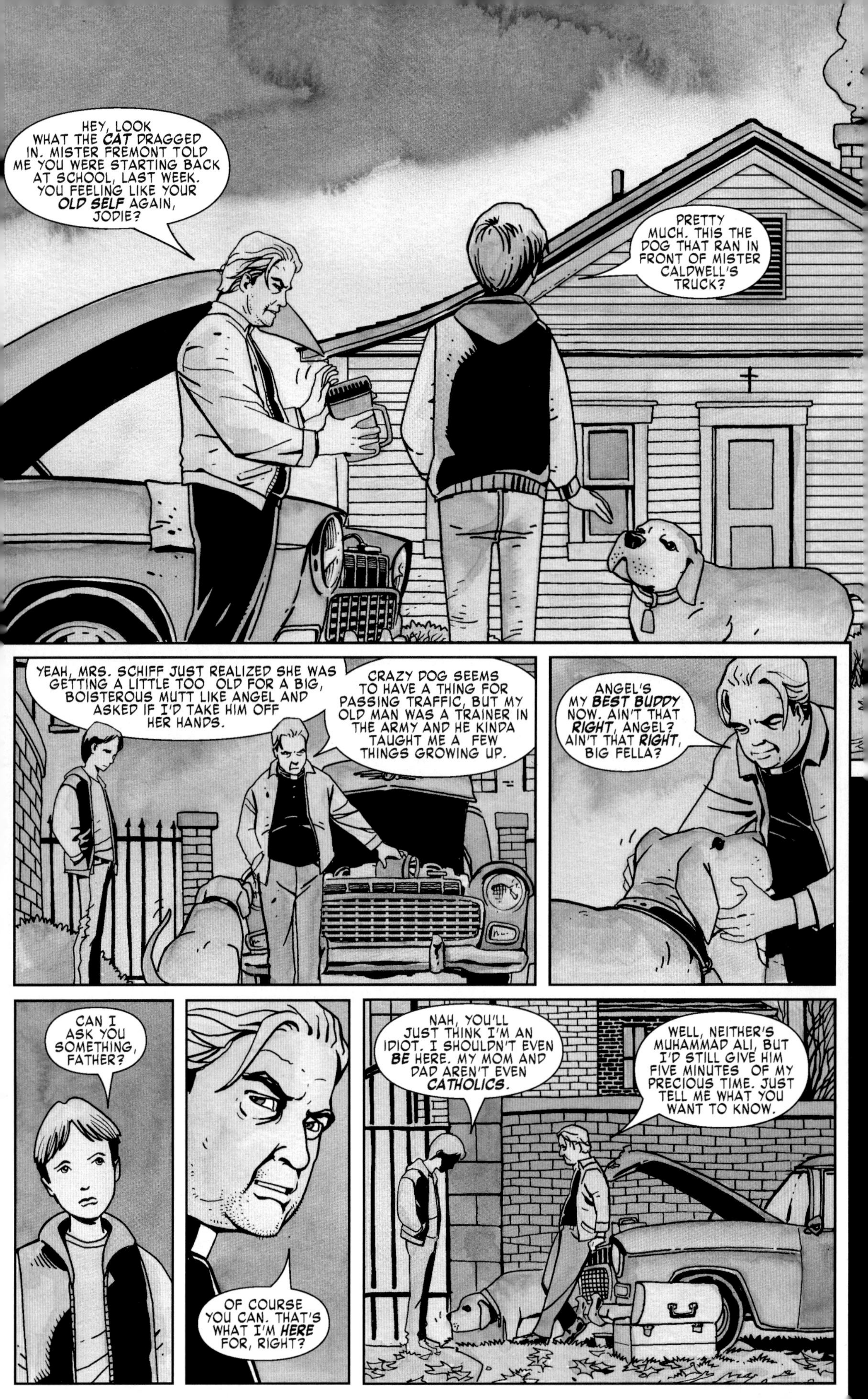
HEY, LOOK WHAT THE CAT DRAGGED IN. MISTER FREMONT TOLD ME YOU WERE STARTING BACK AT SCHOOL, LAST WEEK. YOU FEELING LIKE YOUR OLD SELF AGAIN, JODIE?
PRETTY MUCH. THIS THE DOG THAT RAN IN FRONT OF MISTER CALDWELL'S TRUCK?
YEAH, MRS. SCHIFF JUST REALIZED SHE WAS GETTING A LITTLE TOO OLD FOR A BIG, BOISTEROUS MUTT LIKE ANGEL AND ASKED IF I'D TAKE HIM OFF HER HANDS.
CRAZY DOG SEEMS TO HAVE A THING FOR PASSING TRAFFIC, BUT MY OLD MAN WAS A TRAINER IN THE ARMY AND HE KINDA TAUGHT ME A FEW THINGS GROWING UP.
ANGEL'S MY BEST BUDDY NOW. AIN'T THAT RIGHT, ANGEL? AIN'T THAT RIGHT, BIG FELLA?
CAN I ASK YOU SOMETHING, FATHER?
OF COURSE YOU CAN. THAT'S WHAT I'M HERE FOR, RIGHT?
NAH, YOU'LL JUST THINK I'M AN IDIOT. I SHOULDN'T EVEN BE HERE. MY MOM AND DAD AREN'T EVEN CATHOLICS.
WELL, NEITHER'S MUHAMMAD ALI, BUT I'D STILL GIVE HIM FIVE MINUTES OF MY PRECIOUS TIME. JUST TELL ME WHAT YOU WANT TO KNOW.

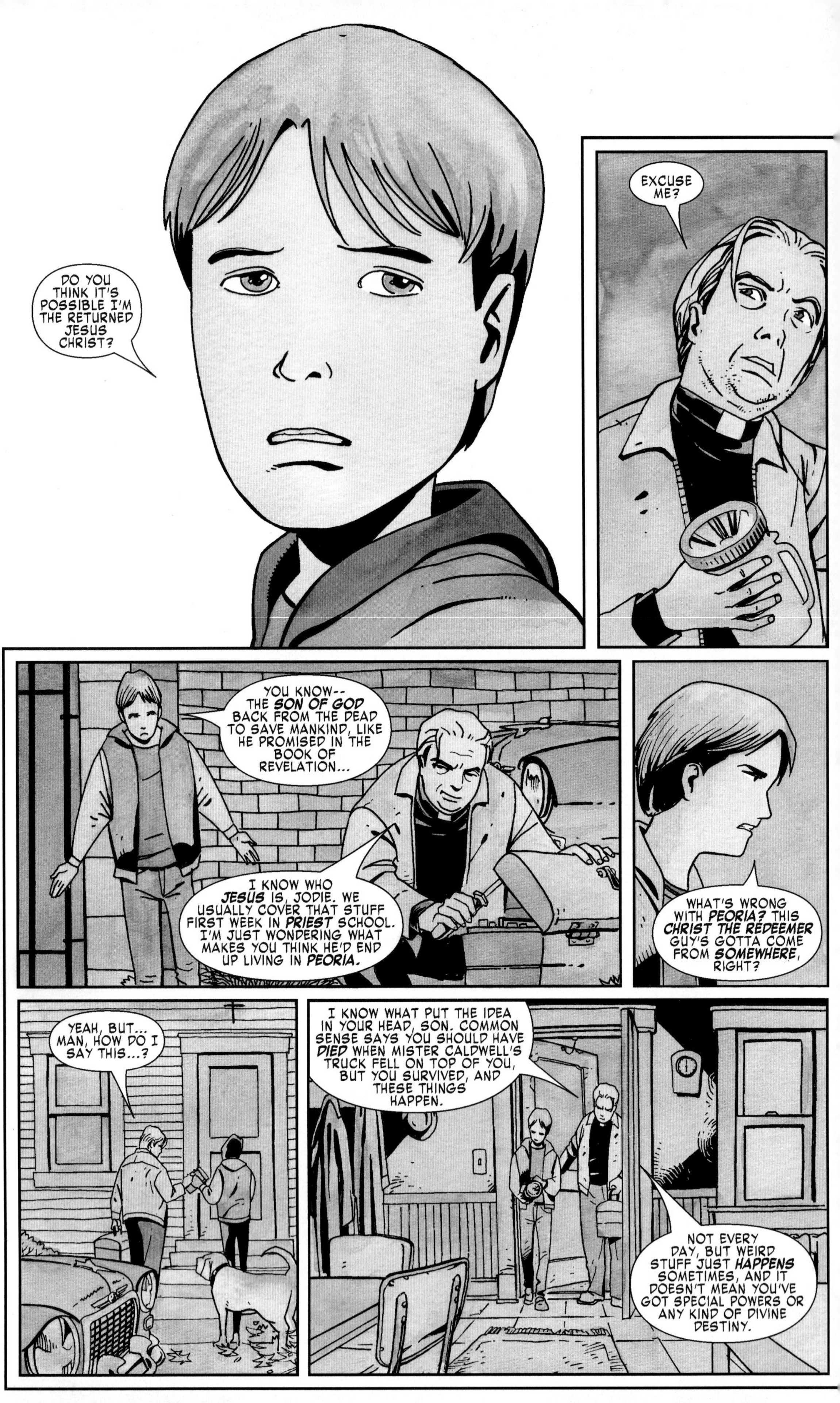
DO YOU THINK IT'S POSSIBLE I'M THE RETURNED JESUS CHRIST?
EXCUSE ME?
YOU KNOW-- THE SON OF GOD BACK FROM THE DEAD TO SAVE MANKIND, LIKE HE PROMISED IN THE BOOK OF REVELATION...
I KNOW WHO JESUS IS, JODIE. WE USUALLY COVER THAT STUFF FIRST WEEK IN PRIEST SCHOOL. I'M JUST WONDERING WHAT MAKES YOU THINK HE'D END UP LIVING IN PEORIA.
WHAT'S WRONG WITH PEORIA? THIS CHRIST THE REDEEMER GUY'S GOTTA COME FROM SOMEWHERE, RIGHT?
YEAH, BUT... MAN, HOW DO I SAY THIS...?
I KNOW WHAT PUT THE IDEA IN YOUR HEAD, SON. COMMON SENSE SAYS YOU SHOULD HAVE DIED WHEN MISTER CALDWELL'S TRUCK FELL ON TOP OF YOU, BUT YOU SURVIVED, AND THESE THINGS HAPPEN.
NOT EVERY DAY, BUT WEIRD STUFF JUST HAPPENS SOMETIMES, AND IT DOESN'T MEAN YOU'VE GOT SPECIAL POWERS OR ANY KIND OF DIVINE DESTINY.

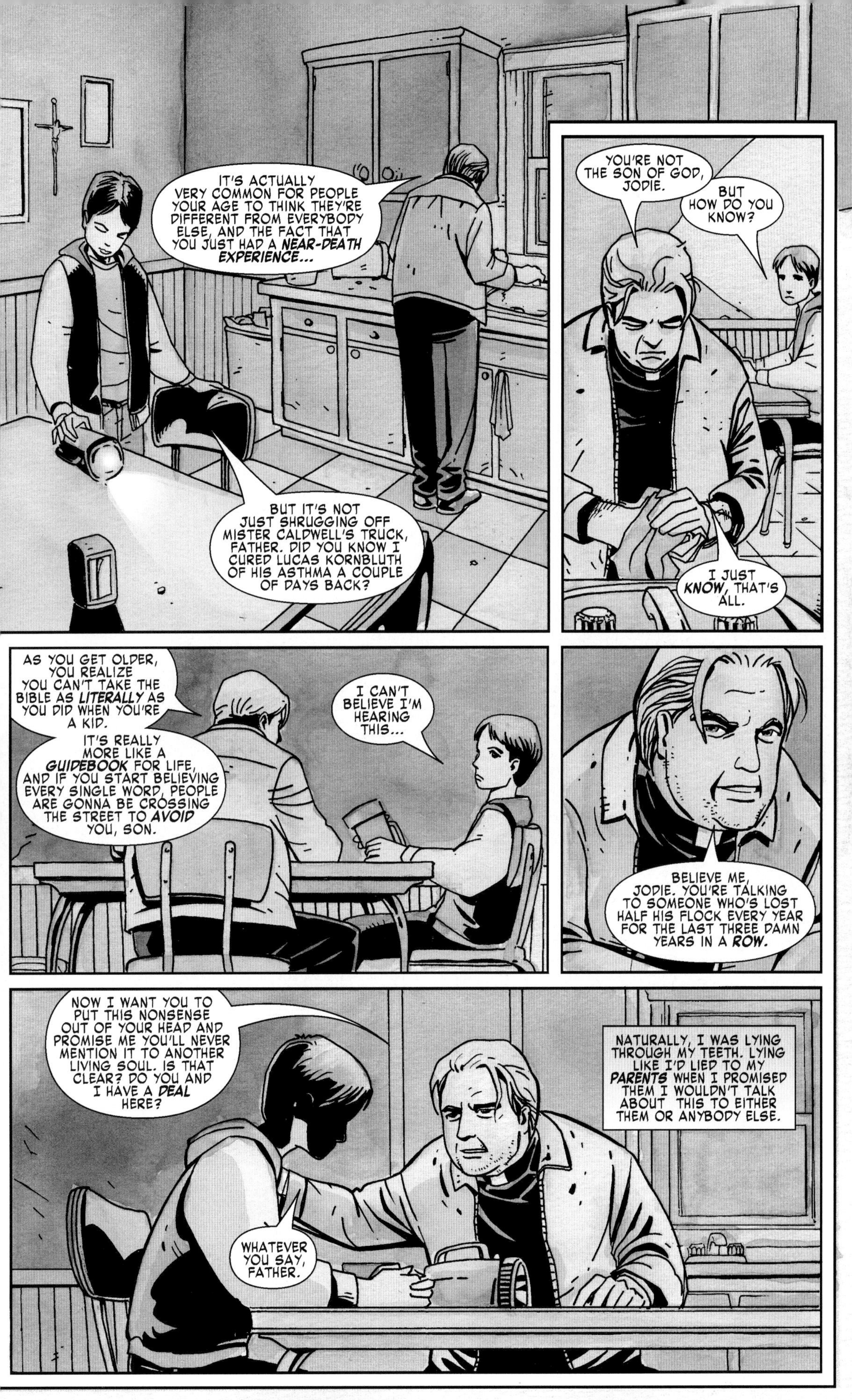
IT'S ACTUALLY VERY COMMON FOR PEOPLE YOUR AGE TO THINK THEY'RE DIFFERENT FROM EVERYBODY ELSE, AND THE FACT THAT YOU JUST HAD A NEAR-DEATH EXPERIENCE...
BUT IT'S NOT JUST SHRUGGING OFF MISTER CALDWELL'S TRUCK, FATHER. DID YOU KNOW I CURED LUCAS KORNBLUTH OF HIS ASTHMA A COUPLE OF DAYS BACK?
YOU'RE NOT THE SON OF GOD, JODIE.
BUT HOW DO YOU KNOW?
I JUST KNOW, THAT'S ALL.
AS YOU GET OLDER, YOU REALIZE YOU CAN'T TAKE THE BIBLE AS LITERALLY AS YOU DID WHEN YOU'RE A KID.
IT'S REALLY MORE LIKE A GUIDEBOOK FOR LIFE, AND IF YOU START BELIEVING EVERY SINGLE WORD, PEOPLE ARE GONNA BE CROSSING THE STREET TO AVOID YOU, SON.
I CAN'T BELIEVE I'M HEARING THIS...
BELIEVE ME, JODIE. YOU'RE TALKING TO SOMEONE WHO'S LOST HALF HIS FLOCK EVERY YEAR FOR THE LAST THREE DAMN YEARS IN A ROW.
NOW I WANT YOU TO PUT THIS NONSENSE OUT OF YOUR HEAD AND PROMISE ME YOU'LL NEVER MENTION IT TO ANOTHER LIVING SOUL. IS THAT CLEAR? DO YOU AND I HAVE A DEAL HERE?
NATURALLY, I WAS LYING THROUGH MY TEETH. LYING LIKE I'D LIED TO MY PARENTS WHEN I PROMISED THEM I WOULDN'T TALK ABOUT THIS TO EITHER THEM OR ANYBODY ELSE.
WHATEVER YOU SAY, FATHER.

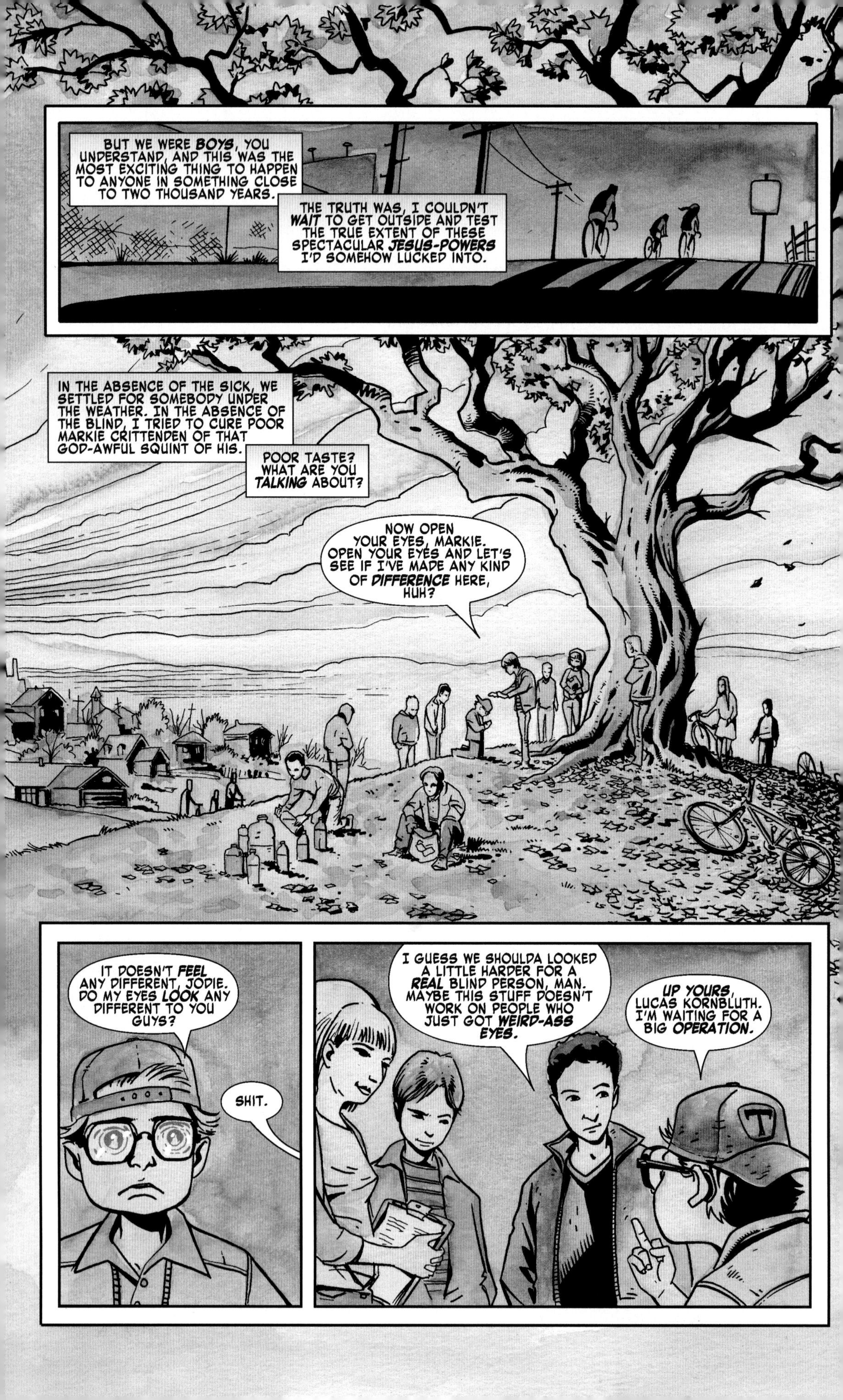
BUT WE WERE BOYS, YOU UNDERSTAND, AND THIS WAS THE MOST EXCITING THING TO HAPPEN TO ANYONE IN SOMETHING CLOSE TO TWO THOUSAND YEARS.
THE TRUTH WAS, I COULDN'T WAIT TO GET OUTSIDE AND TEST THE TRUE EXTENT OF THESE SPECTACULAR JESUS-POWERS I'D SOMEHOW LUCKED INTO.
IN THE ABSENCE OF THE SICK, WE SETTLED FOR SOMEBODY UNDER THE WEATHER. IN THE ABSENCE OF THE BLIND, I TRIED TO CURE POOR MARKIE CRITTENDEN OF THAT GOD-AWFUL SQUINT OF HIS.
POOR TASTE? WHAT ARE YOU TALKING ABOUT?
NOW OPEN YOUR EYES, MARKIE. OPEN YOUR EYES AND LET'S SEE IF I'VE MADE ANY KIND OF DIFFERENCE HERE, HUH?
IT DOESN'T FEEL ANY DIFFERENT, JODIE. DO MY EYES LOOK ANY DIFFERENT TO YOU GUYS?
SHIT.
I GUESS WE SHOULDA LOOKED A LITTLE HARDER FOR A REAL BLIND PERSON, MAN. MAYBE THIS STUFF DOESN'T WORK ON PEOPLE WHO JUST GOT WEIRD-ASS EYES.
UP YOURS, LUCAS KORNBLUTH. I'M WAITING FOR A BIG OPERATION.

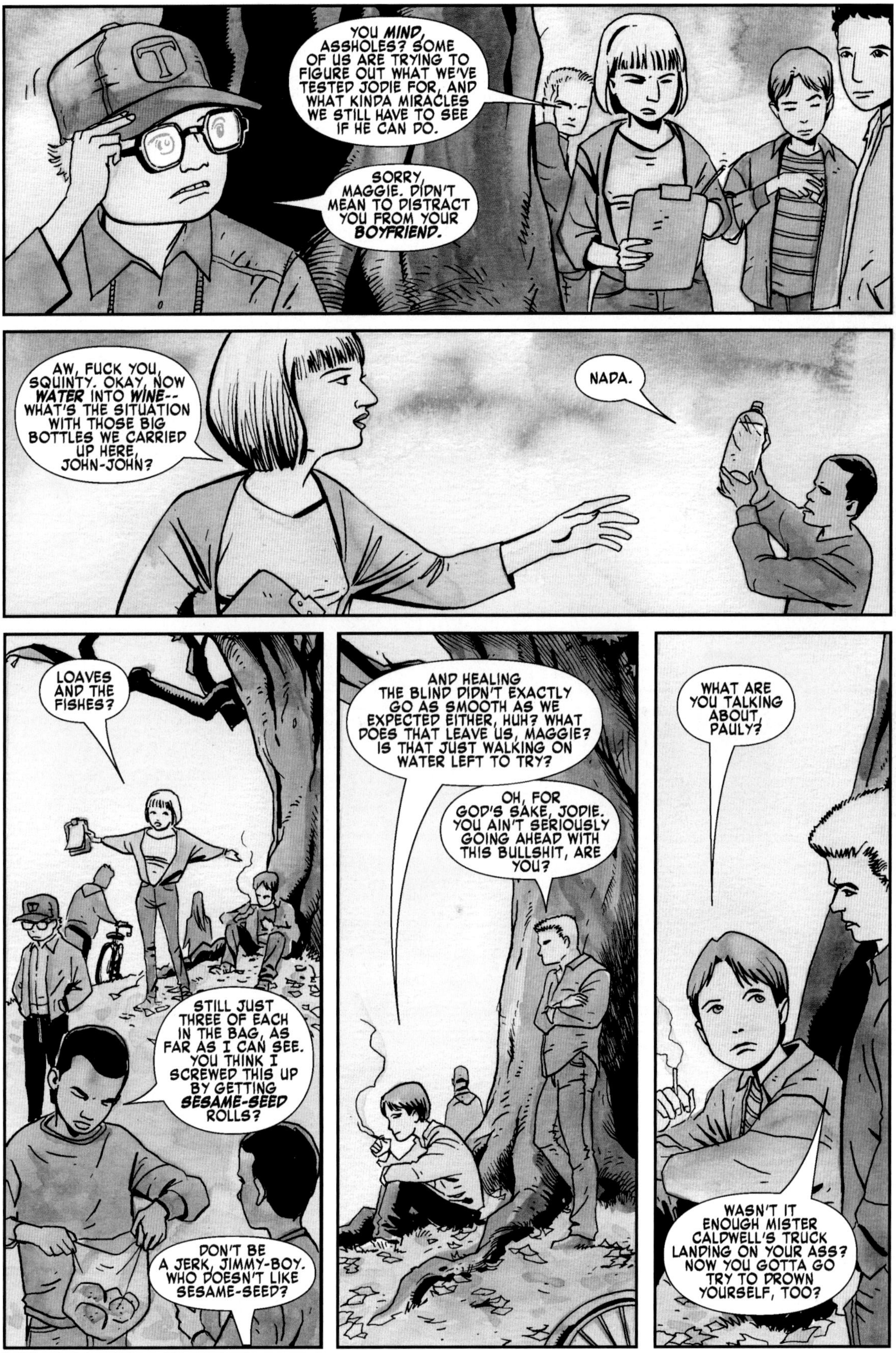
YOU MIND, ASSHOLES? SOME OF US ARE TRYING TO FIGURE OUT WHAT WE'VE TESTED JODIE FOR, AND WHAT KINDA MIRACLES WE STILL HAVE TO SEE IF HE CAN DO.
SORRY, MAGGIE. DIDN'T MEAN TO DISTRACT YOU FROM YOUR BOYFRIEND.
AW, FUCK YOU, SQUINTY. OKAY, NOW WATER INTO WINE-- WHAT'S THE SITUATION WITH THOSE BIG BOTTLES WE CARRIED UP HERE, JOHN-JOHN?
NADA.
LOAVES AND THE FISHES?
STILL JUST THREE OF EACH IN THE BAG, AS FAR AS I CAN SEE. YOU THINK I SCREWED THIS UP BY GETTING SESAME-SEED ROLLS?
DON'T BE A JERK, JIMMY-BOY. WHO DOESN'T LIKE SESAME-SEED?
AND HEALING THE BLIND DIDN'T EXACTLY GO AS SMOOTH AS WE EXPECTED EITHER, HUH? WHAT DOES THAT LEAVE US, MAGGIE? IS THAT JUST WALKING ON WATER LEFT TO TRY?
OH, FOR GOD'S SAKE, JODIE. YOU AIN'T SERIOUSLY GOING AHEAD WITH THIS BULLSHIT, ARE YOU?
WHAT ARE YOU TALKING ABOUT, PAULY?
WASN'T IT ENOUGH MISTER CALDWELL'S TRUCK LANDING ON YOUR ASS? NOW YOU GOTTA GO TRY TO DROWN YOURSELF, TOO?

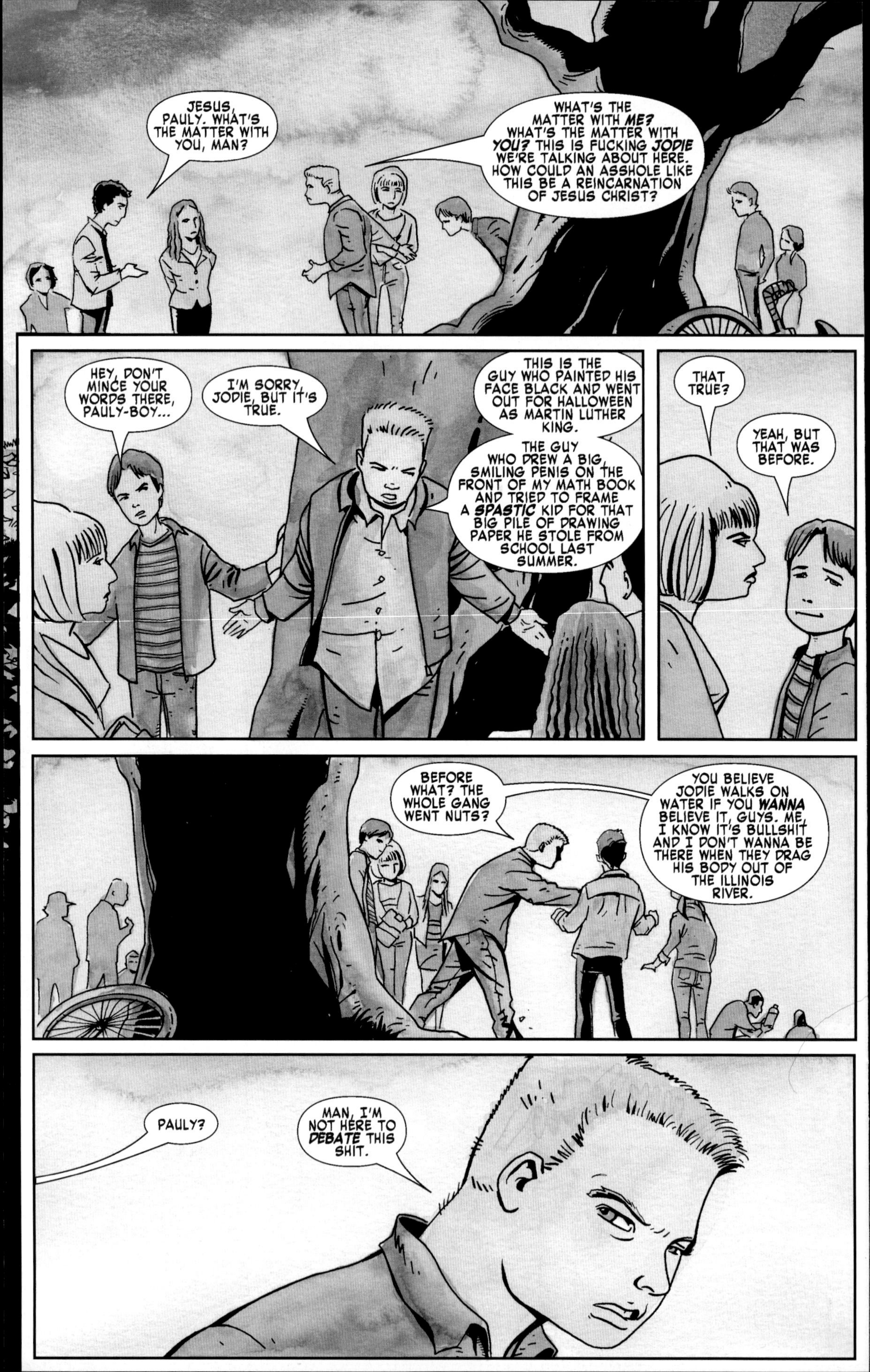
JESUS, PAULY. WHAT'S THE MATTER WITH YOU, MAN?
WHAT'S THE MATTER WITH ME? WHAT'S THE MATTER WITH YOU? THIS IS FUCKING JODIE WE'RE TALKING ABOUT HERE. HOW COULD AN ASSHOLE LIKE THIS BE A REINCARNATION OF JESUS CHRIST?
HEY, DON'T MINCE YOUR WORDS THERE, PAULY-BOY...
I'M SORRY, JODIE, BUT IT'S TRUE.
THIS IS THE GUY WHO PAINTED HIS FACE BLACK AND WENT OUT FOR HALLOWEEN AS MARTIN LUTHER KING.
THE GUY WHO DREW A BIG, SMILING PENIS ON THE FRONT OF MY MATH BOOK AND TRIED TO FRAME A SPASTIC KID FOR THAT BIG PILE OF DRAWING PAPER HE STOLE FROM SCHOOL LAST SUMMER.
THAT TRUE?
YEAH, BUT THAT WAS BEFORE.
BEFORE WHAT? THE WHOLE GANG WENT NUTS?
YOU BELIEVE JODIE WALKS ON WATER IF YOU WANNA BELIEVE IT, GUYS. ME, I KNOW IT'S BULLSHIT AND I DON'T WANNA BE THERE WHEN THEY DRAG HIS BODY OUT OF THE ILLINOIS RIVER.
PAULY?
MAN, I'M NOT HERE TO DEBATE THIS SHIT.

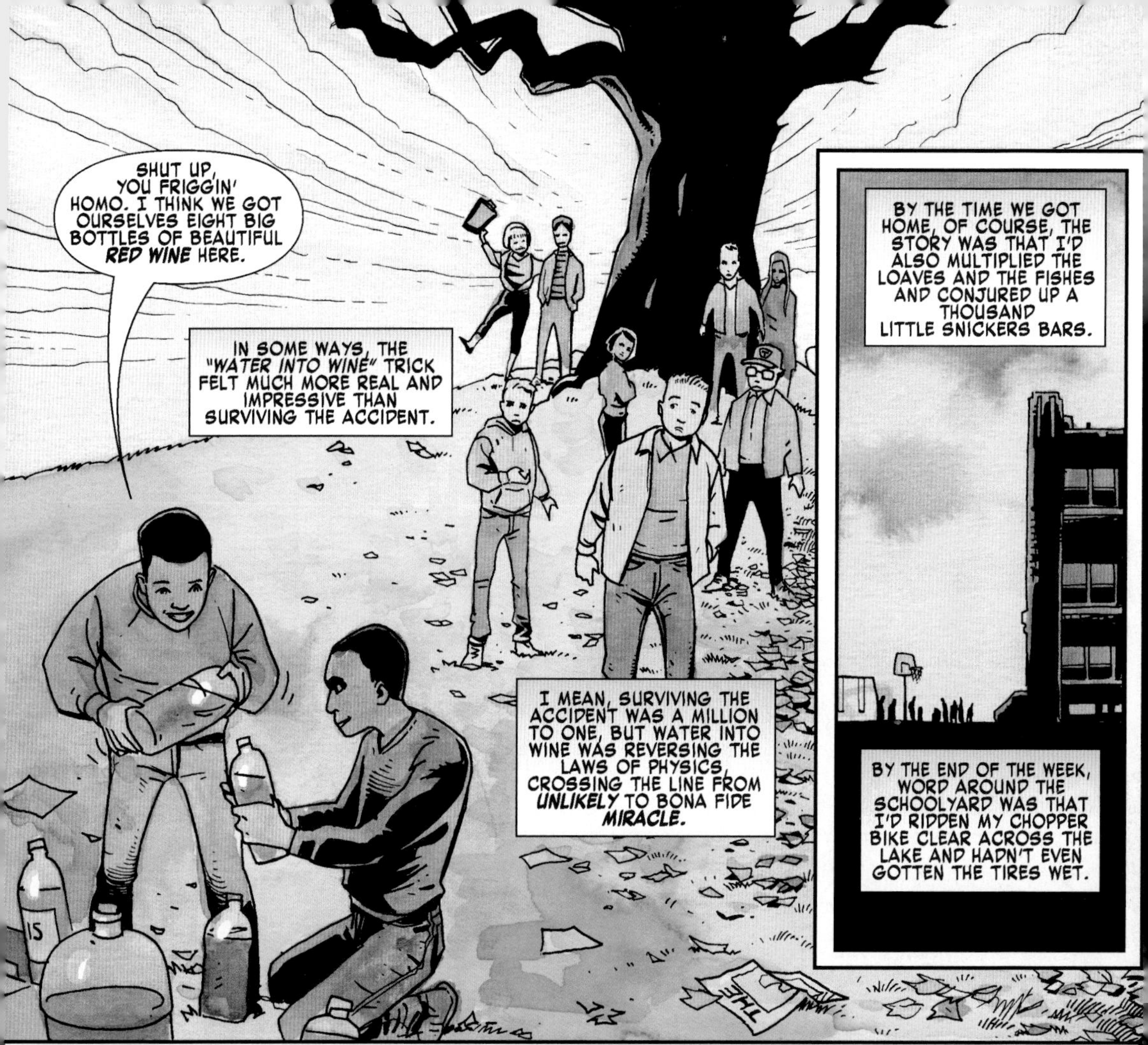
SHUT UP, YOU FRIGGIN' HOMO. I THINK WE GOT OURSELVES EIGHT BIG BOTTLES OF BEAUTIFUL **RED WINE** HERE.
IN SOME WAYS, THE *"WATER INTO WINE"* TRICK FELT MUCH MORE REAL AND IMPRESSIVE THAN SURVIVING THE ACCIDENT.
I MEAN, SURVIVING THE ACCIDENT WAS A MILLION TO ONE, BUT WATER INTO WINE WAS REVERSING THE LAWS OF PHYSICS, CROSSING THE LINE FROM **UNLIKELY** TO BONA FIDE **MIRACLE.**
BY THE TIME WE GOT HOME, OF COURSE, THE STORY WAS THAT I'D ALSO MULTIPLIED THE LOAVES AND THE FISHES AND CONJURED UP A THOUSAND LITTLE SNICKERS BARS.
BY THE END OF THE WEEK, WORD AROUND THE SCHOOLYARD WAS THAT I'D RIDDEN MY CHOPPER BIKE CLEAR ACROSS THE LAKE AND HADN'T EVEN GOTTEN THE TIRES WET.

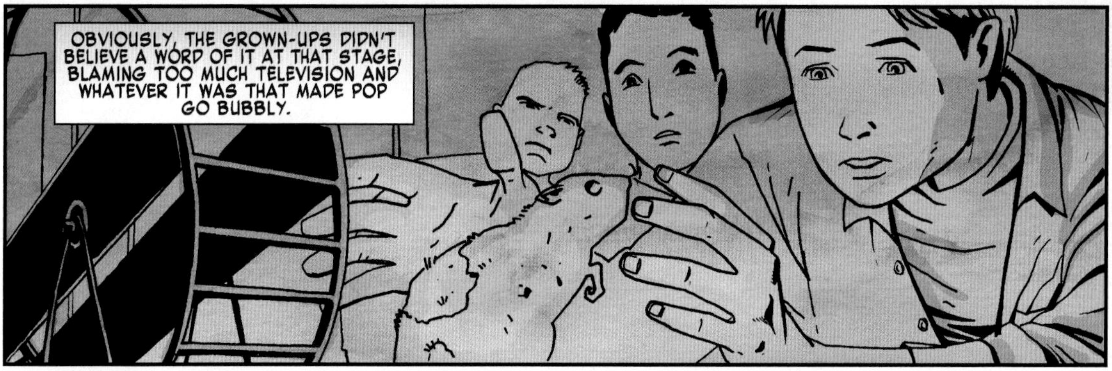
OBVIOUSLY, THE GROWN-UPS DIDN'T BELIEVE A WORD OF IT AT THAT STAGE, BLAMING TOO MUCH TELEVISION AND WHATEVER IT WAS THAT MADE POP GO BUBBLY.

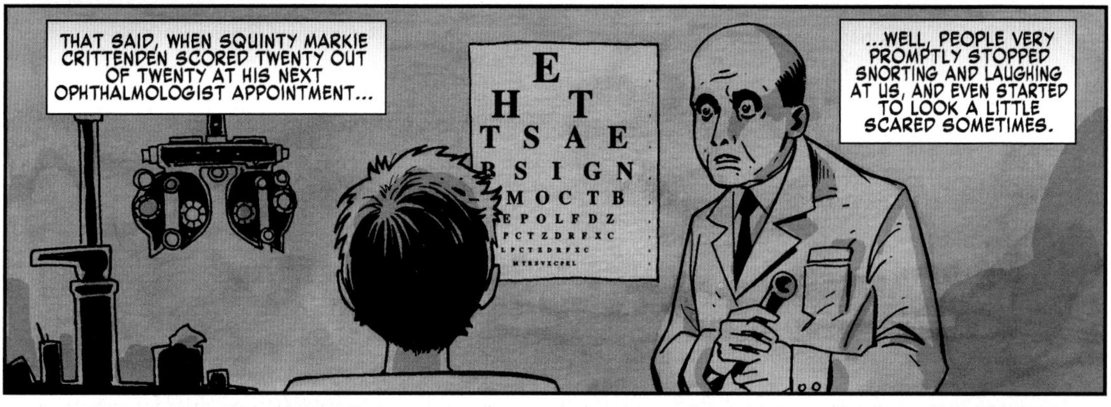
THAT SAID, WHEN SQUINTY MARKIE CRITTENDEN SCORED TWENTY OUT OF TWENTY AT HIS NEXT OPHTHALMOLOGIST APPOINTMENT...
E
H T
T S A E
S I G N
M O C T B
...WELL, PEOPLE VERY PROMPTLY STOPPED SNORTING AND LAUGHING AT US, AND EVEN STARTED TO LOOK A LITTLE SCARED SOMETIMES.

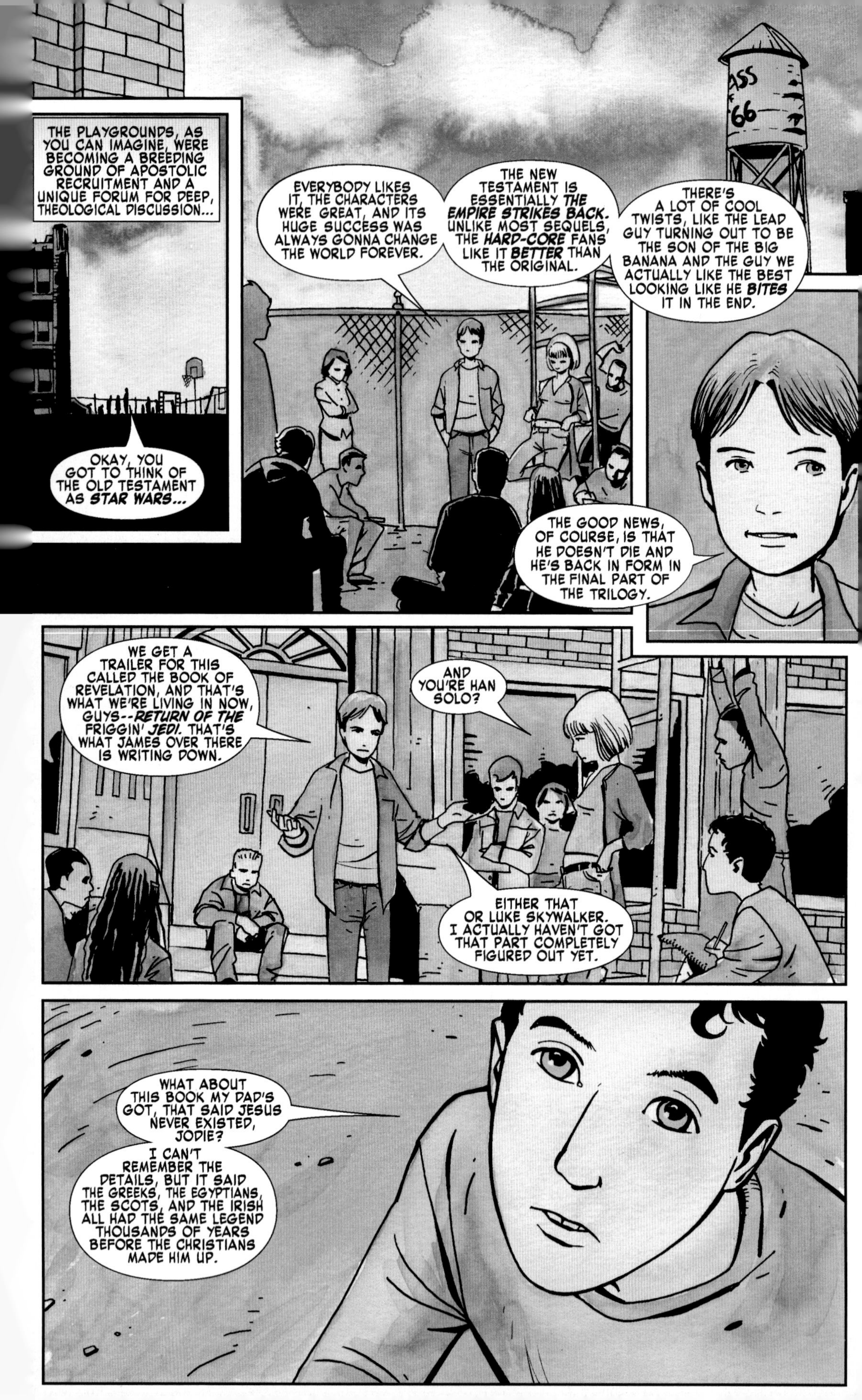
THE PLAYGROUNDS, AS YOU CAN IMAGINE, WERE BECOMING A BREEDING GROUND OF APOSTOLIC RECRUITMENT AND A UNIQUE FORUM FOR DEEP, THEOLOGICAL DISCUSSION...
OKAY, YOU GOT TO THINK OF THE OLD TESTAMENT AS STAR WARS...
EVERYBODY LIKES IT, THE CHARACTERS WERE GREAT, AND ITS HUGE SUCCESS WAS ALWAYS GONNA CHANGE THE WORLD FOREVER.
THE NEW TESTAMENT IS ESSENTIALLY THE EMPIRE STRIKES BACK. UNLIKE MOST SEQUELS, THE HARD-CORE FANS LIKE IT BETTER THAN THE ORIGINAL.
THERE'S A LOT OF COOL TWISTS, LIKE THE LEAD GUY TURNING OUT TO BE THE SON OF THE BIG BANANA AND THE GUY WE ACTUALLY LIKE THE BEST LOOKING LIKE HE BITES IT IN THE END.
THE GOOD NEWS, OF COURSE, IS THAT HE DOESN'T DIE AND HE'S BACK IN FORM IN THE FINAL PART OF THE TRILOGY.
WE GET A TRAILER FOR THIS CALLED THE BOOK OF REVELATION, AND THAT'S WHAT WE'RE LIVING IN NOW, GUYS--RETURN OF THE FRIGGIN' JEDI. THAT'S WHAT JAMES OVER THERE IS WRITING DOWN.
AND YOU'RE HAN SOLO?
EITHER THAT OR LUKE SKYWALKER. I ACTUALLY HAVEN'T GOT THAT PART COMPLETELY FIGURED OUT YET.
WHAT ABOUT THIS BOOK MY DAD'S GOT, THAT SAID JESUS NEVER EXISTED, JODIE?
I CAN'T REMEMBER THE DETAILS, BUT IT SAID THE GREEKS, THE EGYPTIANS, THE SCOTS, AND THE IRISH ALL HAD THE SAME LEGEND THOUSANDS OF YEARS BEFORE THE CHRISTIANS MADE HIM UP.

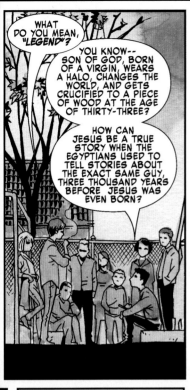

WHAT DO YOU MEAN, *"LEGEND"*?

YOU KNOW-- SON OF GOD, BORN OF A VIRGIN, WEARS A HALO, CHANGES THE WORLD, AND GETS CRUCIFIED TO A PIECE OF WOOD AT THE AGE OF THIRTY-THREE?

HOW CAN JESUS BE A TRUE STORY WHEN THE EGYPTIANS USED TO TELL STORIES ABOUT THE EXACT SAME GUY, THREE THOUSAND YEARS BEFORE JESUS WAS EVEN BORN?

I DUNNO.

WHAT ABOUT ALL THE OTHER BIG RELIGIONS, JODIE? WHAT DO YOU SAY TO ALL THE MILLIONS OF MUSLIMS AND JEWS AND HINDUS AND WHATEVER YOU CALL THOSE GUYS WHO WEAR THE TURBANS, MAN?

YEAH, DOES THE FACT THAT YOU EXIST MEAN THEIR RELIGIONS DON'T *COUNT* ANYMORE?

NOT MY FAULT THOSE GUYS ALL BACKED THE WRONG HORSE.

UNFORTUNATELY, NOT EVERYBODY SEEMED TO THINK THE SUN SHONE OUT OF MY SKINNY LITTLE POSTERIOR BACK IN THOSE DAYS.

YOU SEE THIS KID? RECOGNIZE THE FACE? THIS IS PETEY CALDWELL, OLDEST SON OF THAT CERTAIN *MISTER* CALDWELL WHO DROPPED HIS TRUCK ON MY HEAD SOME WEEKS BEFORE.

EVERYBODY KNEW IT WASN'T *MY* FAULT HIS DAD WAS LYING IN A COMA, BUT PETEY NEEDED SOMEBODY TO BLAME FOR THE FACT THAT HE WAS EATING SPAGHETTI-O'S FOR DINNER EVERY NIGHT.

WHAT'S THE *MATTER*, JESUS? YOU NOT GONNA TURN THE *OTHER* CHEEK? YOU NOT GONNA LET US KICK THE OTHER HALF'A YOUR ASS WHILE WE'RE HERE?

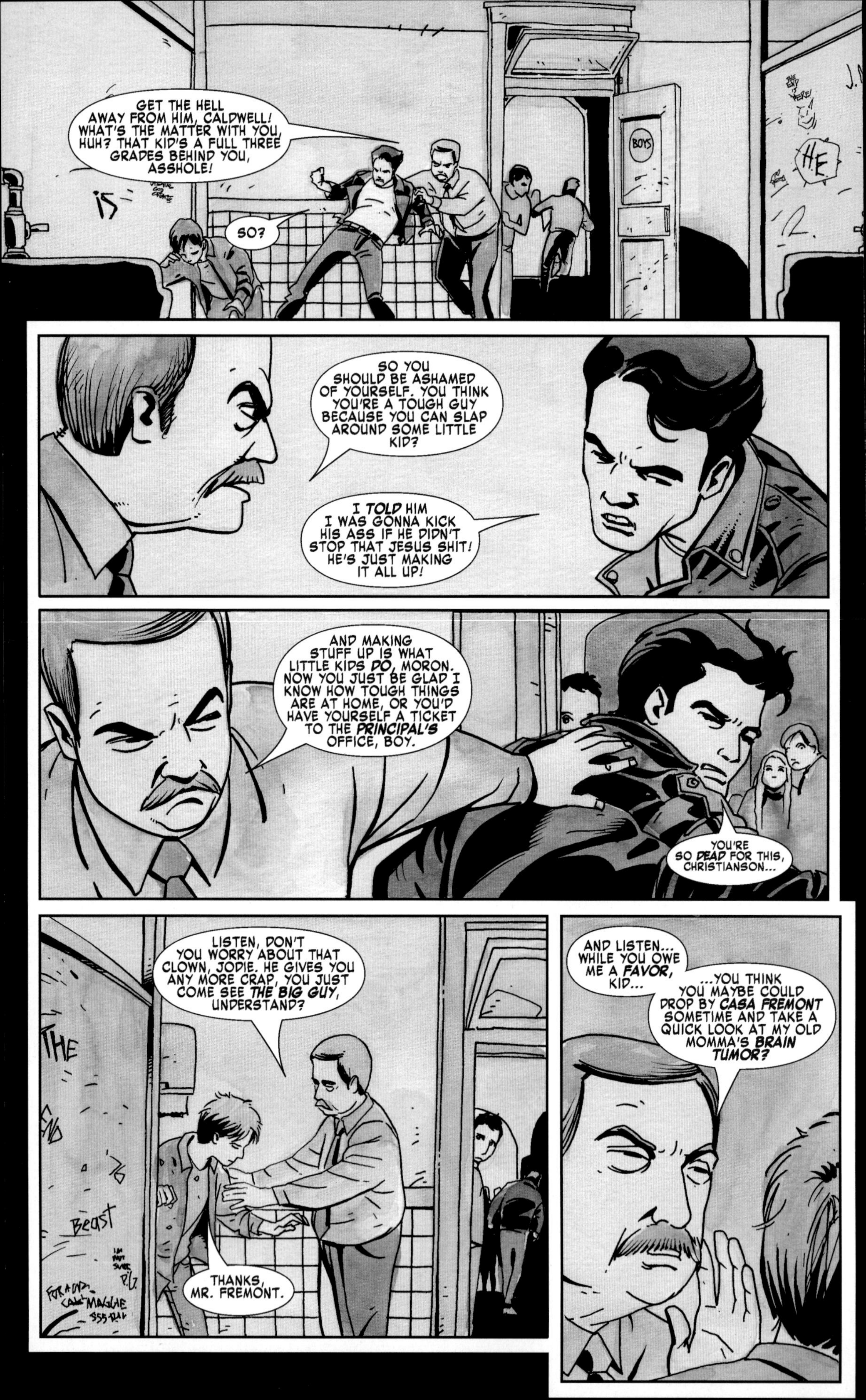

GET THE HELL AWAY FROM HIM, CALDWELL! WHAT'S THE MATTER WITH YOU, HUH? THAT KID'S A FULL THREE GRADES BEHIND YOU, ASSHOLE!
SO?
SO YOU SHOULD BE ASHAMED OF YOURSELF. YOU THINK YOU'RE A TOUGH GUY BECAUSE YOU CAN SLAP AROUND SOME LITTLE KID?
I TOLD HIM I WAS GONNA KICK HIS ASS IF HE DIDN'T STOP THAT JESUS SHIT! HE'S JUST MAKING IT ALL UP!
AND MAKING STUFF UP IS WHAT LITTLE KIDS DO, MORON. NOW YOU JUST BE GLAD I KNOW HOW TOUGH THINGS ARE AT HOME, OR YOU'D HAVE YOURSELF A TICKET TO THE PRINCIPAL'S OFFICE, BOY.
YOU'RE SO DEAD FOR THIS, CHRISTIANSON...
LISTEN, DON'T YOU WORRY ABOUT THAT CLOWN, JODIE. HE GIVES YOU ANY MORE CRAP, YOU JUST COME SEE THE BIG GUY, UNDERSTAND?
THANKS, MR. FREMONT.
AND LISTEN... WHILE YOU OWE ME A FAVOR, KID...
...YOU THINK YOU MAYBE COULD DROP BY CASA FREMONT SOMETIME AND TAKE A QUICK LOOK AT MY OLD MOMMA'S BRAIN TUMOR?

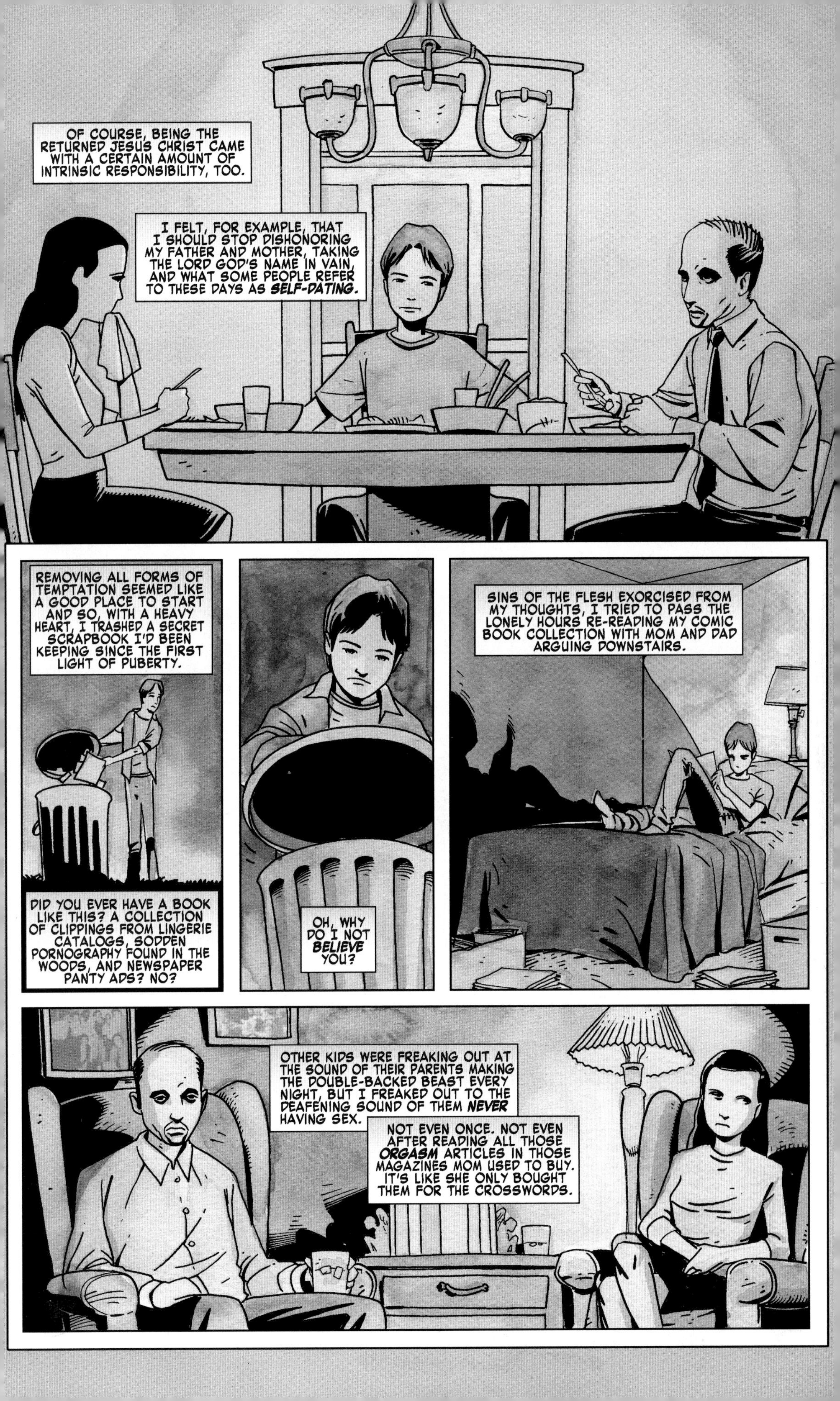
OF COURSE, BEING THE RETURNED JESUS CHRIST CAME WITH A CERTAIN AMOUNT OF INTRINSIC RESPONSIBILITY, TOO.
I FELT, FOR EXAMPLE, THAT I SHOULD STOP DISHONORING MY FATHER AND MOTHER, TAKING THE LORD GOD'S NAME IN VAIN, AND WHAT SOME PEOPLE REFER TO THESE DAYS AS SELF-DATING.
REMOVING ALL FORMS OF TEMPTATION SEEMED LIKE A GOOD PLACE TO START AND SO, WITH A HEAVY HEART, I TRASHED A SECRET SCRAPBOOK I'D BEEN KEEPING SINCE THE FIRST LIGHT OF PUBERTY.
DID YOU EVER HAVE A BOOK LIKE THIS? A COLLECTION OF CLIPPINGS FROM LINGERIE CATALOGS, SODDEN PORNOGRAPHY FOUND IN THE WOODS, AND NEWSPAPER PANTY ADS? NO?
OH, WHY DO I NOT BELIEVE YOU?
SINS OF THE FLESH EXORCISED FROM MY THOUGHTS, I TRIED TO PASS THE LONELY HOURS RE-READING MY COMIC BOOK COLLECTION WITH MOM AND DAD ARGUING DOWNSTAIRS.
OTHER KIDS WERE FREAKING OUT AT THE SOUND OF THEIR PARENTS MAKING THE DOUBLE-BACKED BEAST EVERY NIGHT, BUT I FREAKED OUT TO THE DEAFENING SOUND OF THEM NEVER HAVING SEX.
NOT EVEN ONCE. NOT EVEN AFTER READING ALL THOSE ORGASM ARTICLES IN THOSE MAGAZINES MOM USED TO BUY. IT'S LIKE SHE ONLY BOUGHT THEM FOR THE CROSSWORDS.

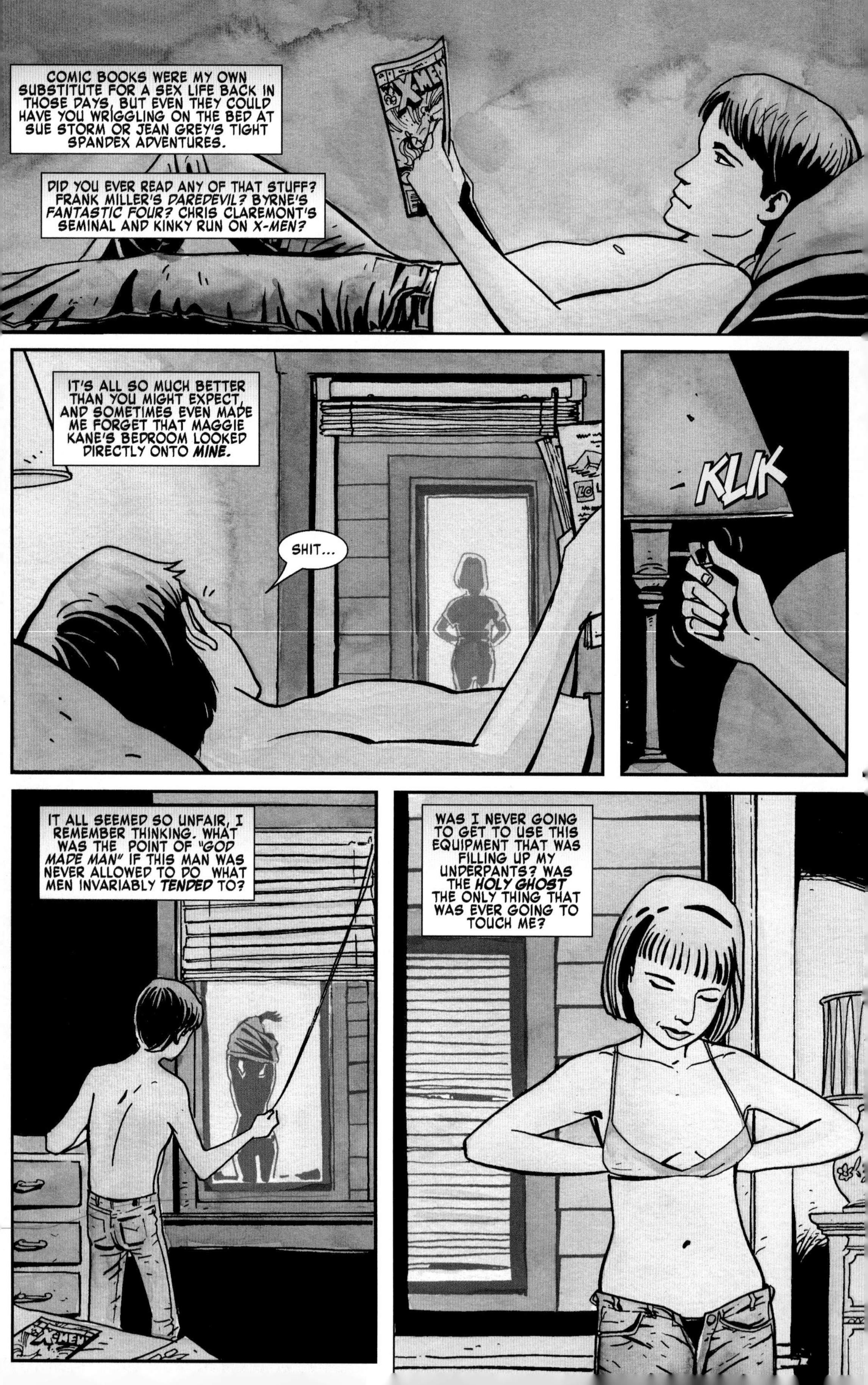
COMIC BOOKS WERE MY OWN SUBSTITUTE FOR A SEX LIFE BACK IN THOSE DAYS, BUT EVEN THEY COULD HAVE YOU WRIGGLING ON THE BED AT SUE STORM OR JEAN GREY'S TIGHT SPANDEX ADVENTURES.
DID YOU EVER READ ANY OF THAT STUFF? FRANK MILLER'S *DAREDEVIL?* BYRNE'S *FANTASTIC FOUR?* CHRIS CLAREMONT'S SEMINAL AND KINKY RUN ON *X-MEN?*
X-MEN
IT'S ALL SO MUCH BETTER THAN YOU MIGHT EXPECT, AND SOMETIMES EVEN MADE ME FORGET THAT MAGGIE KANE'S BEDROOM LOOKED DIRECTLY ONTO *MINE.*
SHIT...
KLIK
IT ALL SEEMED SO UNFAIR, I REMEMBER THINKING. WHAT WAS THE POINT OF *"GOD MADE MAN"* IF THIS MAN WAS NEVER ALLOWED TO DO WHAT MEN INVARIABLY *TENDED* TO?
WAS I NEVER GOING TO GET TO USE THIS EQUIPMENT THAT WAS FILLING UP MY UNDERPANTS? WAS THE *HOLY GHOST* THE ONLY THING THAT WAS EVER GOING TO TOUCH ME?
X-MEN

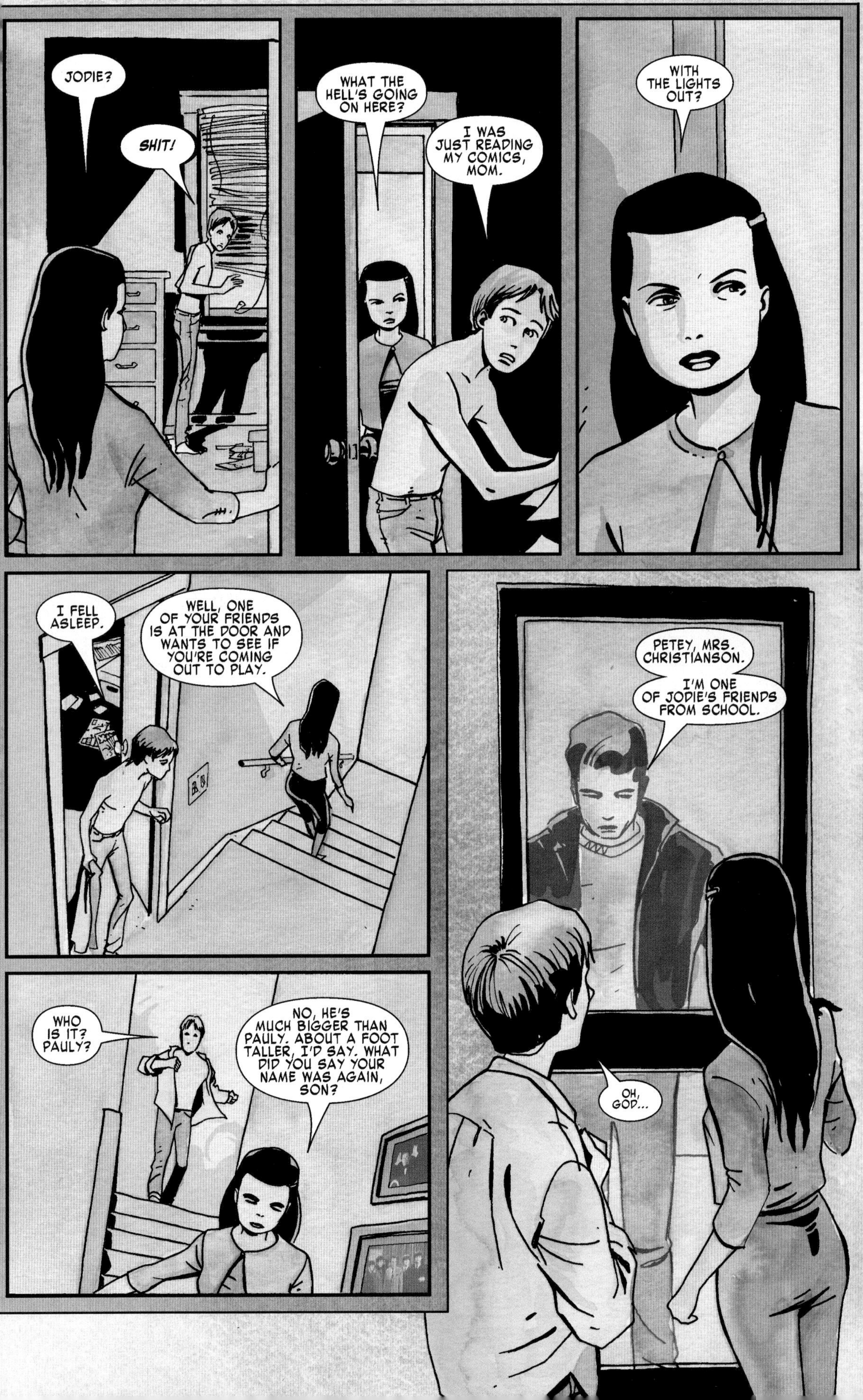
JODIE?
SHIT!
WHAT THE HELL'S GOING ON HERE?
I WAS JUST READING MY COMICS, MOM.
WITH THE LIGHTS OUT?
I FELL ASLEEP.
WELL, ONE OF YOUR FRIENDS IS AT THE DOOR AND WANTS TO SEE IF YOU'RE COMING OUT TO PLAY.
WHO IS IT? PAULY?
NO, HE'S MUCH BIGGER THAN PAULY. ABOUT A FOOT TALLER, I'D SAY. WHAT DID YOU SAY YOUR NAME WAS AGAIN, SON?
PETEY, MRS. CHRISTIANSON.
I'M ONE OF JODIE'S FRIENDS FROM SCHOOL.
OH, GOD...

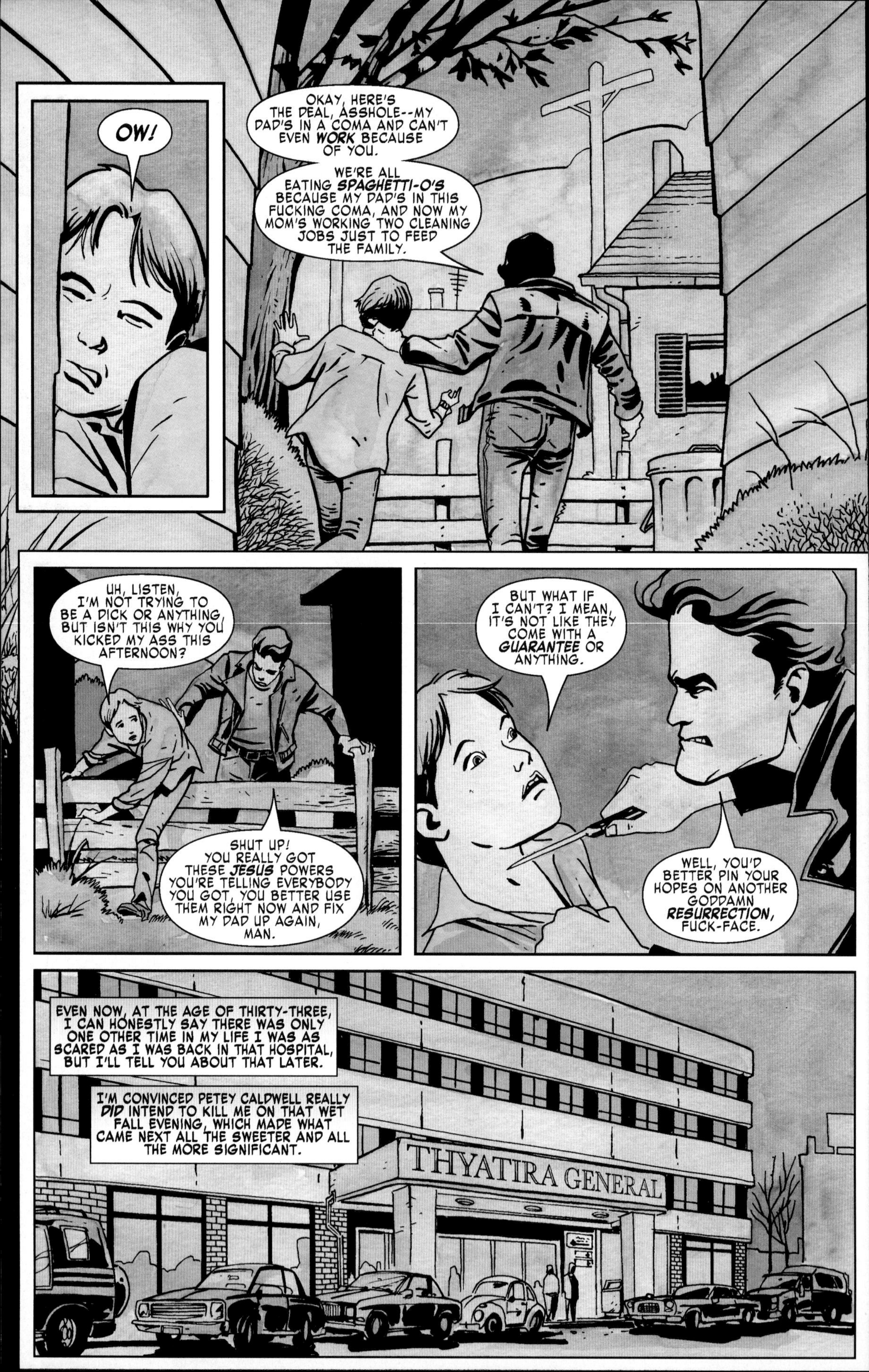
OW!
OKAY, HERE'S THE DEAL, ASSHOLE--MY DAD'S IN A COMA AND CAN'T EVEN WORK BECAUSE OF YOU.
WE'RE ALL EATING SPAGHETTI-O'S BECAUSE MY DAD'S IN THIS FUCKING COMA, AND NOW MY MOM'S WORKING TWO CLEANING JOBS JUST TO FEED THE FAMILY.
UH, LISTEN, I'M NOT TRYING TO BE A DICK OR ANYTHING, BUT ISN'T THIS WHY YOU KICKED MY ASS THIS AFTERNOON?
SHUT UP! YOU REALLY GOT THESE JESUS POWERS YOU'RE TELLING EVERYBODY YOU GOT, YOU BETTER USE THEM RIGHT NOW AND FIX MY DAD UP AGAIN, MAN.
BUT WHAT IF I CAN'T? I MEAN, IT'S NOT LIKE THEY COME WITH A GUARANTEE OR ANYTHING.
WELL, YOU'D BETTER PIN YOUR HOPES ON ANOTHER GODDAMN RESURRECTION, FUCK-FACE.
EVEN NOW, AT THE AGE OF THIRTY-THREE, I CAN HONESTLY SAY THERE WAS ONLY ONE OTHER TIME IN MY LIFE I WAS AS SCARED AS I WAS BACK IN THAT HOSPITAL, BUT I'LL TELL YOU ABOUT THAT LATER.
I'M CONVINCED PETEY CALDWELL REALLY DID INTEND TO KILL ME ON THAT WET FALL EVENING, WHICH MADE WHAT CAME NEXT ALL THE SWEETER AND ALL THE MORE SIGNIFICANT.
THYATIRA GENERAL

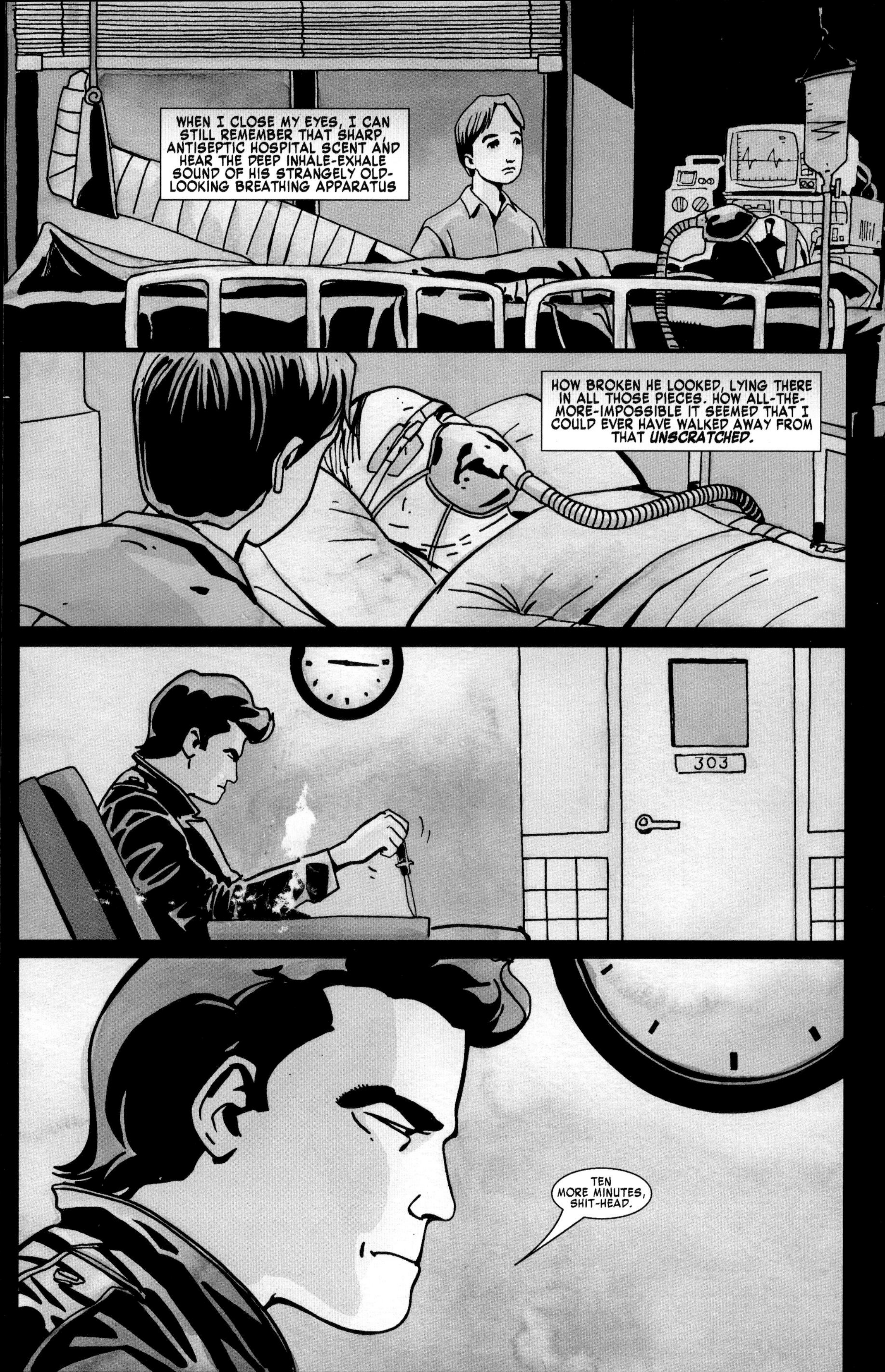
WHEN I CLOSE MY EYES, I CAN STILL REMEMBER THAT SHARP, ANTISEPTIC HOSPITAL SCENT AND HEAR THE DEEP INHALE-EXHALE SOUND OF HIS STRANGELY OLD-LOOKING BREATHING APPARATUS
HOW BROKEN HE LOOKED, LYING THERE IN ALL THOSE PIECES. HOW ALL-THE-MORE-IMPOSSIBLE IT SEEMED THAT I COULD EVER HAVE WALKED AWAY FROM THAT UNSCRATCHED.
303
TEN MORE MINUTES, SHIT-HEAD.

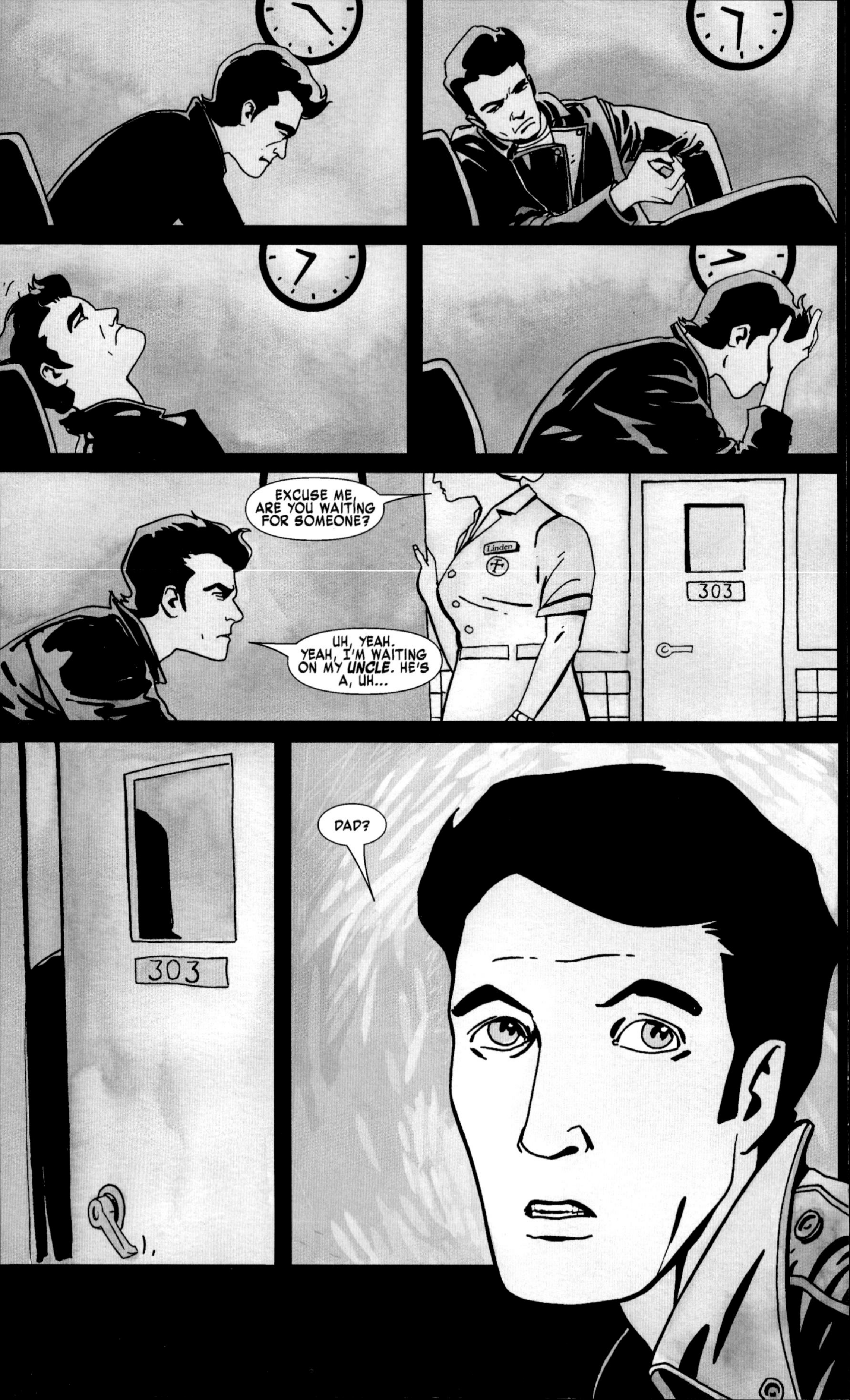
EXCUSE ME, ARE YOU WAITING FOR SOMEONE?
UH, YEAH. YEAH, I'M WAITING ON MY UNCLE. HE'S A, UH...
Linden
303
303
DAD?

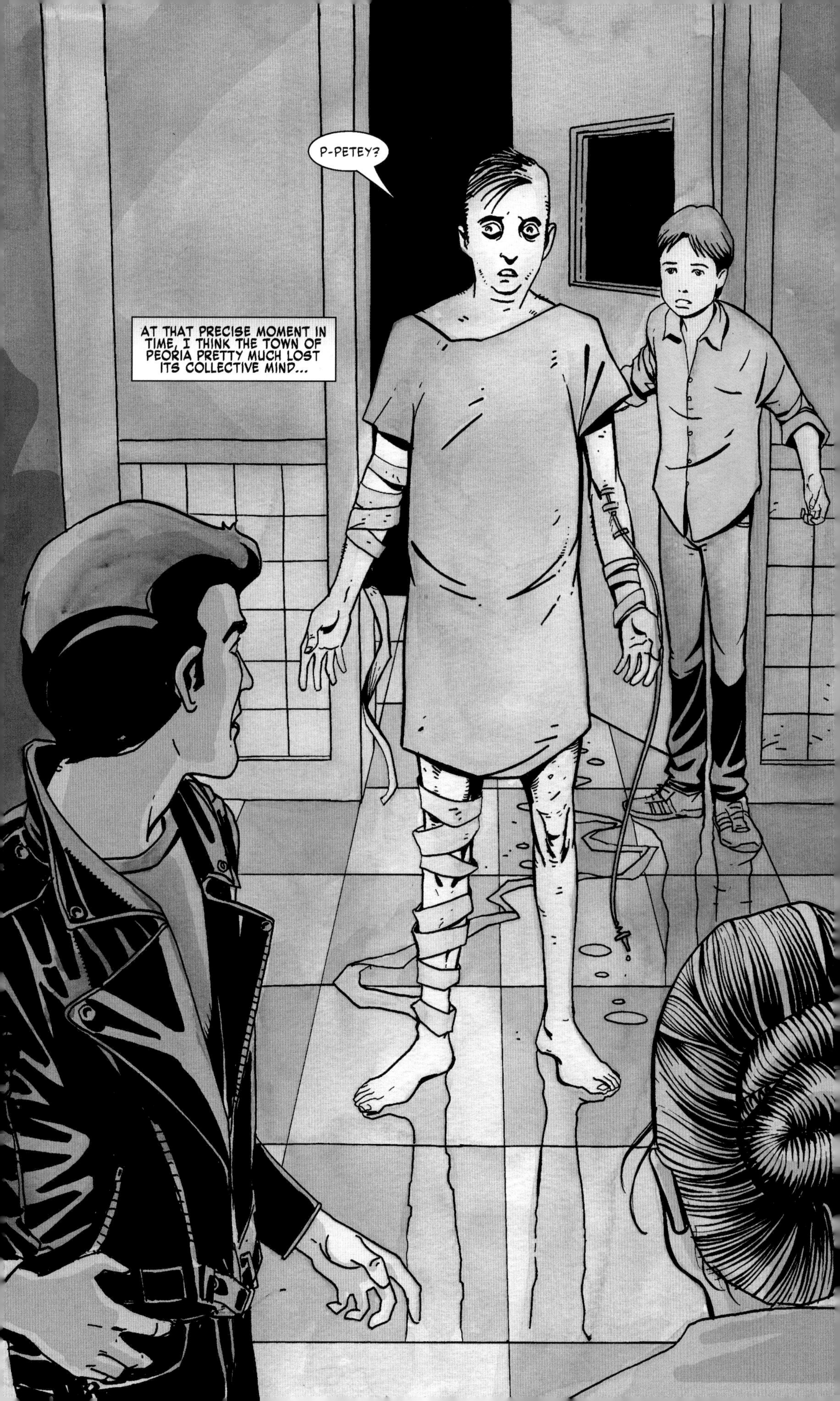
AT THAT PRECISE MOMENT IN TIME, I THINK THE TOWN OF PEORIA PRETTY MUCH LOST ITS COLLECTIVE MIND...
P-PETEY?

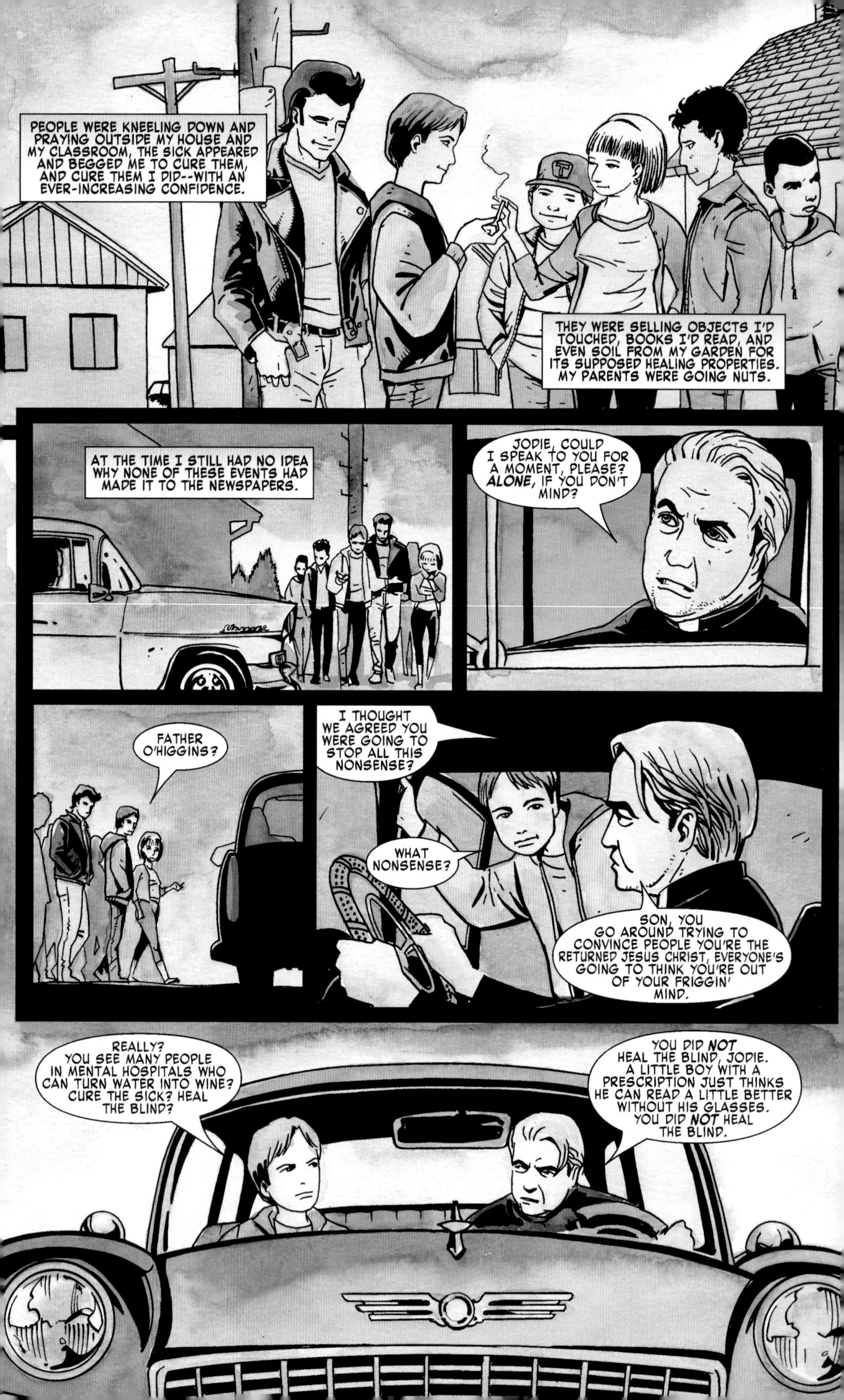
PEOPLE WERE KNEELING DOWN AND PRAYING OUTSIDE MY HOUSE AND MY CLASSROOM, THE SICK APPEARED AND BEGGED ME TO CURE THEM, AND CURE THEM I DID--WITH AN EVER-INCREASING CONFIDENCE.
THEY WERE SELLING OBJECTS I'D TOUCHED, BOOKS I'D READ, AND EVEN SOIL FROM MY GARDEN FOR ITS SUPPOSED HEALING PROPERTIES. MY PARENTS WERE GOING NUTS.
AT THE TIME I STILL HAD NO IDEA WHY NONE OF THESE EVENTS HAD MADE IT TO THE NEWSPAPERS.
JODIE, COULD I SPEAK TO YOU FOR A MOMENT, PLEASE? ALONE, IF YOU DON'T MIND?
FATHER O'HIGGINS?
I THOUGHT WE AGREED YOU WERE GOING TO STOP ALL THIS NONSENSE?
WHAT NONSENSE?
SON, YOU GO AROUND TRYING TO CONVINCE PEOPLE YOU'RE THE RETURNED JESUS CHRIST, EVERYONE'S GOING TO THINK YOU'RE OUT OF YOUR FRIGGIN' MIND.
REALLY? YOU SEE MANY PEOPLE IN MENTAL HOSPITALS WHO CAN TURN WATER INTO WINE? CURE THE SICK? HEAL THE BLIND?
YOU DID NOT HEAL THE BLIND, JODIE. A LITTLE BOY WITH A PRESCRIPTION JUST THINKS HE CAN READ A LITTLE BETTER WITHOUT HIS GLASSES. YOU DID NOT HEAL THE BLIND.

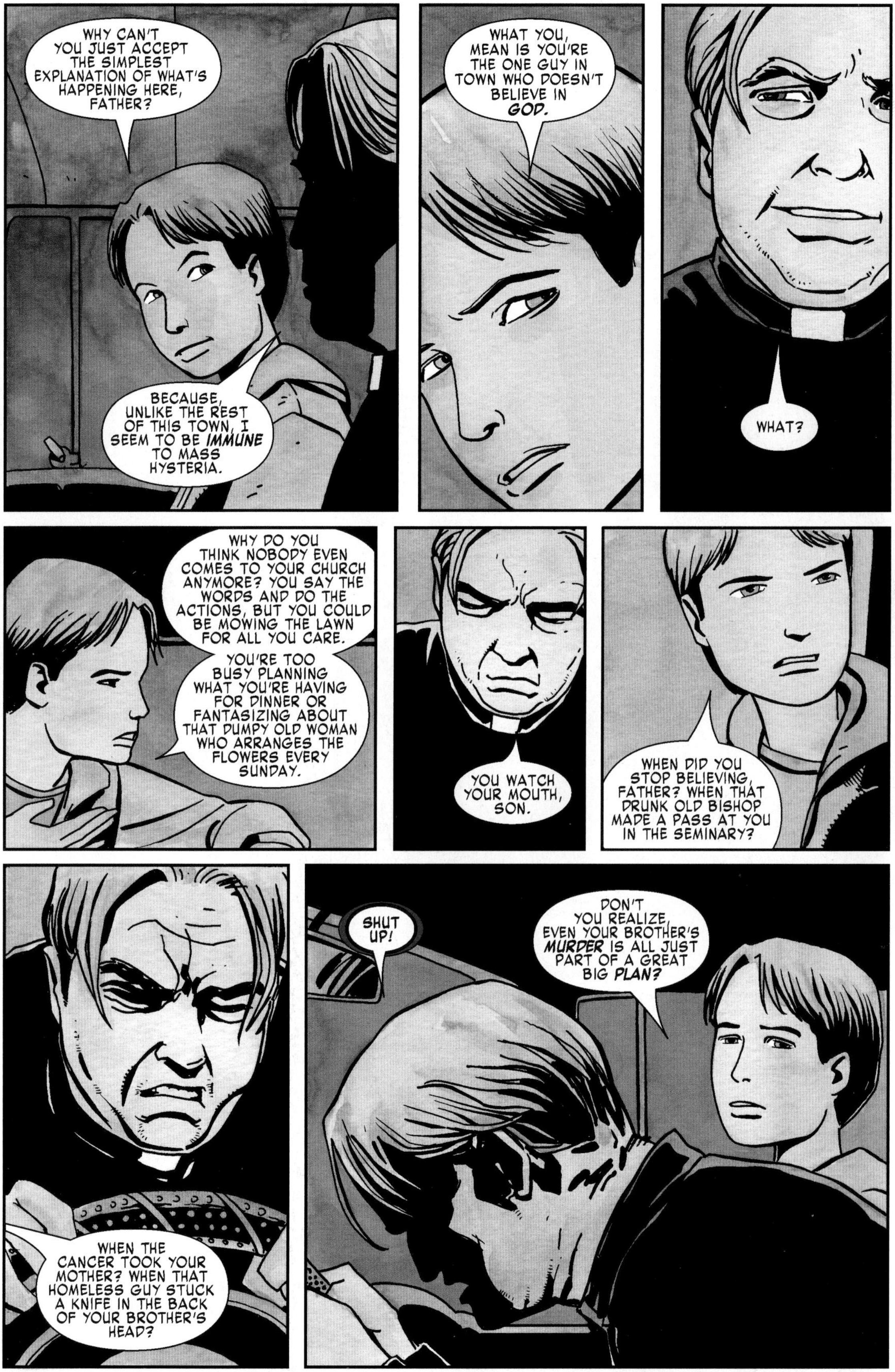
WHY CAN'T YOU JUST ACCEPT THE SIMPLEST EXPLANATION OF WHAT'S HAPPENING HERE, FATHER?
BECAUSE, UNLIKE THE REST OF THIS TOWN, I SEEM TO BE IMMUNE TO MASS HYSTERIA.
WHAT YOU, MEAN IS YOU'RE THE ONE GUY IN TOWN WHO DOESN'T BELIEVE IN GOD.
WHAT?
WHY DO YOU THINK NOBODY EVEN COMES TO YOUR CHURCH ANYMORE? YOU SAY THE WORDS AND DO THE ACTIONS, BUT YOU COULD BE MOWING THE LAWN FOR ALL YOU CARE.
YOU'RE TOO BUSY PLANNING WHAT YOU'RE HAVING FOR DINNER OR FANTASIZING ABOUT THAT DUMPY OLD WOMAN WHO ARRANGES THE FLOWERS EVERY SUNDAY.
YOU WATCH YOUR MOUTH, SON.
WHEN DID YOU STOP BELIEVING, FATHER? WHEN THAT DRUNK OLD BISHOP MADE A PASS AT YOU IN THE SEMINARY?
WHEN THE CANCER TOOK YOUR MOTHER? WHEN THAT HOMELESS GUY STUCK A KNIFE IN THE BACK OF YOUR BROTHER'S HEAD?
SHUT UP!
DON'T YOU REALIZE, EVEN YOUR BROTHER'S MURDER IS ALL JUST PART OF A GREAT BIG PLAN?

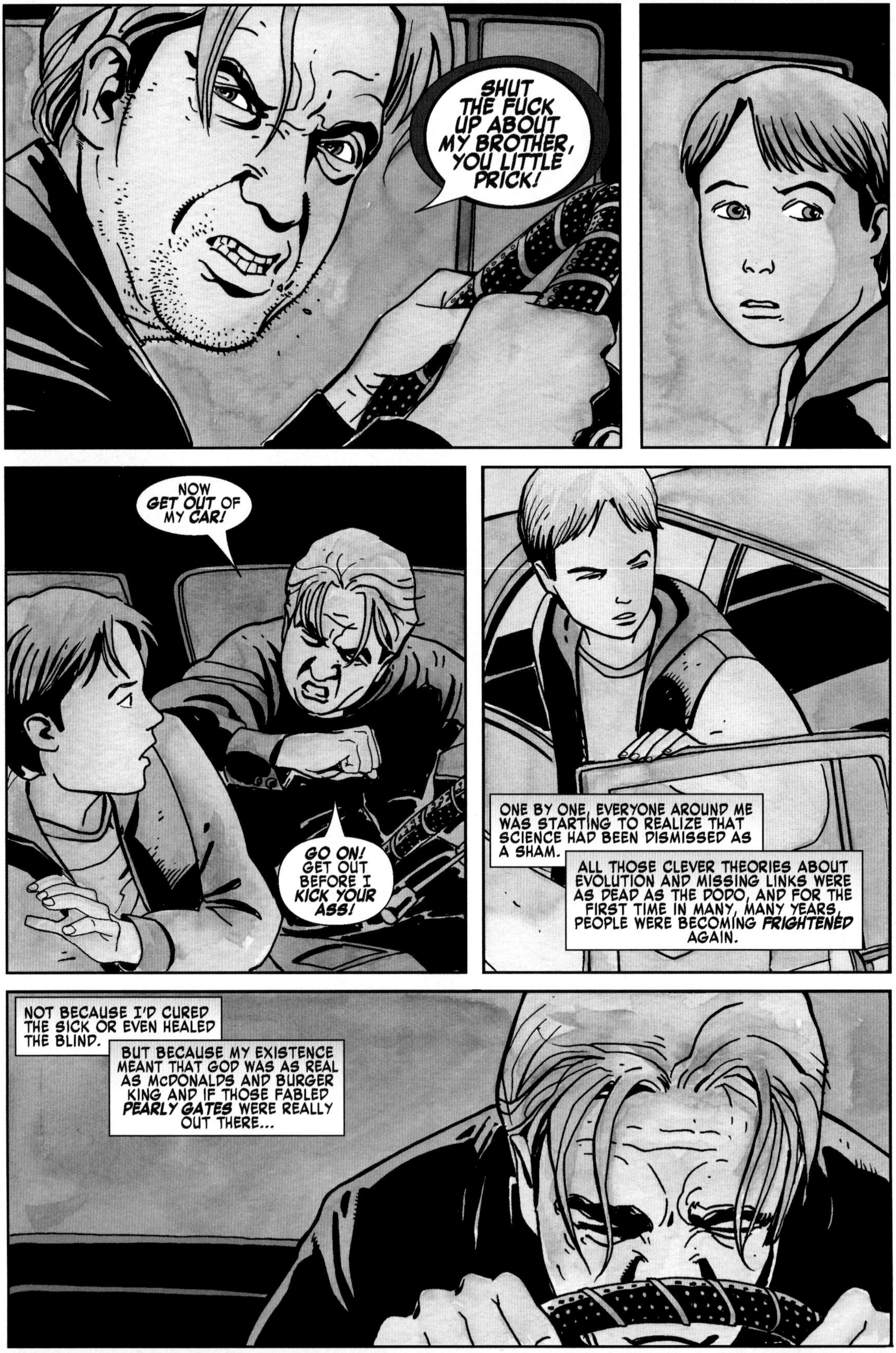
SHUT THE FUCK UP ABOUT MY BROTHER, YOU LITTLE PRICK!
NOW GET OUT OF MY CAR!
GO ON! GET OUT BEFORE I KICK YOUR ASS!
ONE BY ONE, EVERYONE AROUND ME WAS STARTING TO REALIZE THAT SCIENCE HAD BEEN DISMISSED AS A SHAM.
ALL THOSE CLEVER THEORIES ABOUT EVOLUTION AND MISSING LINKS WERE AS DEAD AS THE DODO, AND FOR THE FIRST TIME IN MANY, MANY YEARS, PEOPLE WERE BECOMING FRIGHTENED AGAIN.
NOT BECAUSE I'D CURED THE SICK OR EVEN HEALED THE BLIND.
BUT BECAUSE MY EXISTENCE MEANT THAT GOD WAS AS REAL AS McDONALDS AND BURGER KING AND IF THOSE FABLED PEARLY GATES WERE REALLY OUT THERE...

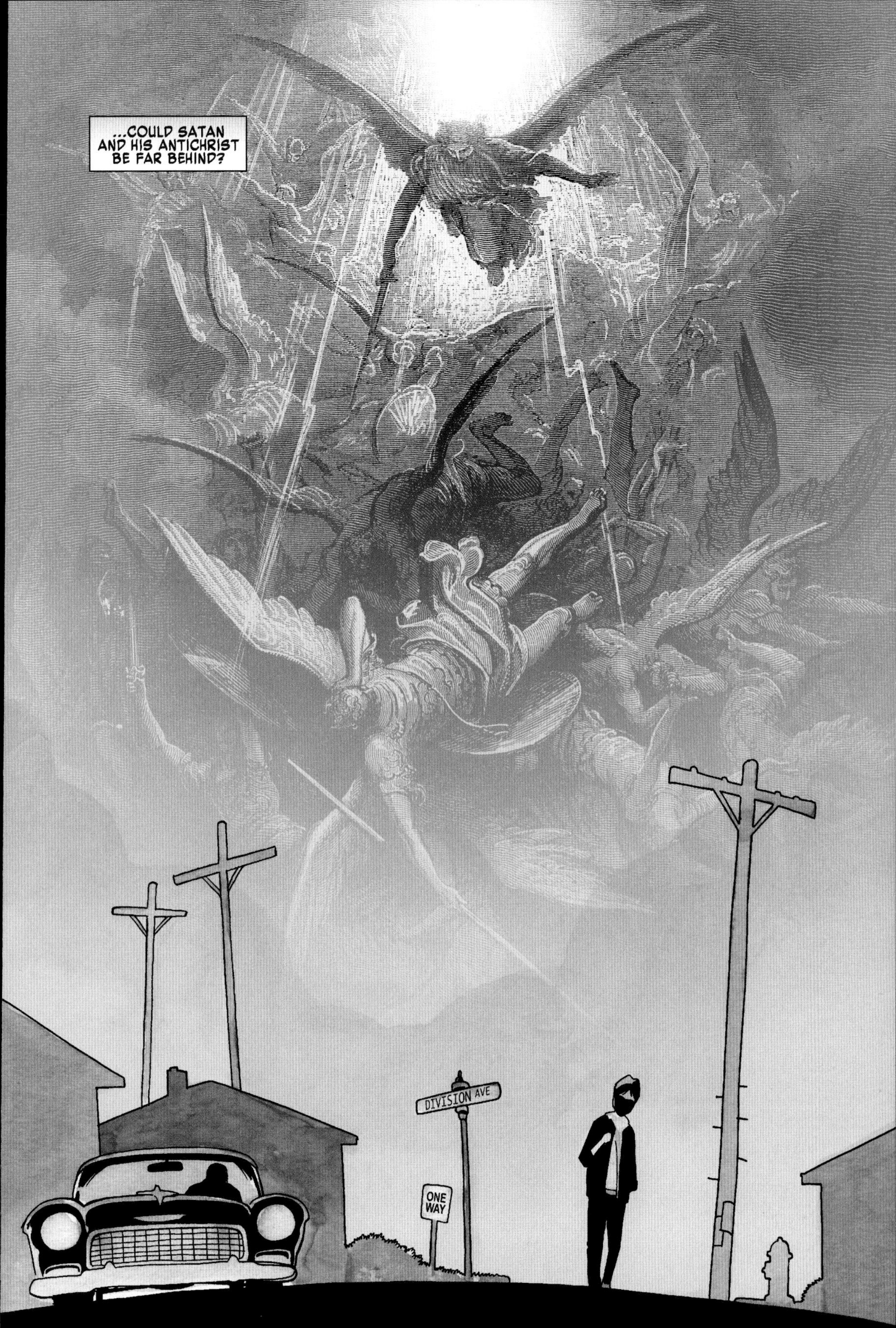
...COULD SATAN AND HIS ANTICHRIST BE FAR BEHIND?
DIVISION AVE
ONE WAY

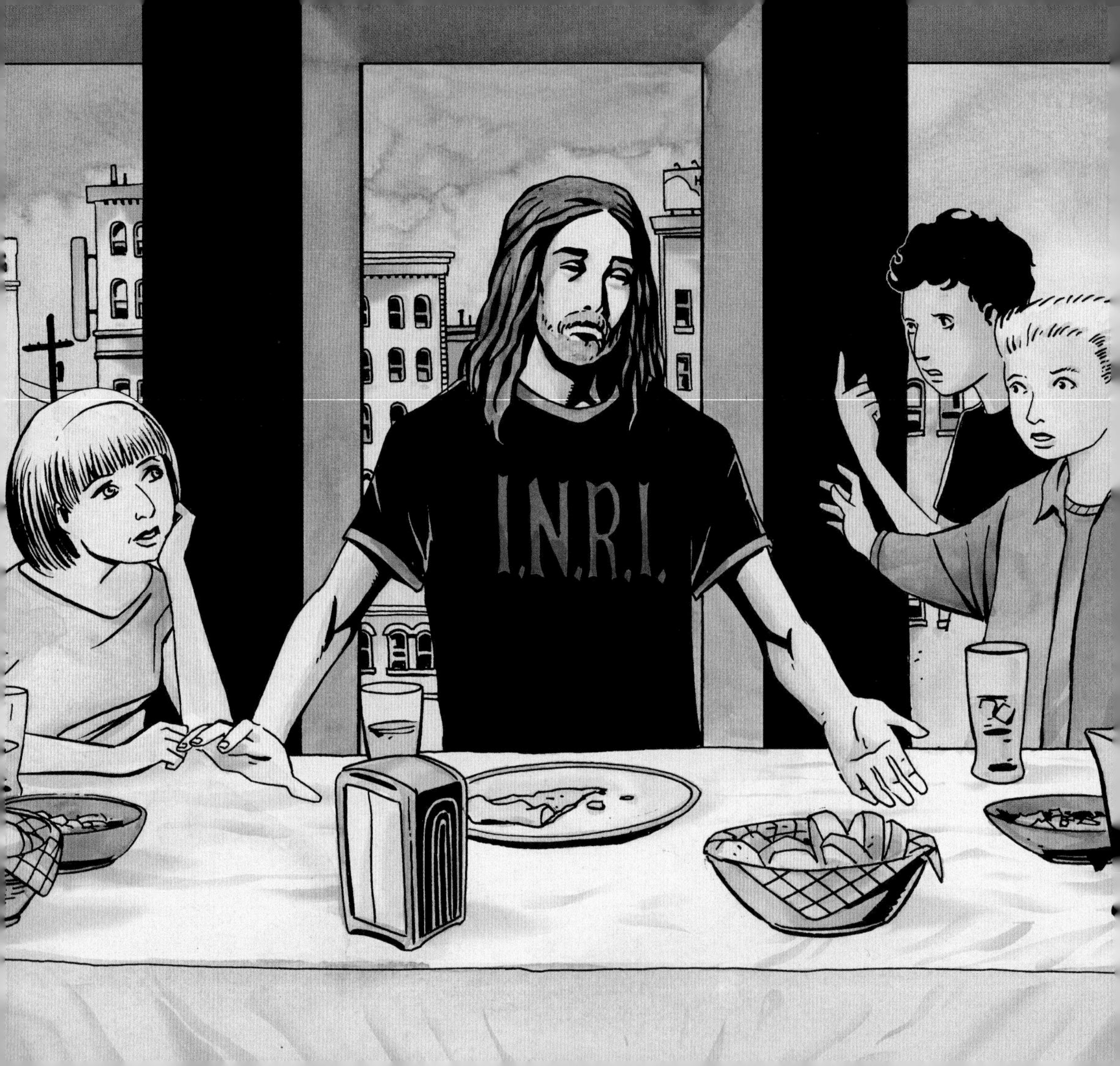
I.N.R.I.

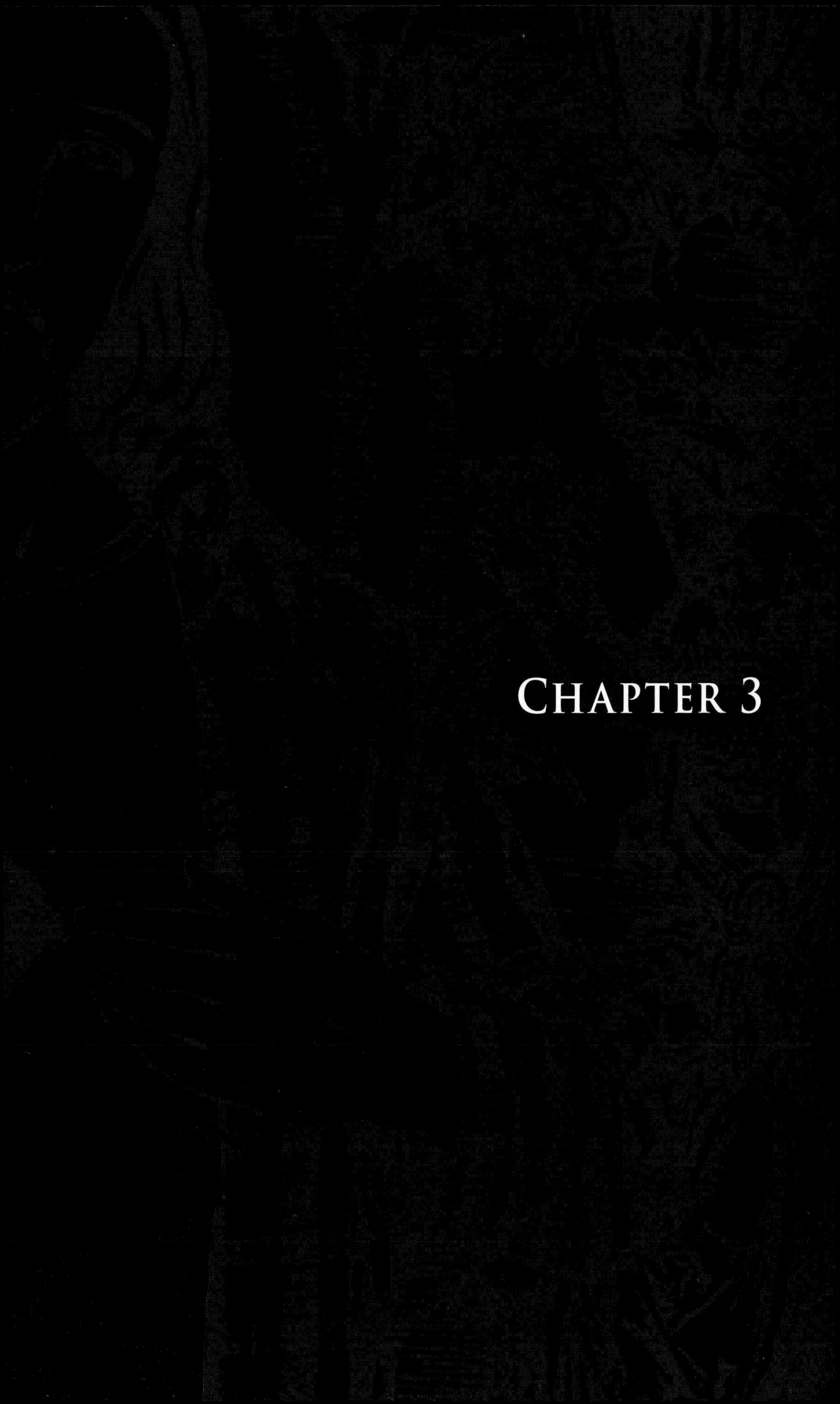

CHAPTER 3

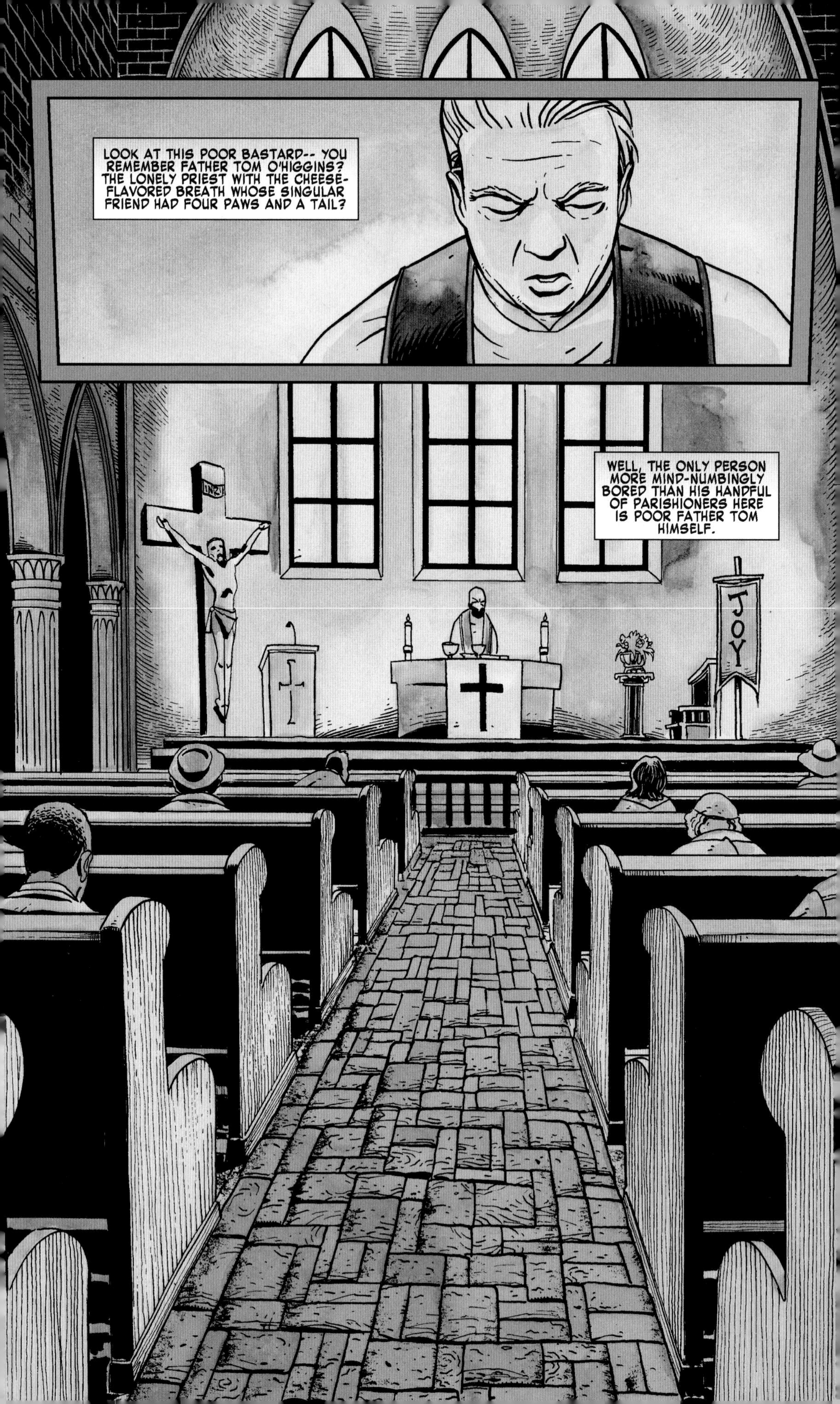
LOOK AT THIS POOR BASTARD-- YOU REMEMBER FATHER TOM O'HIGGINS? THE LONELY PRIEST WITH THE CHEESE-FLAVORED BREATH WHOSE SINGULAR FRIEND HAD FOUR PAWS AND A TAIL?
WELL, THE ONLY PERSON MORE MIND-NUMBINGLY BORED THAN HIS HANDFUL OF PARISHIONERS HERE IS POOR FATHER TOM HIMSELF.
INRI
JOY

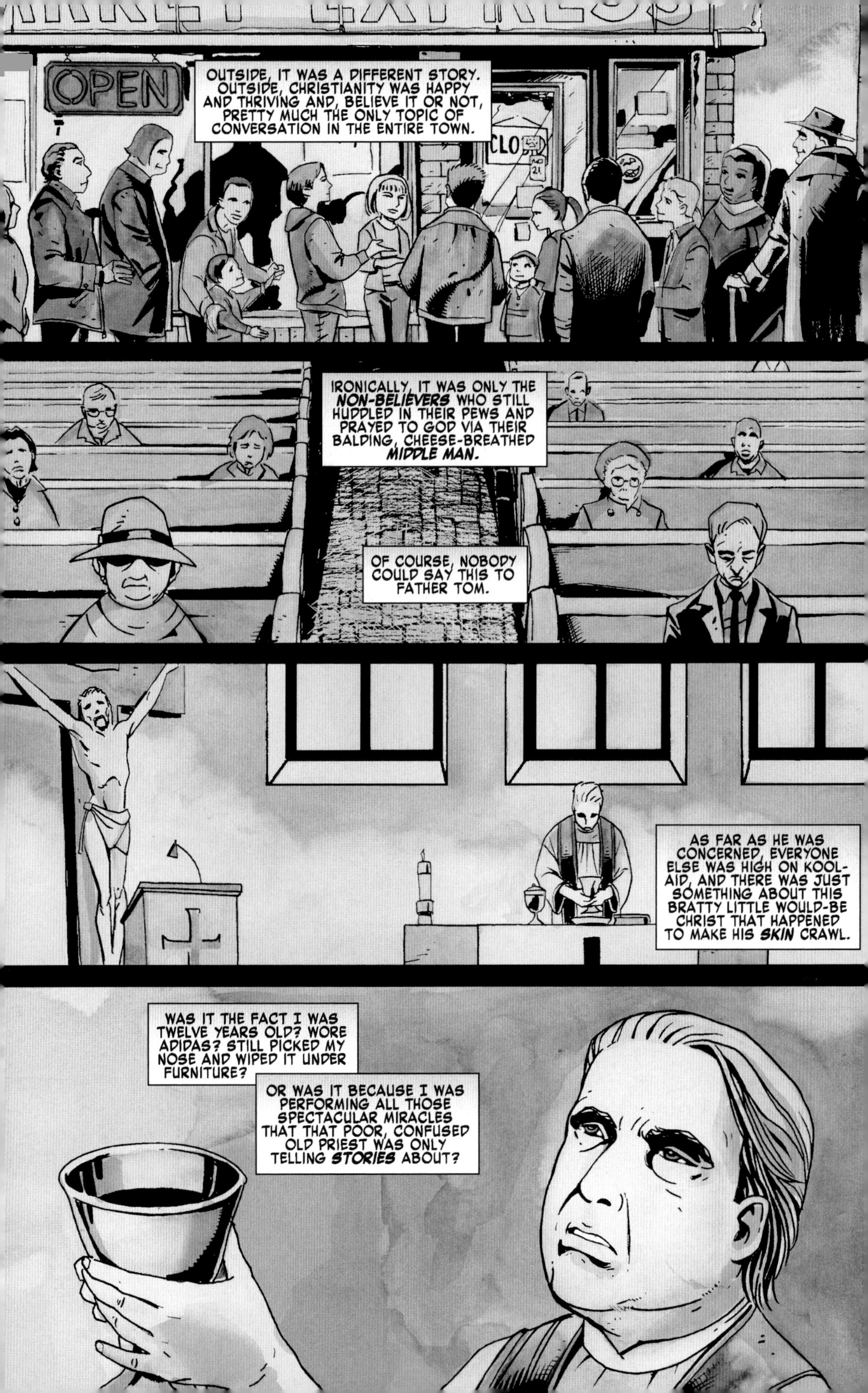
OUTSIDE, IT WAS A DIFFERENT STORY. OUTSIDE, CHRISTIANITY WAS HAPPY AND THRIVING AND, BELIEVE IT OR NOT, PRETTY MUCH THE ONLY TOPIC OF CONVERSATION IN THE ENTIRE TOWN.
OPEN
IRONICALLY, IT WAS ONLY THE NON-BELIEVERS WHO STILL HUDDLED IN THEIR PEWS AND PRAYED TO GOD VIA THEIR BALDING, CHEESE-BREATHED MIDDLE MAN.
OF COURSE, NOBODY COULD SAY THIS TO FATHER TOM.
AS FAR AS HE WAS CONCERNED, EVERYONE ELSE WAS HIGH ON KOOL-AID, AND THERE WAS JUST SOMETHING ABOUT THIS BRATTY LITTLE WOULD-BE CHRIST THAT HAPPENED TO MAKE HIS SKIN CRAWL.
WAS IT THE FACT I WAS TWELVE YEARS OLD? WORE ADIDAS? STILL PICKED MY NOSE AND WIPED IT UNDER FURNITURE?
OR WAS IT BECAUSE I WAS PERFORMING ALL THOSE SPECTACULAR MIRACLES THAT THAT POOR, CONFUSED OLD PRIEST WAS ONLY TELLING STORIES ABOUT?

WHATEVER IRKED HIM ABOUT ME, HE TOLD MY TEACHER IN NO UNCERTAIN TERMS HE WAS *INSANE* TO LET ME NEAR HIS PRUNE-FACED AND CANCEROUS, DARLING OLD MOTHER...

YOU SURE I CAN'T GET YOU ANYTHING, JODIE?

HONESTLY, I'M FINE, MISTER FREMONT. YOUR MOM AND I HAVE JUST BEEN HAVING A LITTLE TALK HERE, BUT WE'RE FINISHED UP NOW ANYWAY, SIR.

WHAT D'YOU RECKON, SON? YOU THINK YOU CAN FIX HER?

OF *COURSE* I CAN FIX HER. I COULD GIVE HER ANOTHER FIVE YEARS IF I WANTED TO. MAYBE EVEN TEN, BUT THAT DOESN'T MEAN IT'S THE RIGHT THING TO *DO* HERE.

WHAT ARE YOU TALKING ABOUT?

I'M READY TO LET GO, BENNY. I'M SICK OF ALL THE BED-BATHS AND PILLS AND COUGHING MY GUTS UP IN THE MIDDLE OF THE NIGHT.

I WANT TO STOP ALL THIS HORRIBLE MEDICATION NOW AND JUST LET NATURE TAKE ITS COURSE, SWEETHEART.

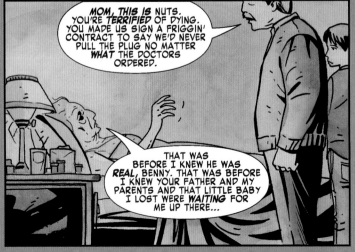

MOM, *THIS IS* NUTS. YOU'RE *TERRIFIED* OF DYING. YOU MADE US SIGN A FRIGGIN' CONTRACT TO SAY WE'D NEVER PULL THE PLUG NO MATTER *WHAT* THE DOCTORS ORDERED.

THAT WAS BEFORE I KNEW HE WAS *REAL*, BENNY. THAT WAS BEFORE I KNEW YOUR FATHER AND MY PARENTS AND THAT LITTLE BABY I LOST WERE *WAITING* FOR ME UP THERE...

...JUST LIKE I'LL BE UP THERE WAITING FOR YOU TOO, HONEY. OH, BENNY, YOU SHOULD HEAR THE WAY HE TALKS ABOUT WHAT'S *AFTER* ALL THIS MISERY AND HEARTACHE. YOU'LL NEVER BE SCARED OF ANYTHING *AGAIN*.

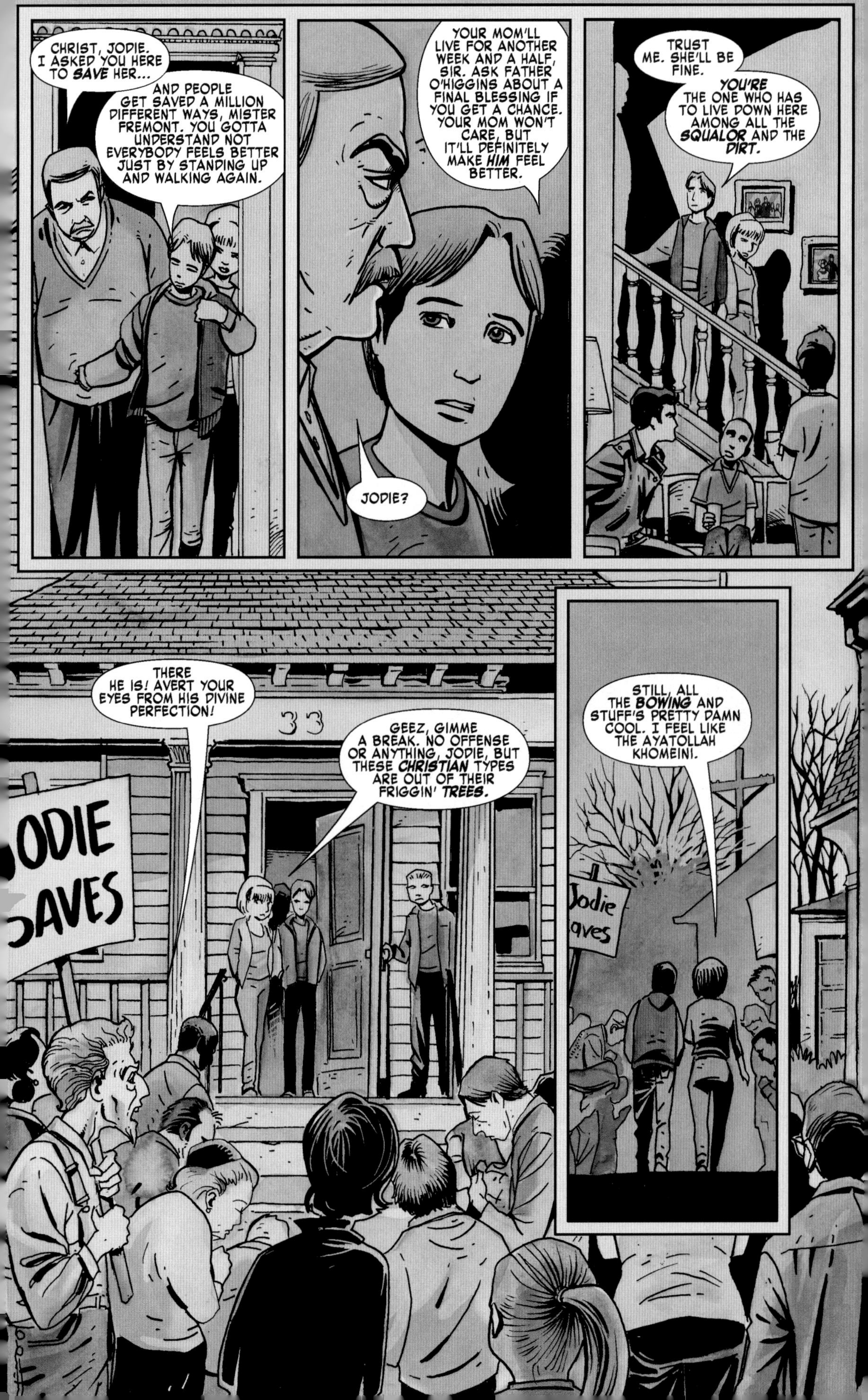
CHRIST, JODIE. I ASKED YOU HERE TO SAVE HER...
AND PEOPLE GET SAVED A MILLION DIFFERENT WAYS, MISTER FREMONT. YOU GOTTA UNDERSTAND NOT EVERYBODY FEELS BETTER JUST BY STANDING UP AND WALKING AGAIN.
YOUR MOM'LL LIVE FOR ANOTHER WEEK AND A HALF, SIR. ASK FATHER O'HIGGINS ABOUT A FINAL BLESSING IF YOU GET A CHANCE. YOUR MOM WON'T CARE, BUT IT'LL DEFINITELY MAKE HIM FEEL BETTER.
JODIE?
TRUST ME. SHE'LL BE FINE.
YOU'RE THE ONE WHO HAS TO LIVE DOWN HERE AMONG ALL THE SQUALOR AND THE DIRT.
THERE HE IS! AVERT YOUR EYES FROM HIS DIVINE PERFECTION!
33
ODIE SAVES
GEEZ, GIMME A BREAK. NO OFFENSE OR ANYTHING, JODIE, BUT THESE CHRISTIAN TYPES ARE OUT OF THEIR FRIGGIN' TREES.
STILL, ALL THE BOWING AND STUFF'S PRETTY DAMN COOL. I FEEL LIKE THE AYATOLLAH KHOMEINI.
Jodie aves

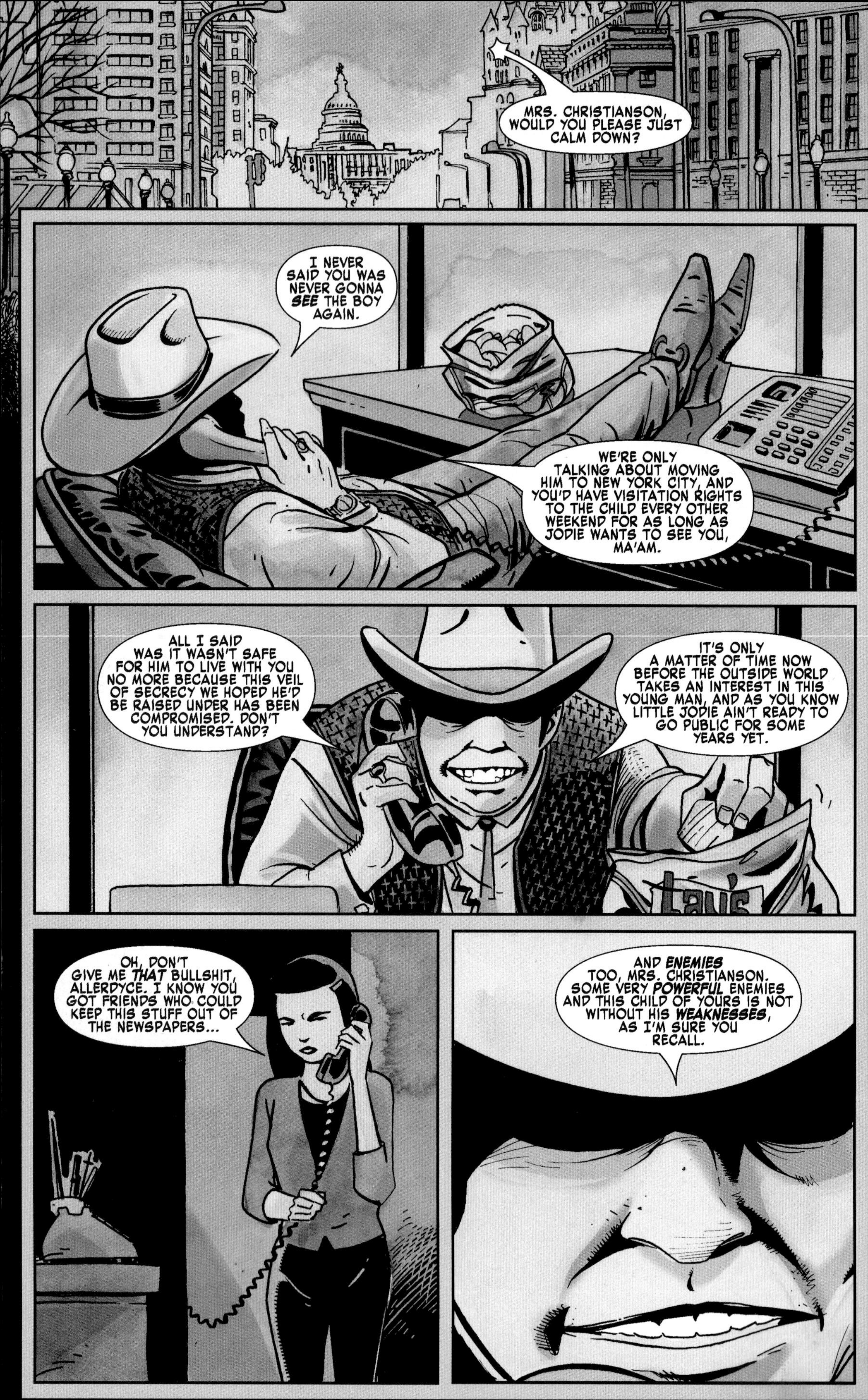
MRS. CHRISTIANSON, WOULD YOU PLEASE JUST CALM DOWN?
I NEVER SAID YOU WAS NEVER GONNA SEE THE BOY AGAIN.
WE'RE ONLY TALKING ABOUT MOVING HIM TO NEW YORK CITY, AND YOU'D HAVE VISITATION RIGHTS TO THE CHILD EVERY OTHER WEEKEND FOR AS LONG AS JODIE WANTS TO SEE YOU, MA'AM.
ALL I SAID WAS IT WASN'T SAFE FOR HIM TO LIVE WITH YOU NO MORE BECAUSE THIS VEIL OF SECRECY WE HOPED HE'D BE RAISED UNDER HAS BEEN COMPROMISED. DON'T YOU UNDERSTAND?
IT'S ONLY A MATTER OF TIME NOW BEFORE THE OUTSIDE WORLD TAKES AN INTEREST IN THIS YOUNG MAN, AND AS YOU KNOW LITTLE JODIE AIN'T READY TO GO PUBLIC FOR SOME YEARS YET.
OH, DON'T GIVE ME THAT BULLSHIT, ALLERDYCE. I KNOW YOU GOT FRIENDS WHO COULD KEEP THIS STUFF OUT OF THE NEWSPAPERS...
AND ENEMIES TOO, MRS. CHRISTIANSON. SOME VERY POWERFUL ENEMIES AND THIS CHILD OF YOURS IS NOT WITHOUT HIS WEAKNESSES, AS I'M SURE YOU RECALL.

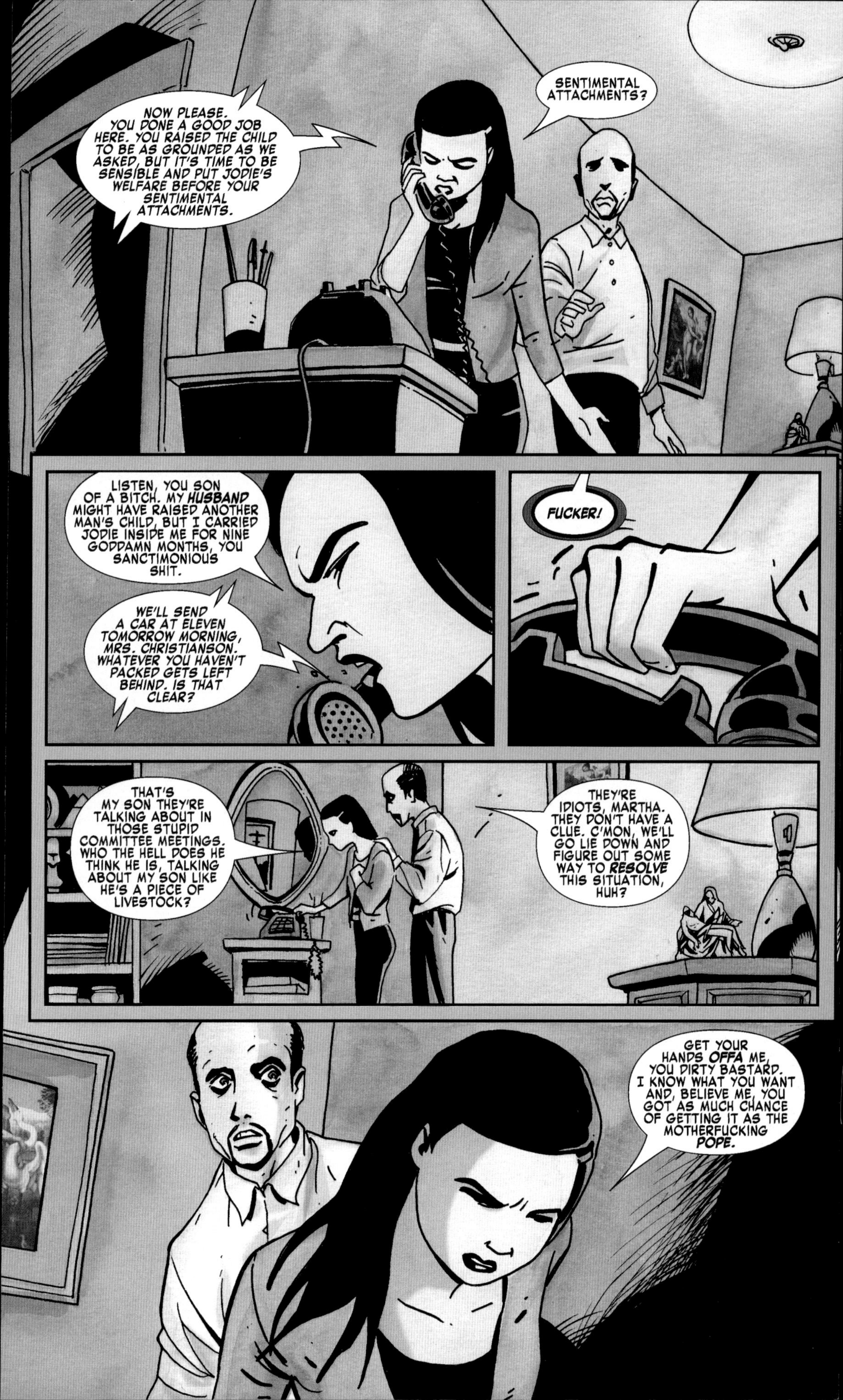
NOW PLEASE. YOU DONE A GOOD JOB HERE. YOU RAISED THE CHILD TO BE AS GROUNDED AS WE ASKED, BUT IT'S TIME TO BE SENSIBLE AND PUT JODIE'S WELFARE BEFORE YOUR SENTIMENTAL ATTACHMENTS.
SENTIMENTAL ATTACHMENTS?
LISTEN, YOU SON OF A BITCH. MY HUSBAND MIGHT HAVE RAISED ANOTHER MAN'S CHILD, BUT I CARRIED JODIE INSIDE ME FOR NINE GODDAMN MONTHS, YOU SANCTIMONIOUS SHIT.
WE'LL SEND A CAR AT ELEVEN TOMORROW MORNING, MRS. CHRISTIANSON. WHATEVER YOU HAVEN'T PACKED GETS LEFT BEHIND. IS THAT CLEAR?
FUCKER!
THAT'S MY SON THEY'RE TALKING ABOUT IN THOSE STUPID COMMITTEE MEETINGS. WHO THE HELL DOES HE THINK HE IS, TALKING ABOUT MY SON LIKE HE'S A PIECE OF LIVESTOCK?
THEY'RE IDIOTS, MARTHA. THEY DON'T HAVE A CLUE. C'MON, WE'LL GO LIE DOWN AND FIGURE OUT SOME WAY TO RESOLVE THIS SITUATION, HUH?
GET YOUR HANDS OFFA ME, YOU DIRTY BASTARD. I KNOW WHAT YOU WANT AND, BELIEVE ME, YOU GOT AS MUCH CHANCE OF GETTING IT AS THE MOTHERFUCKING POPE.

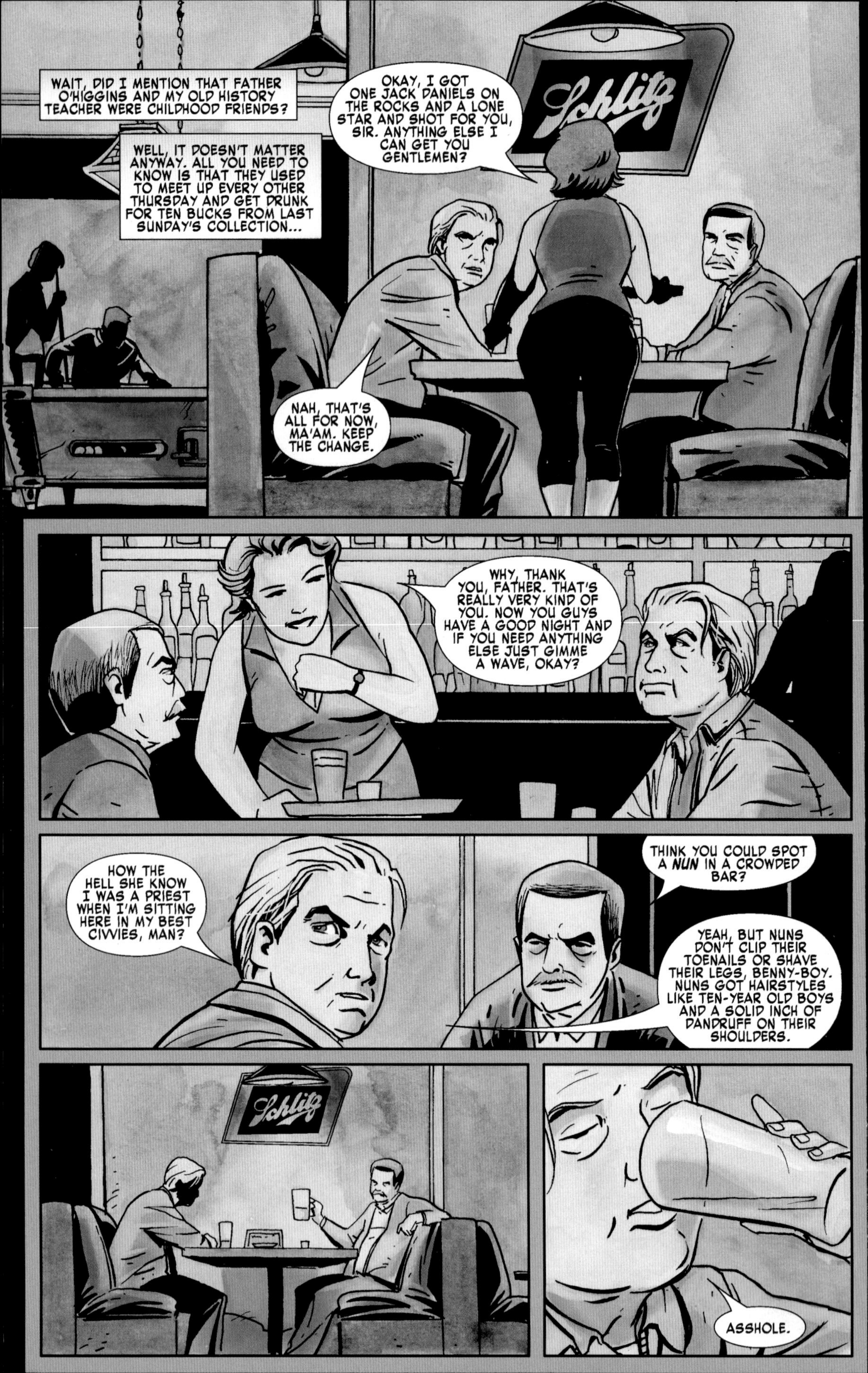
WAIT, DID I MENTION THAT FATHER O'HIGGINS AND MY OLD HISTORY TEACHER WERE CHILDHOOD FRIENDS?
WELL, IT DOESN'T MATTER ANYWAY. ALL YOU NEED TO KNOW IS THAT THEY USED TO MEET UP EVERY OTHER THURSDAY AND GET DRUNK FOR TEN BUCKS FROM LAST SUNDAY'S COLLECTION...
OKAY, I GOT ONE JACK DANIELS ON THE ROCKS AND A LONE STAR AND SHOT FOR YOU, SIR. ANYTHING ELSE I CAN GET YOU GENTLEMEN?
Schlitz
NAH, THAT'S ALL FOR NOW, MA'AM. KEEP THE CHANGE.
WHY, THANK YOU, FATHER. THAT'S REALLY VERY KIND OF YOU. NOW YOU GUYS HAVE A GOOD NIGHT AND IF YOU NEED ANYTHING ELSE JUST GIMME A WAVE, OKAY?
HOW THE HELL SHE KNOW I WAS A PRIEST WHEN I'M SITTING HERE IN MY BEST CIVVIES, MAN?
THINK YOU COULD SPOT A *NUN* IN A CROWDED BAR?
YEAH, BUT NUNS DON'T CLIP THEIR TOENAILS OR SHAVE THEIR LEGS, BENNY-BOY. NUNS GOT HAIRSTYLES LIKE TEN-YEAR OLD BOYS AND A SOLID INCH OF DANDRUFF ON THEIR SHOULDERS.
Schlitz
ASSHOLE.

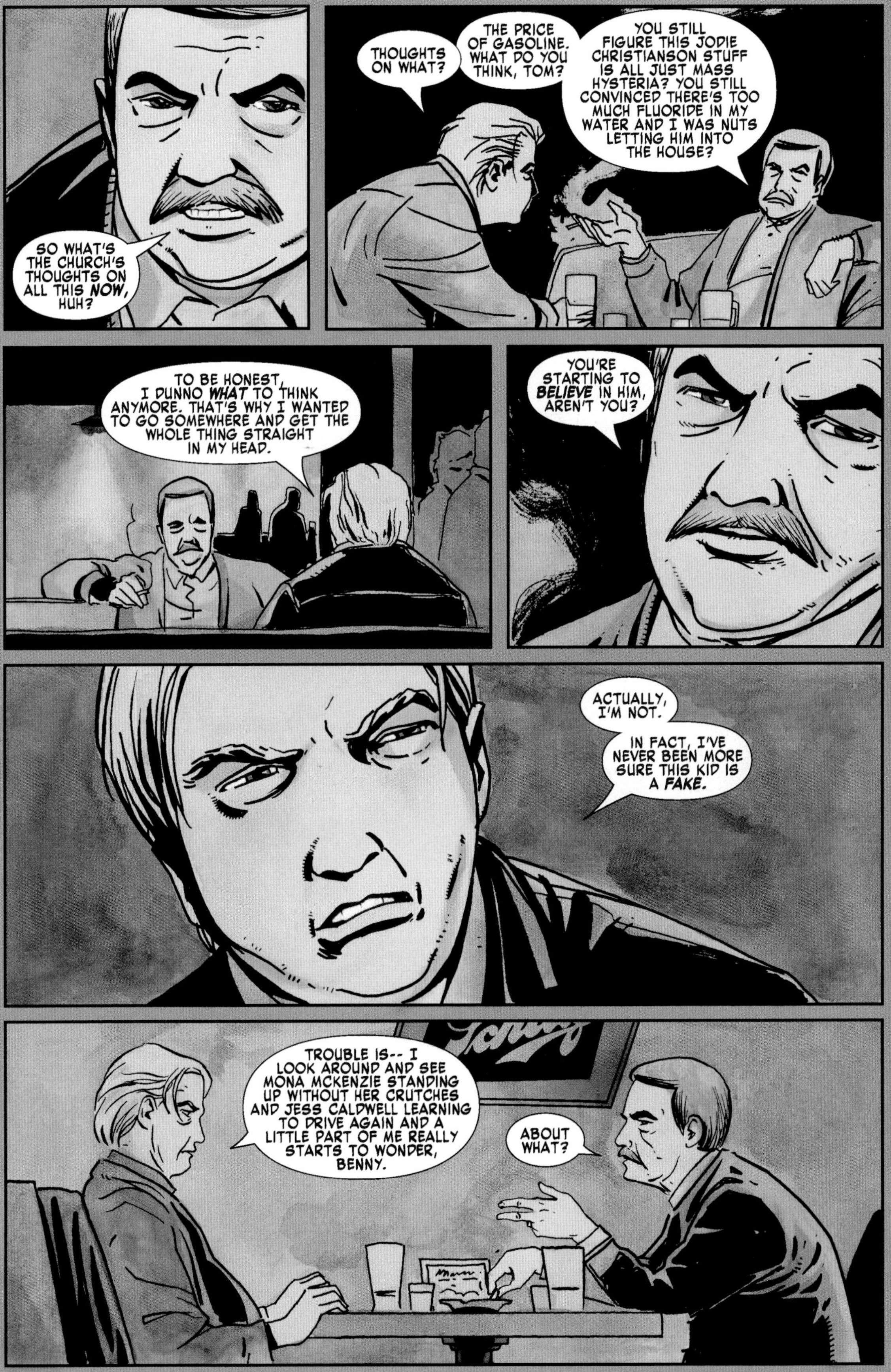
SO WHAT'S THE CHURCH'S THOUGHTS ON ALL THIS *NOW*, HUH?
THOUGHTS ON WHAT?
THE PRICE OF GASOLINE. WHAT DO YOU THINK, TOM?
YOU STILL FIGURE THIS JODIE CHRISTIANSON STUFF IS ALL JUST MASS HYSTERIA? YOU STILL CONVINCED THERE'S TOO MUCH FLUORIDE IN MY WATER AND I WAS NUTS LETTING HIM INTO THE HOUSE?
TO BE HONEST, I DUNNO *WHAT* TO THINK ANYMORE. THAT'S WHY I WANTED TO GO SOMEWHERE AND GET THE WHOLE THING STRAIGHT IN MY HEAD.
YOU'RE STARTING TO *BELIEVE* IN HIM, AREN'T YOU?
ACTUALLY, I'M NOT.
IN FACT, I'VE NEVER BEEN MORE SURE THIS KID IS A *FAKE.*
TROUBLE IS-- I LOOK AROUND AND SEE MONA MCKENZIE STANDING UP WITHOUT HER CRUTCHES AND JESS CALDWELL LEARNING TO DRIVE AGAIN AND A LITTLE PART OF ME REALLY STARTS TO WONDER, BENNY.
ABOUT WHAT?

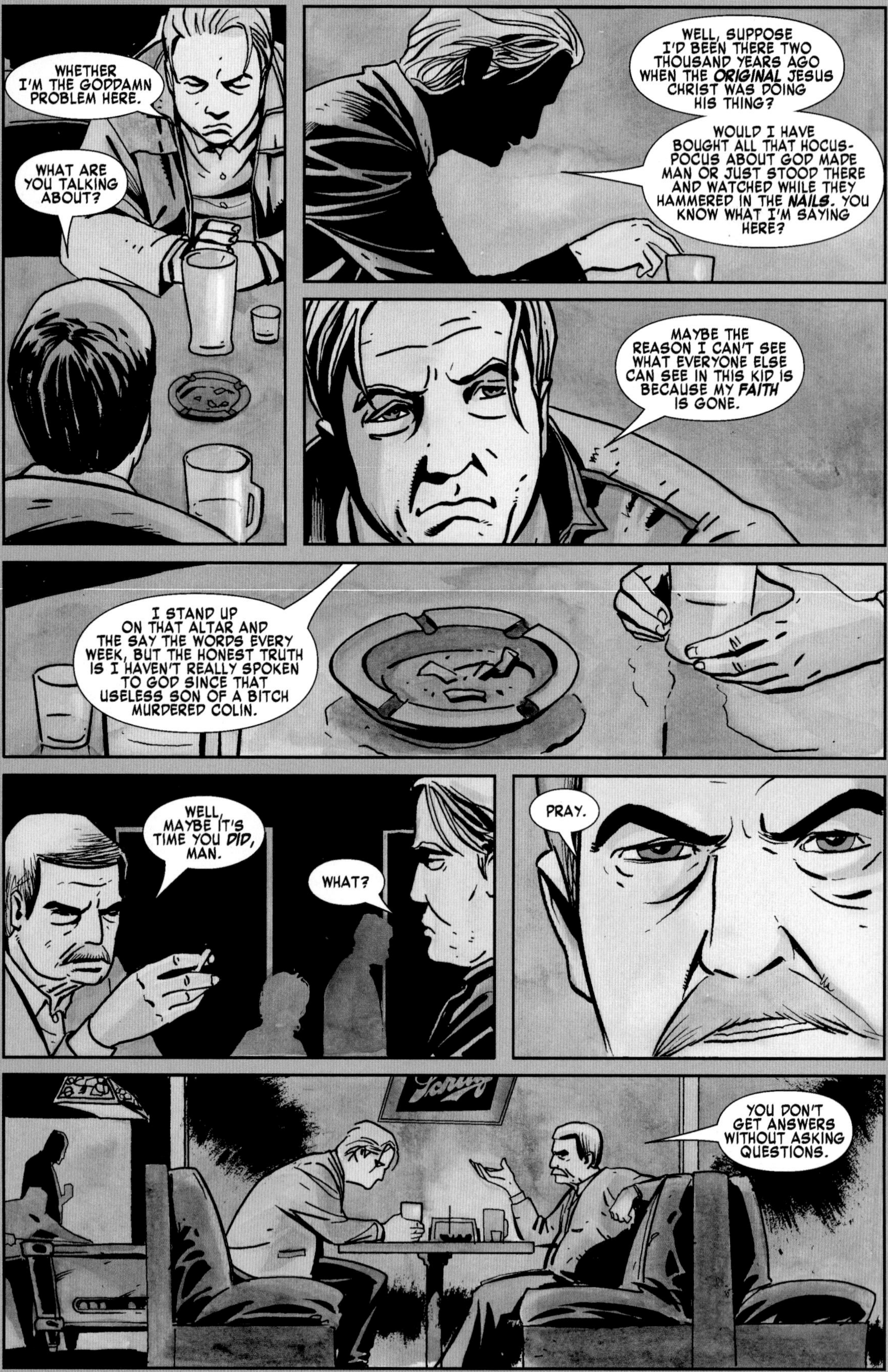
WHETHER I'M THE GODDAMN PROBLEM HERE.
WHAT ARE YOU TALKING ABOUT?
WELL, SUPPOSE I'D BEEN THERE TWO THOUSAND YEARS AGO WHEN THE ORIGINAL JESUS CHRIST WAS DOING HIS THING?
WOULD I HAVE BOUGHT ALL THAT HOCUS-POCUS ABOUT GOD MADE MAN OR JUST STOOD THERE AND WATCHED WHILE THEY HAMMERED IN THE NAILS. YOU KNOW WHAT I'M SAYING HERE?
MAYBE THE REASON I CAN'T SEE WHAT EVERYONE ELSE CAN SEE IN THIS KID IS BECAUSE MY FAITH IS GONE.
I STAND UP ON THAT ALTAR AND THE SAY THE WORDS EVERY WEEK, BUT THE HONEST TRUTH IS I HAVEN'T REALLY SPOKEN TO GOD SINCE THAT USELESS SON OF A BITCH MURDERED COLIN.
WELL, MAYBE IT'S TIME YOU DID, MAN.
WHAT?
PRAY.
YOU DON'T GET ANSWERS WITHOUT ASKING QUESTIONS.

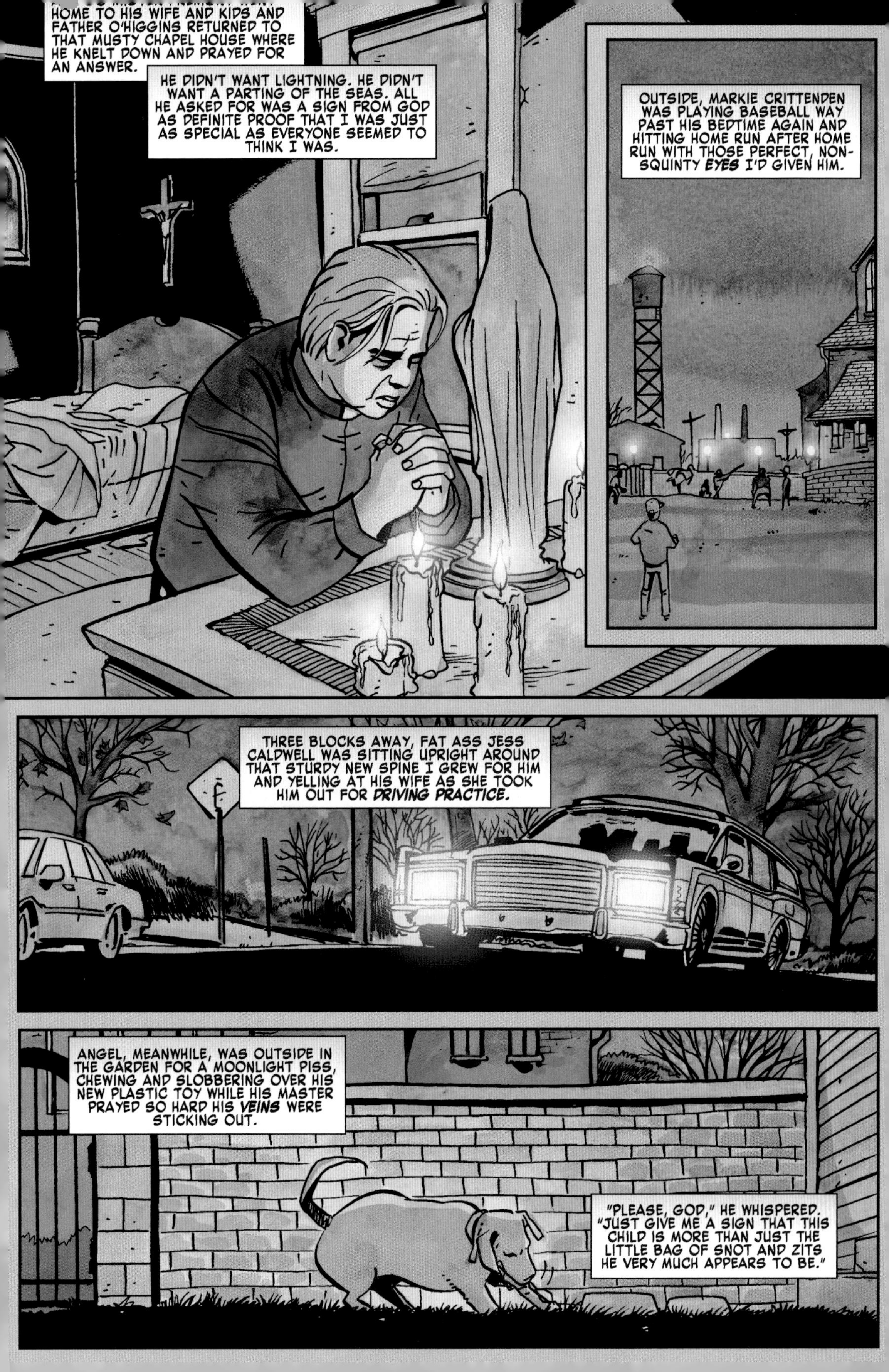

HOME TO HIS WIFE AND KIDS AND FATHER O'HIGGINS RETURNED TO THAT MUSTY CHAPEL HOUSE WHERE HE KNELT DOWN AND PRAYED FOR AN ANSWER.
HE DIDN'T WANT LIGHTNING. HE DIDN'T WANT A PARTING OF THE SEAS. ALL HE ASKED FOR WAS A SIGN FROM GOD AS DEFINITE PROOF THAT I WAS JUST AS SPECIAL AS EVERYONE SEEMED TO THINK I WAS.
OUTSIDE, MARKIE CRITTENDEN WAS PLAYING BASEBALL WAY PAST HIS BEDTIME AGAIN AND HITTING HOME RUN AFTER HOME RUN WITH THOSE PERFECT, NON-SQUINTY *EYES* I'D GIVEN HIM.
THREE BLOCKS AWAY, FAT ASS JESS CALDWELL WAS SITTING UPRIGHT AROUND THAT STURDY NEW SPINE I GREW FOR HIM AND YELLING AT HIS WIFE AS SHE TOOK HIM OUT FOR *DRIVING PRACTICE.*
ANGEL, MEANWHILE, WAS OUTSIDE IN THE GARDEN FOR A MOONLIGHT PISS, CHEWING AND SLOBBERING OVER HIS NEW PLASTIC TOY WHILE HIS MASTER PRAYED SO HARD HIS *VEINS* WERE STICKING OUT.
"PLEASE, GOD," HE WHISPERED. "JUST GIVE ME A SIGN THAT THIS CHILD IS MORE THAN JUST THE LITTLE BAG OF SNOT AND ZITS HE VERY MUCH APPEARS TO BE."

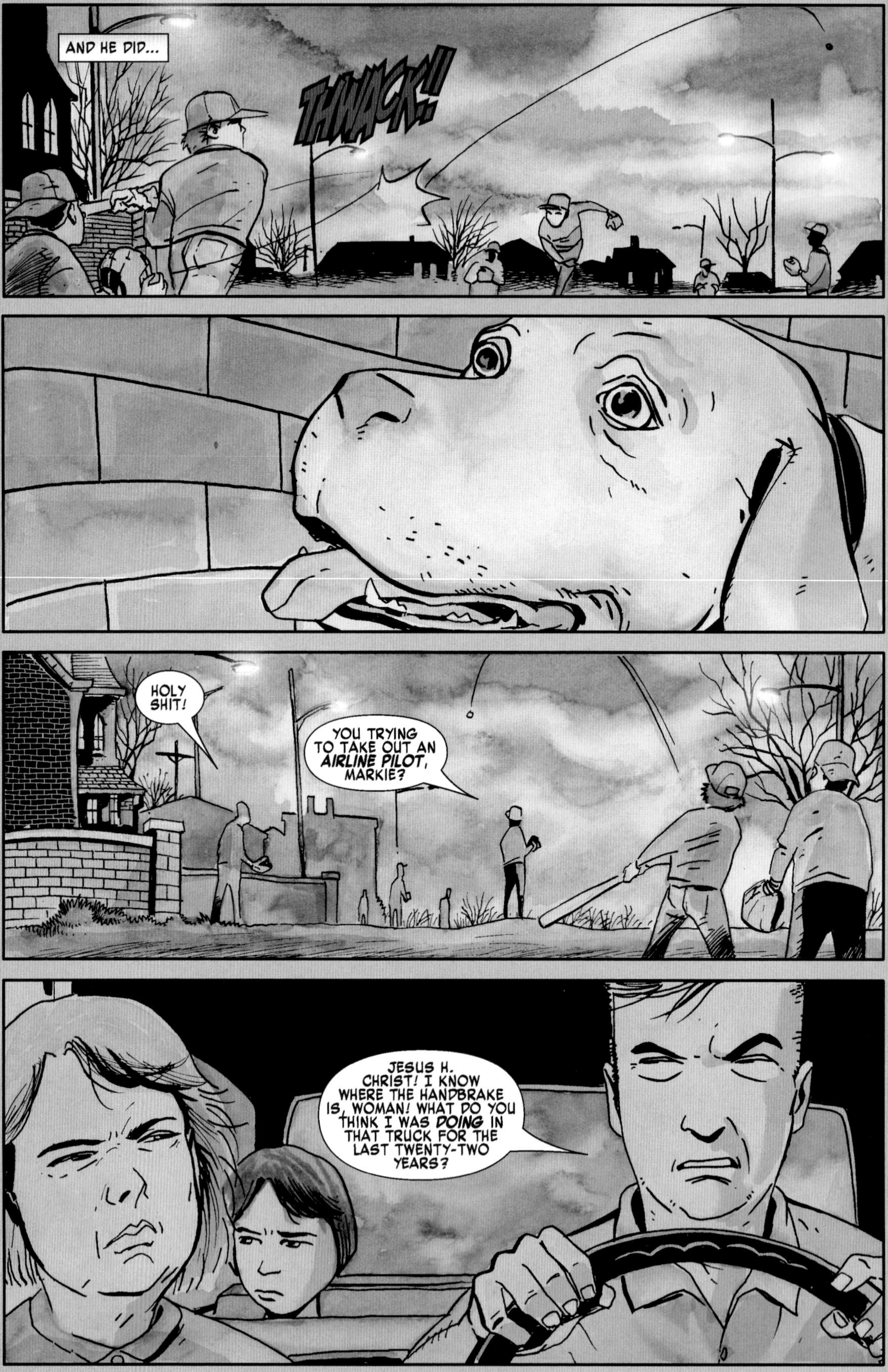
AND HE DID...
THWACK!!
HOLY SHIT!
YOU TRYING TO TAKE OUT AN AIRLINE PILOT, MARKIE?
JESUS H. CHRIST! I KNOW WHERE THE HANDBRAKE IS, WOMAN! WHAT DO YOU THINK I WAS DOING IN THAT TRUCK FOR THE LAST TWENTY-TWO YEARS?

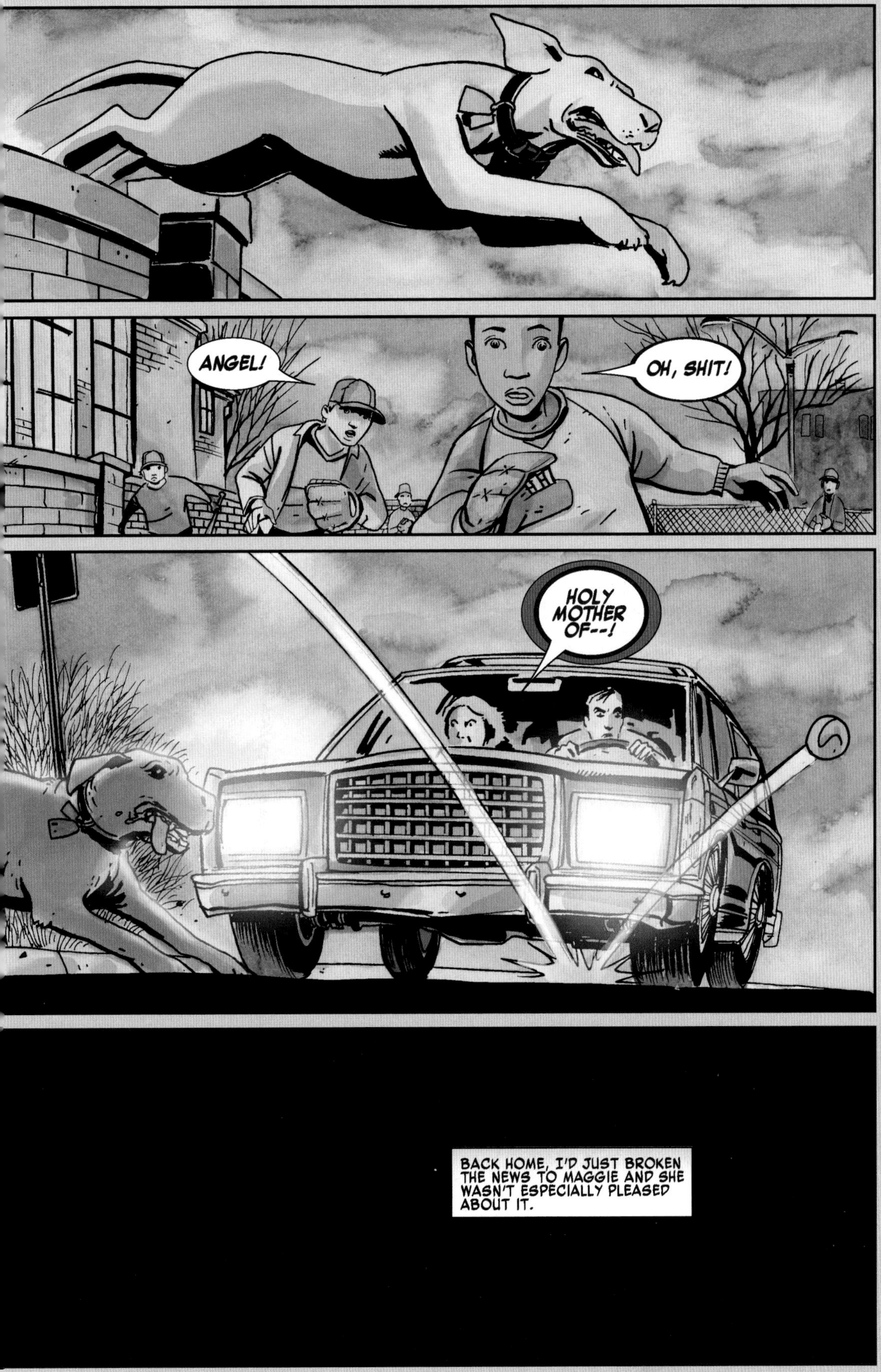
ANGEL!
OH, SHIT!
HOLY MOTHER OF--!
BACK HOME, I'D JUST BROKEN THE NEWS TO MAGGIE AND SHE WASN'T ESPECIALLY PLEASED ABOUT IT.

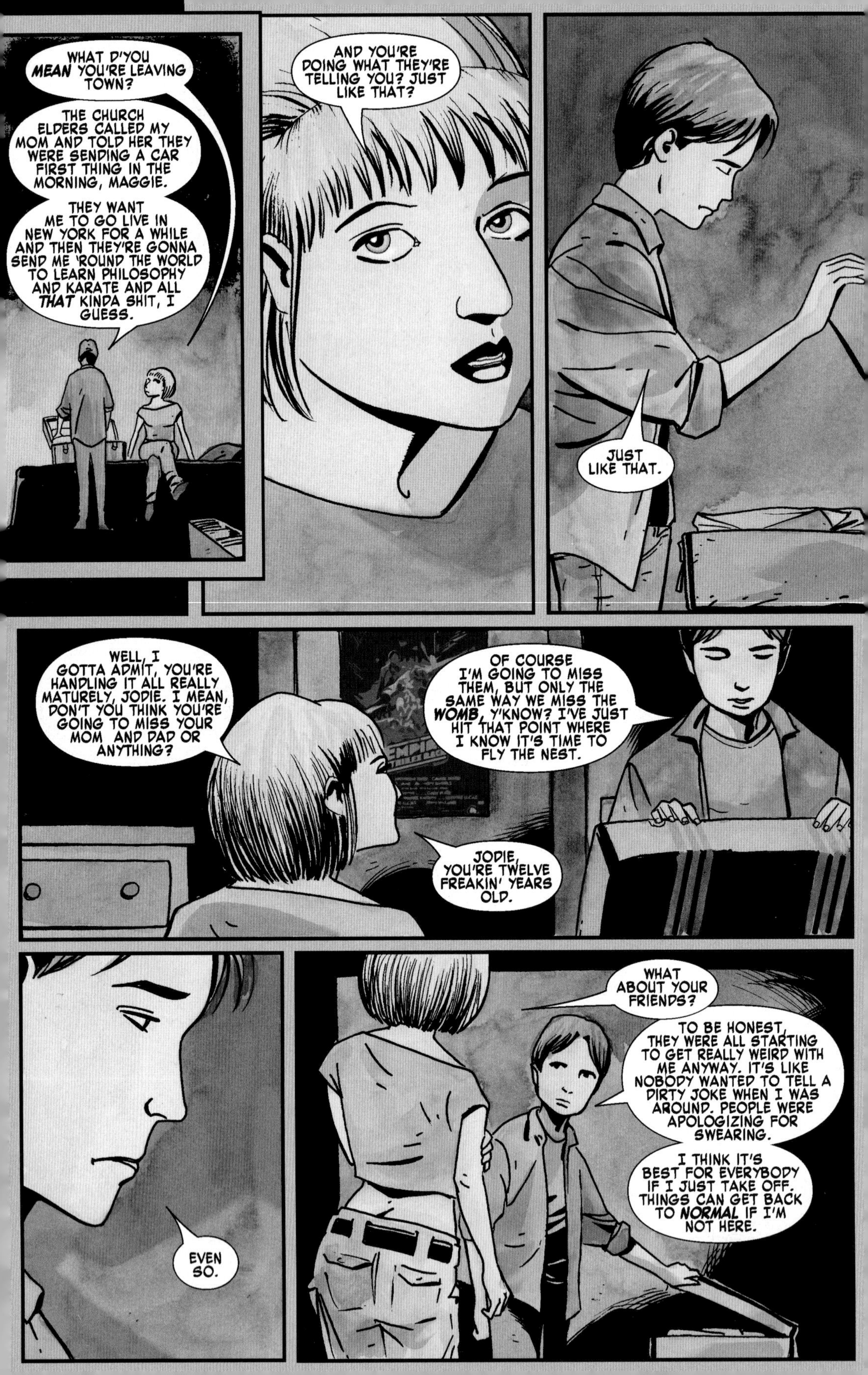
WHAT D'YOU MEAN YOU'RE LEAVING TOWN?
THE CHURCH ELDERS CALLED MY MOM AND TOLD HER THEY WERE SENDING A CAR FIRST THING IN THE MORNING, MAGGIE.
THEY WANT ME TO GO LIVE IN NEW YORK FOR A WHILE AND THEN THEY'RE GONNA SEND ME 'ROUND THE WORLD TO LEARN PHILOSOPHY AND KARATE AND ALL THAT KINDA SHIT, I GUESS.
AND YOU'RE DOING WHAT THEY'RE TELLING YOU? JUST LIKE THAT?
JUST LIKE THAT.
WELL, I GOTTA ADMIT, YOU'RE HANDLING IT ALL REALLY MATURELY, JODIE. I MEAN, DON'T YOU THINK YOU'RE GOING TO MISS YOUR MOM AND DAD OR ANYTHING?
OF COURSE I'M GOING TO MISS THEM, BUT ONLY THE SAME WAY WE MISS THE WOMB, Y'KNOW? I'VE JUST HIT THAT POINT WHERE I KNOW IT'S TIME TO FLY THE NEST.
JODIE, YOU'RE TWELVE FREAKIN' YEARS OLD.
EVEN SO.
WHAT ABOUT YOUR FRIENDS?
TO BE HONEST, THEY WERE ALL STARTING TO GET REALLY WEIRD WITH ME ANYWAY. IT'S LIKE NOBODY WANTED TO TELL A DIRTY JOKE WHEN I WAS AROUND. PEOPLE WERE APOLOGIZING FOR SWEARING.
I THINK IT'S BEST FOR EVERYBODY IF I JUST TAKE OFF. THINGS CAN GET BACK TO NORMAL IF I'M NOT HERE.

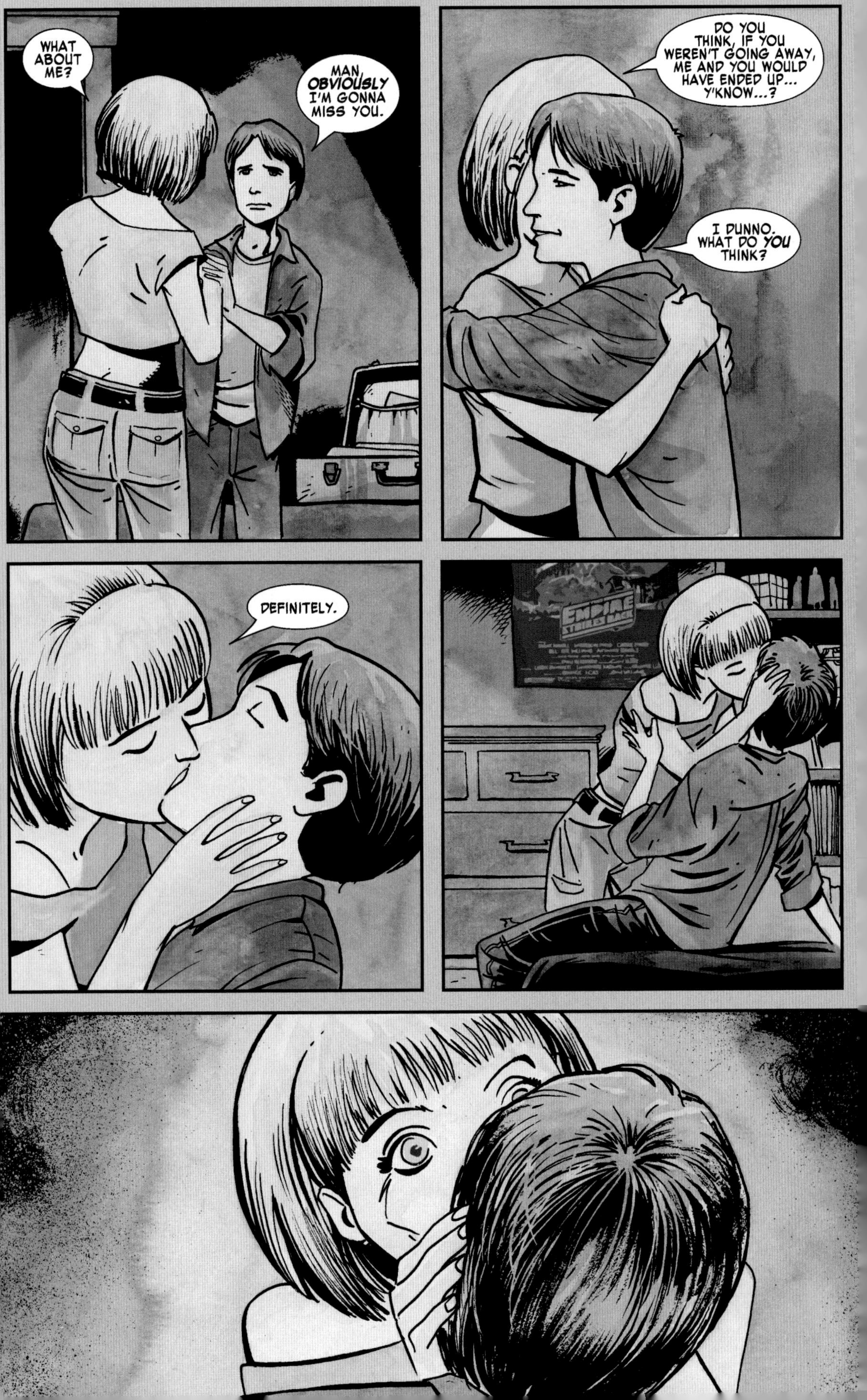
WHAT ABOUT ME?
MAN, OBVIOUSLY I'M GONNA MISS YOU.
DO YOU THINK, IF YOU WEREN'T GOING AWAY, ME AND YOU WOULD HAVE ENDED UP... Y'KNOW...?
I DUNNO. WHAT DO YOU THINK?
DEFINITELY.
EMPIRE STRIKES BACK

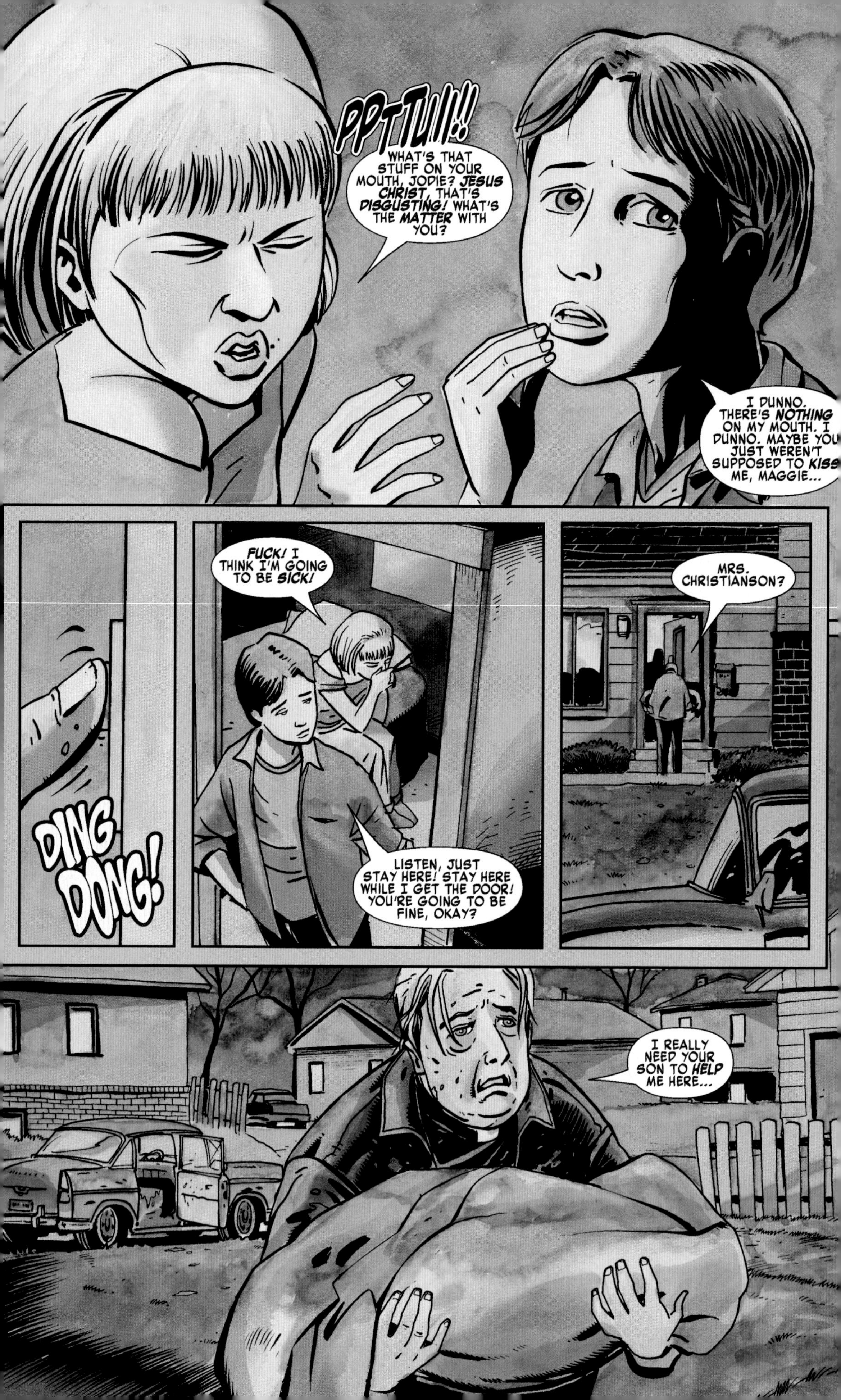
PPTTUI!!!!
WHAT'S THAT STUFF ON YOUR MOUTH, JODIE? JESUS CHRIST, THAT'S DISGUSTING! WHAT'S THE MATTER WITH YOU?
I DUNNO. THERE'S NOTHING ON MY MOUTH. I DUNNO. MAYBE YOU JUST WEREN'T SUPPOSED TO KISS ME, MAGGIE...
DING DONG!
FUCK! I THINK I'M GOING TO BE SICK!
LISTEN, JUST STAY HERE! STAY HERE WHILE I GET THE DOOR! YOU'RE GOING TO BE FINE, OKAY?
MRS. CHRISTIANSON?
I REALLY NEED YOUR SON TO HELP ME HERE...

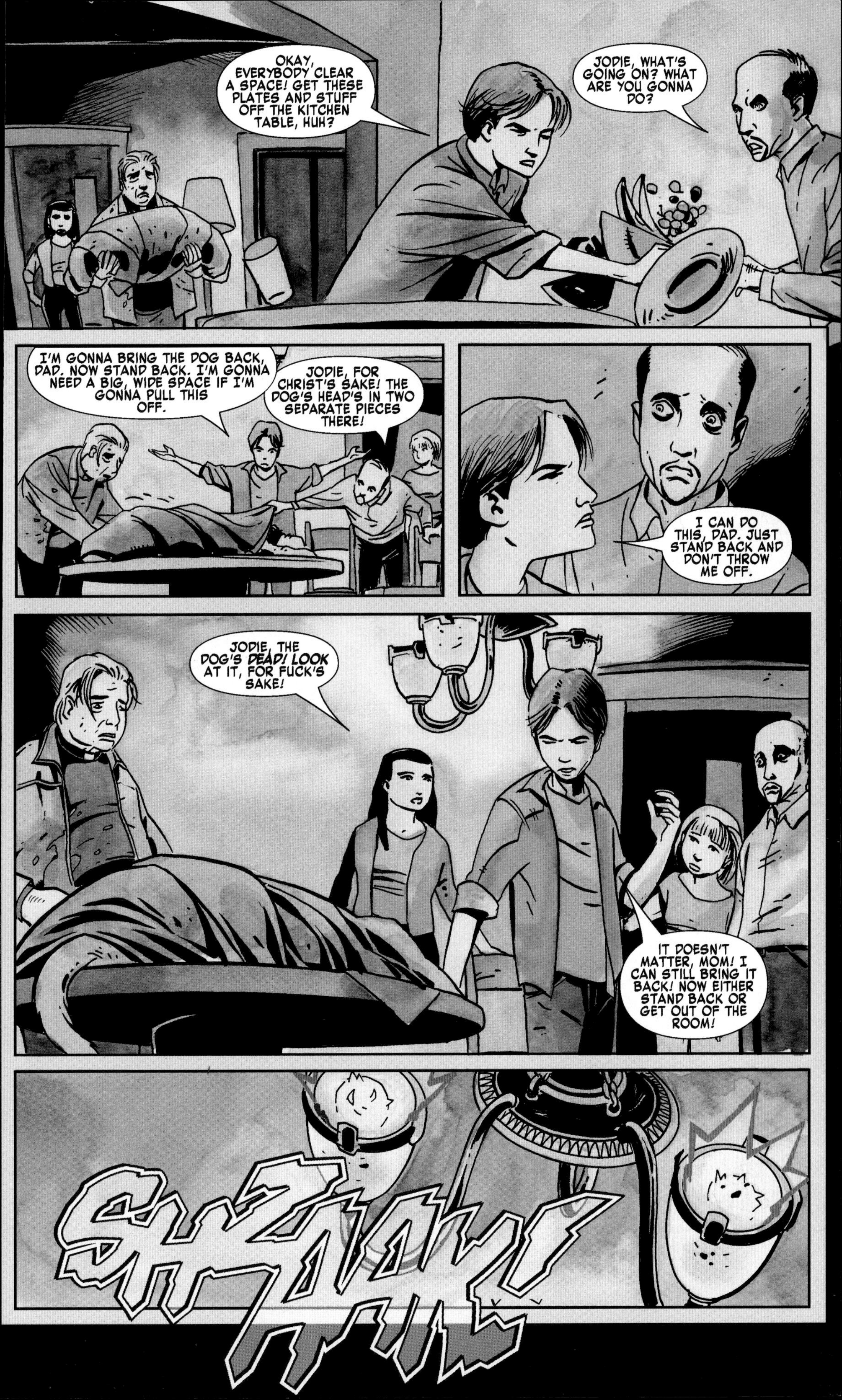
OKAY, EVERYBODY CLEAR A SPACE! GET THESE PLATES AND STUFF OFF THE KITCHEN TABLE, HUH?
JODIE, WHAT'S GOING ON? WHAT ARE YOU GONNA DO?
I'M GONNA BRING THE DOG BACK, DAD. NOW STAND BACK. I'M GONNA NEED A BIG, WIDE SPACE IF I'M GONNA PULL THIS OFF.
JODIE, FOR CHRIST'S SAKE! THE DOG'S HEAD'S IN TWO SEPARATE PIECES THERE!
I CAN DO THIS, DAD. JUST STAND BACK AND DON'T THROW ME OFF.
JODIE, THE DOG'S DEAD! LOOK AT IT, FOR FUCK'S SAKE!
IT DOESN'T MATTER, MOM! I CAN STILL BRING IT BACK! NOW EITHER STAND BACK OR GET OUT OF THE ROOM!

JODIE?

QUIET! I NEED *TOTAL CONCENTRATION* HERE! NOBODY TOUCH ME AND GET AWAY FROM THE DOG, TOO! I DON'T WANT ANYBODY GETTING *HURT!*

OUTSIDE, IT WAS LIKE SOMEBODY TURNED THE STREETLIGHTS UP UNTIL THEY JUST COULDN'T TAKE IT ANYMORE AND POPPED LIKE FIRECRACKERS FROM ONE END OF TOWN TO THE OTHER.

EVERY BULB, EVERY FUSE, EVERY CABLE AND EVERY TINY TRANSISTOR BURNED WHITE-HOT FOR A FRACTION OF A SECOND AND THEN DIED JUST AS QUICKLY, THEIR ENERGIES ROCKETING ELSEWHERE.

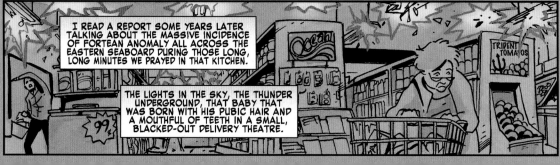

I READ A REPORT SOME YEARS LATER TALKING ABOUT THE MASSIVE INCIDENCE OF FORTEAN ANOMALY ALL ACROSS THE EASTERN SEABOARD DURING THOSE LONG, LONG MINUTES WE PRAYED IN THAT KITCHEN.

THE LIGHTS IN THE SKY, THE THUNDER UNDERGROUND, THAT BABY THAT WAS BORN WITH HIS PUBIC HAIR AND A MOUTHFUL OF TEETH IN A SMALL, BLACKED-OUT DELIVERY THEATRE.

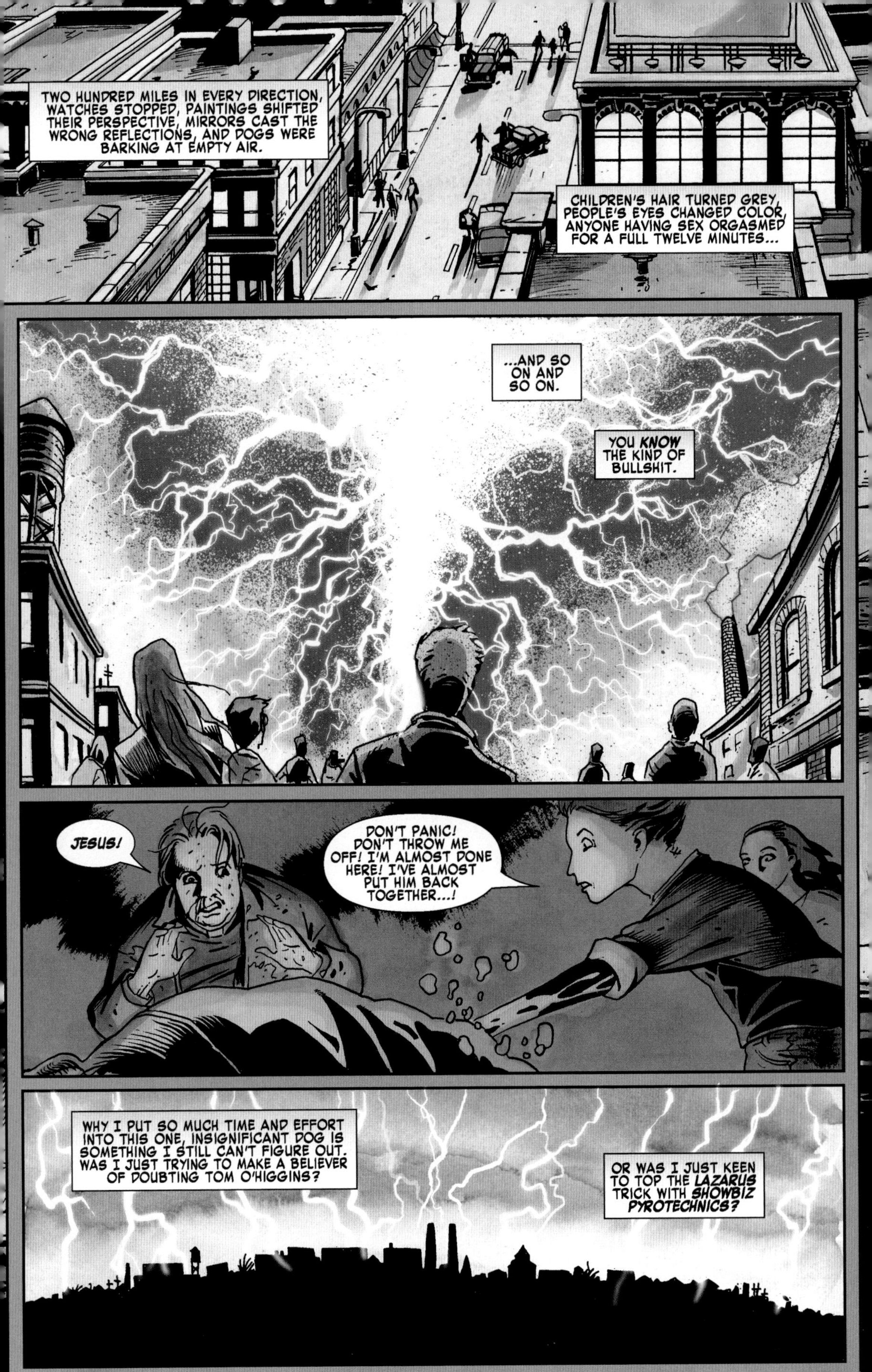
TWO HUNDRED MILES IN EVERY DIRECTION, WATCHES STOPPED, PAINTINGS SHIFTED THEIR PERSPECTIVE, MIRRORS CAST THE WRONG REFLECTIONS, AND DOGS WERE BARKING AT EMPTY AIR.
CHILDREN'S HAIR TURNED GREY, PEOPLE'S EYES CHANGED COLOR, ANYONE HAVING SEX ORGASMED FOR A FULL TWELVE MINUTES...
...AND SO ON AND SO ON.
YOU *KNOW* THE KIND OF BULLSHIT.
JESUS!
DON'T PANIC! DON'T THROW ME OFF! I'M ALMOST DONE HERE! I'VE ALMOST PUT HIM BACK TOGETHER...!
WHY I PUT SO MUCH TIME AND EFFORT INTO THIS ONE, INSIGNIFICANT DOG IS SOMETHING I STILL CAN'T FIGURE OUT. WAS I JUST TRYING TO MAKE A BELIEVER OF DOUBTING TOM O'HIGGINS?
OR WAS I JUST KEEN TO TOP THE *LAZARUS* TRICK WITH *SHOWBIZ PYROTECHNICS?*

I ASKED FOR A SIGN AND HE SENT ME A SIGN. THE CRITTENDEN BOY, JESS CALDWELL, ALL THOSE UNIMPORTANT DETAILS...

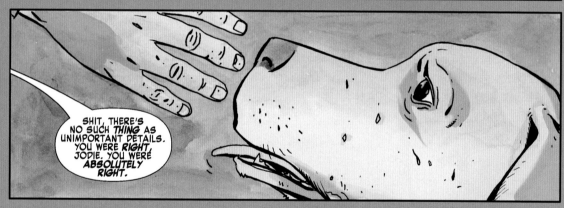

SHIT, THERE'S NO SUCH THING AS UNIMPORTANT DETAILS. YOU WERE RIGHT, JODIE. YOU WERE ABSOLUTELY RIGHT.

YOU JUST LOST SIGHT OF THE BIG PICTURE FOR A WHILE THERE, TOM.

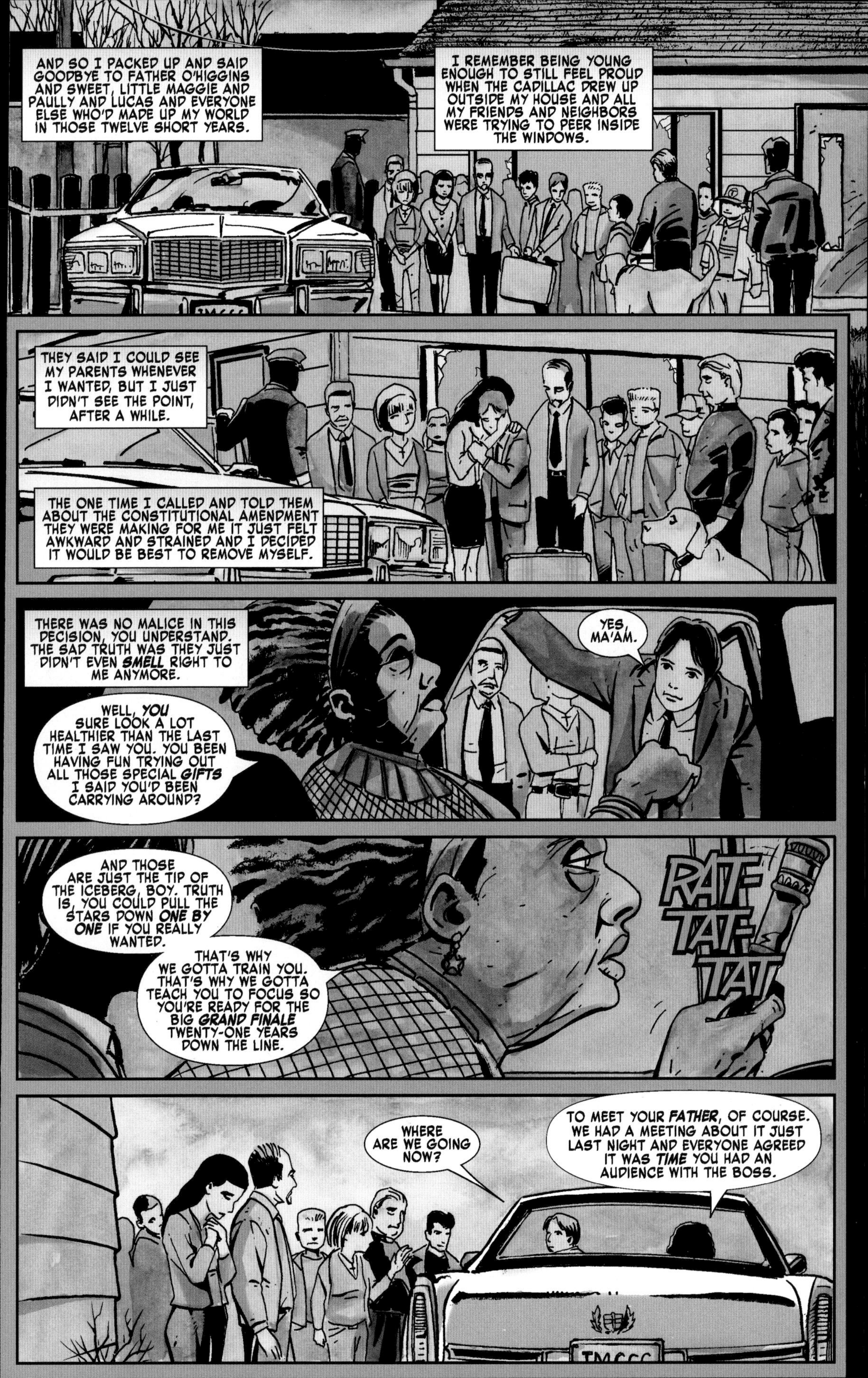

AND SO I PACKED UP AND SAID GOODBYE TO FATHER O'HIGGINS AND SWEET, LITTLE MAGGIE AND PAULLY AND LUCAS AND EVERYONE ELSE WHO'D MADE UP MY WORLD IN THOSE TWELVE SHORT YEARS.
I REMEMBER BEING YOUNG ENOUGH TO STILL FEEL PROUD WHEN THE CADILLAC DREW UP OUTSIDE MY HOUSE AND ALL MY FRIENDS AND NEIGHBORS WERE TRYING TO PEER INSIDE THE WINDOWS.
THEY SAID I COULD SEE MY PARENTS WHENEVER I WANTED, BUT I JUST DIDN'T SEE THE POINT, AFTER A WHILE.
THE ONE TIME I CALLED AND TOLD THEM ABOUT THE CONSTITUTIONAL AMENDMENT THEY WERE MAKING FOR ME IT JUST FELT AWKWARD AND STRAINED AND I DECIDED IT WOULD BE BEST TO REMOVE MYSELF.
THERE WAS NO MALICE IN THIS DECISION, YOU UNDERSTAND. THE SAD TRUTH WAS THEY JUST DIDN'T EVEN SMELL RIGHT TO ME ANYMORE.
YES, MA'AM.
WELL, YOU SURE LOOK A LOT HEALTHIER THAN THE LAST TIME I SAW YOU. YOU BEEN HAVING FUN TRYING OUT ALL THOSE SPECIAL GIFTS I SAID YOU'D BEEN CARRYING AROUND?
AND THOSE ARE JUST THE TIP OF THE ICEBERG, BOY. TRUTH IS, YOU COULD PULL THE STARS DOWN ONE BY ONE IF YOU REALLY WANTED.
RAT-TAT-TAT
THAT'S WHY WE GOTTA TRAIN YOU. THAT'S WHY WE GOTTA TEACH YOU TO FOCUS SO YOU'RE READY FOR THE BIG GRAND FINALE TWENTY-ONE YEARS DOWN THE LINE.
WHERE ARE WE GOING NOW?
TO MEET YOUR FATHER, OF COURSE. WE HAD A MEETING ABOUT IT JUST LAST NIGHT AND EVERYONE AGREED IT WAS TIME YOU HAD AN AUDIENCE WITH THE BOSS.

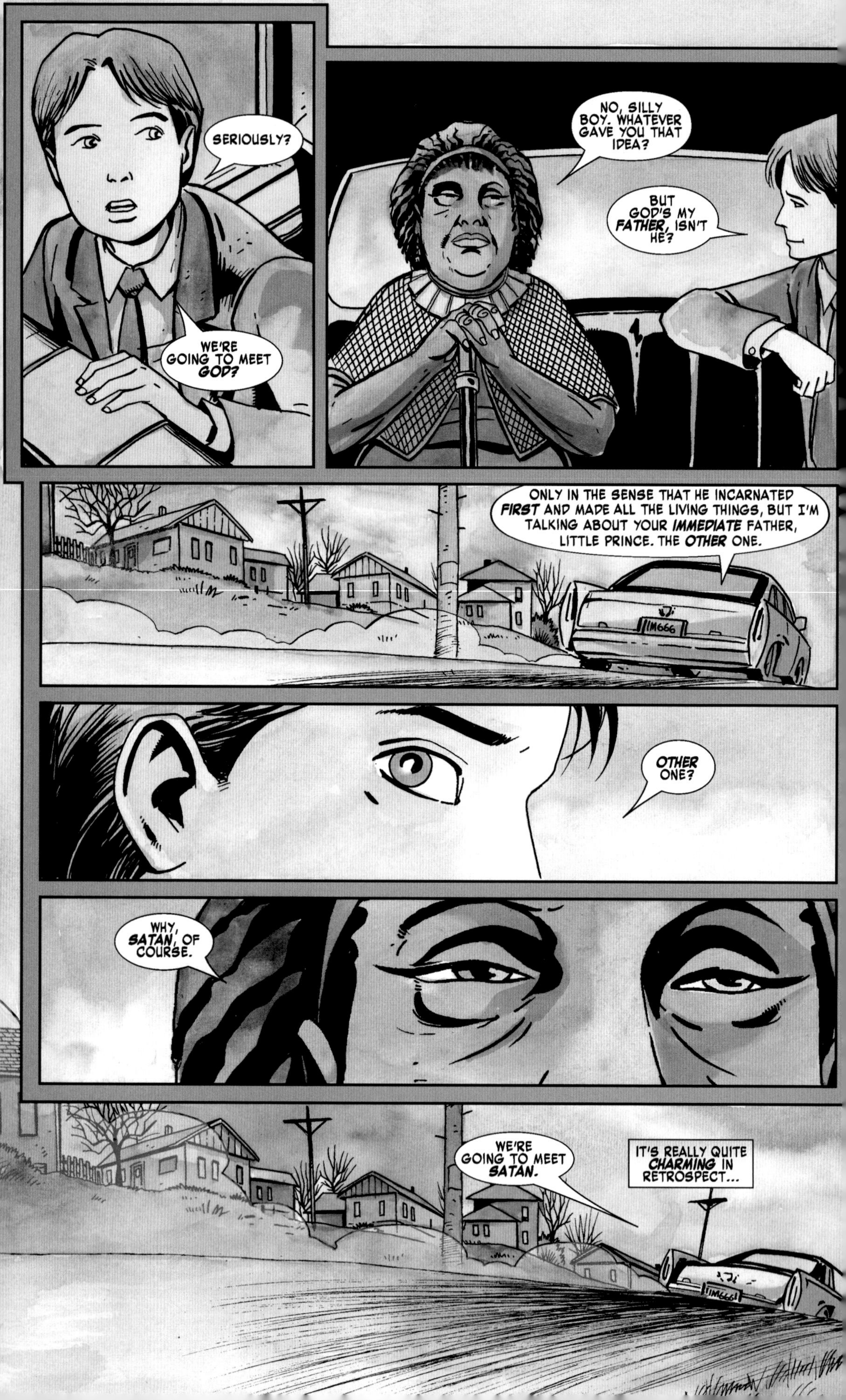

SERIOUSLY?
WE'RE GOING TO MEET *GOD?*
NO, SILLY BOY. WHATEVER GAVE YOU THAT IDEA?
BUT GOD'S MY *FATHER*, ISN'T HE?
ONLY IN THE SENSE THAT HE INCARNATED *FIRST* AND MADE ALL THE LIVING THINGS, BUT I'M TALKING ABOUT YOUR *IMMEDIATE* FATHER, LITTLE PRINCE. THE *OTHER* ONE.
IM666
OTHER ONE?
WHY, *SATAN*, OF COURSE.
WE'RE GOING TO MEET *SATAN.*
IT'S REALLY QUITE *CHARMING* IN RETROSPECT...
IM666

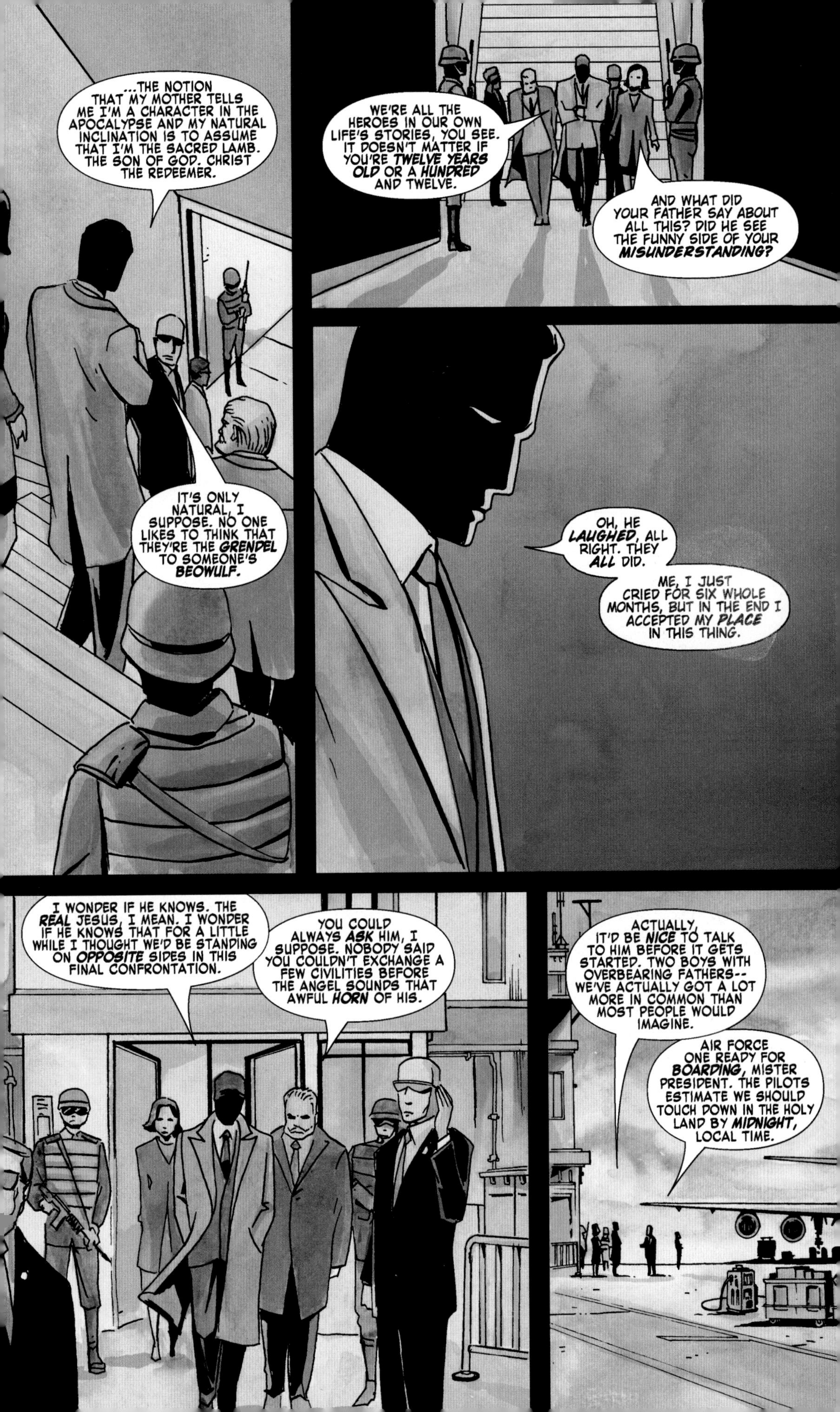
...THE NOTION THAT MY MOTHER TELLS ME I'M A CHARACTER IN THE APOCALYPSE AND MY NATURAL INCLINATION IS TO ASSUME THAT I'M THE SACRED LAMB. THE SON OF GOD. CHRIST THE REDEEMER.
IT'S ONLY NATURAL, I SUPPOSE. NO ONE LIKES TO THINK THAT THEY'RE THE GRENDEL TO SOMEONE'S BEOWULF.
WE'RE ALL THE HEROES IN OUR OWN LIFE'S STORIES, YOU SEE. IT DOESN'T MATTER IF YOU'RE TWELVE YEARS OLD OR A HUNDRED AND TWELVE.
AND WHAT DID YOUR FATHER SAY ABOUT ALL THIS? DID HE SEE THE FUNNY SIDE OF YOUR MISUNDERSTANDING?
OH, HE LAUGHED, ALL RIGHT. THEY ALL DID.
ME, I JUST CRIED FOR SIX WHOLE MONTHS, BUT IN THE END I ACCEPTED MY PLACE IN THIS THING.
I WONDER IF HE KNOWS. THE REAL JESUS, I MEAN. I WONDER IF HE KNOWS THAT FOR A LITTLE WHILE I THOUGHT WE'D BE STANDING ON OPPOSITE SIDES IN THIS FINAL CONFRONTATION.
YOU COULD ALWAYS ASK HIM, I SUPPOSE. NOBODY SAID YOU COULDN'T EXCHANGE A FEW CIVILITIES BEFORE THE ANGEL SOUNDS THAT AWFUL HORN OF HIS.
ACTUALLY, IT'D BE NICE TO TALK TO HIM BEFORE IT GETS STARTED. TWO BOYS WITH OVERBEARING FATHERS-- WE'VE ACTUALLY GOT A LOT MORE IN COMMON THAN MOST PEOPLE WOULD IMAGINE.
AIR FORCE ONE READY FOR BOARDING, MISTER PRESIDENT. THE PILOTS ESTIMATE WE SHOULD TOUCH DOWN IN THE HOLY LAND BY MIDNIGHT, LOCAL TIME.

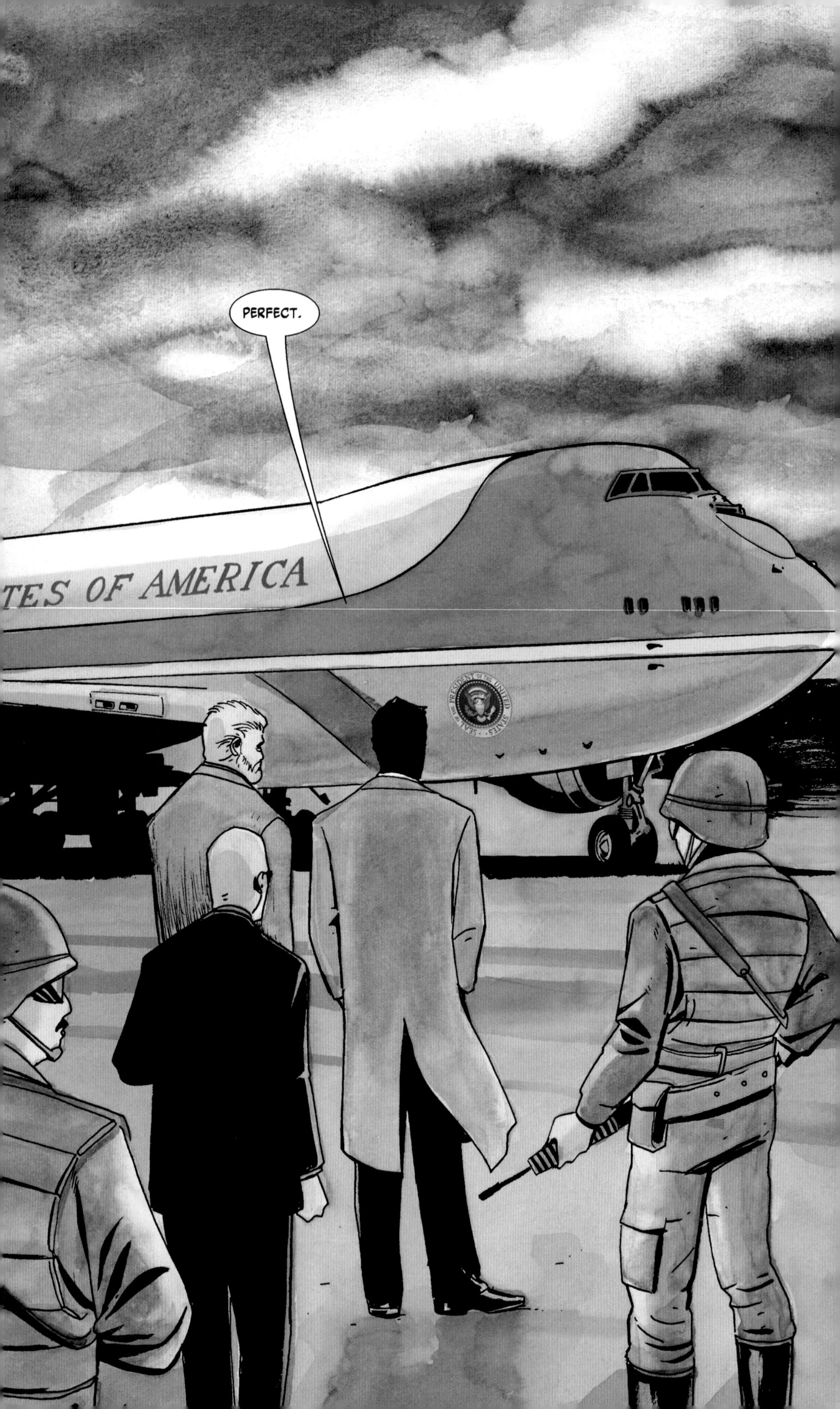
PERFECT.
TES OF AMERICA

End of Book One

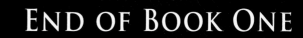

The Gospel According to Millar and Gross
Occult Symbols and Hidden Meanings

Peter Gross: I'm going to start you off talking about *American Jesus: Chosen* —— Tell me how and what the inspiration was.

Mark Millar: I'd had the idea for *American Jesus: Chosen* rattling around in my head for a long time. I grew up in a religious part of a religious country, and this still plays a big part in my adult life—whether it's going to Mass on Sundays or sending my daughter to a Catholic school. That notion of Catholicism you see in movies with nuns beating the shit out of people is absolutely nothing like Catholic life for 99.9% of Scottish Catholics. The church was just a part of the community as much as a the school or the local doctor, and the priests in my own parish were just three big friendly guys who'll have a drink with your dad or drop by and have their dinner at your house because they didn't have wives or any idea how to cook their own meals. I really have nothing but happy memories of growing up as a Catholic, and I wanted to do a book about faith that *wasn't* about child-molesting priests or all the usual shit you get when we liberals write stories about the Church. I wanted to write something about the Church without taking the piss out of it, and writing something about Jesus that wasn't judgmental or mocking.

PG: What prompted you to ask me to get involved?

MM: I can't remember if I told you this, but you coming onto *Chosen* was a fortunate accident and a brainwave for which our former editor Stuart Moore should get full credit. The original guy I had in mind was Mike Wieringo. I've always like Ringo's stuff and had wanted to work with him, and the fact that he and Mark Waid were briefly fired from *The Fantastic Four* seemed like the perfect opportunity to make the best of a sad situation. For about ten minutes, the stars were aligned and everything looked set and we were about to announce the whole Millarworld line at San Diego Comic Con '03, but then Ringo was un-fired. He was re-hired for *The Fantastic Four* and there was a huge kiss-and-make-up at Marvel, and I suddenly found myself with a press release and no artist. I was complaining about all this to Stuart when he suddenly remembered that you, Mister Peter Gross, were both great and fast [well, *reasonably* fast]. I'd loved what you'd done on *Books of Magic*, and that was exactly the kind of atmosphere I wanted on this book. The original pitch was *Harry Potter* for fundamentalist Christians, and you tapped into that whole Peter Straub/Stephen King/J.K. Rowling thing really well. It really was serendipity because you gave the book a quiet tone and a realistic atmosphere that made everything very fairy tale, but also very natural. People just looked like people, and there was a beautiful verisimilitude brought to Jodie's world. I couldn't be happier with how the book turned out, and I knew you were the guy the second I saw those first few pages coming through the fax machine. Jodie and his friends just looked like real kids.

PG: Thanks for the kind words—but you weren't at San Diego in '03, were you? The way I remember it, I was having breakfast with Stuart at one of those bayside San Diego restaurants and he was obsessed with checking his email with his Treo, and he got an email from you asking how to get a hold of me. He emailed you back and forth and got the briefest description of *American Jesus: Chosen* and I had a day or so to decide if I wanted to do it [with not a mention in the emails from you what the ending to *Chosen* would be]. I ran it by Shelly Bond [my *Lucifer* editor] and she was probably none too pleased, and I got the contract details and hopped on board the next day.   Up until then, the only brief experience I had working with you was when you wrote the infamous Tim Hunter/*Teen Titans* parody in a *Books of Magic Annual* during my run as writer on the book. It was so fucking hilarious [especially with Phil Jimenez doing his best George Perez style on the art] that I knew working with you on a story about Jesus and Revelation would be an experience I had to jump at.

MM: Yeah, that's right. I was weeping in Glasgow and Stuart was getting emails from me at the San Diego Con. I was basically firing emails out to everyone I knew and asking if they had heard of anyone good who might be available. I'd also forgotten how tight-lipped I was about the ending. Dark Horse kept asking me for an actual outline before they coughed up both cash and contract, and I kept saying they were being unreasonable [which is pretty hilarious in hindsight]. Mike Richardson, Randy Stradley and Dave Land just kept dropping these really polite emails asking what the book was going to be about, and I kept telling them not to worry and it was going to be great, which must have sounded insanely vague to them. My big fear was that someone would mention the ending to someone else. I don't think I even told *you* the ending until I was writing the third issue. This twist was actually the first thing that came to me. I wanted to write a book about Jesus, a book about the Antichrist, and a book about the moment they both actually faced one another. It was always loosely planned as a three-issue miniseries and I wanted to do something with the Antichrist that was a little different than the traditional take we've seen a million time since the [brilliant] take in *The Omen*. I just liked the idea that nobody thinks of themselves as a bad guy and, if you grow up watching *Star Wars* and *Superman* and having all the experiences Jodie would have had at that age, the last thing you're going to assume is that you're the most famous villain in history. You're always the hero of your own story, and this seemed like an interesting take on the character to me. I had the ending and just worked my way back from there. I genuinely wrote the whole thing backwards.

PG: Working backwards gave us a huge opportunity to sprinkle clues throughout the book, teasing about the twist at the end without actually giving the game away. I don't think anyone's ever actually found all the little clues we planted in each issue.

MM: The *Star Wars* visuals throughout the story really made me smile. Luke's dark and sinister secret dad was one of the biggest twists in movie history, and was a nice foreshadowing of what was coming up. We should probably detail some of the other clues we threw in there. I'd like to leave out some of the numerological ones because I'd like crazies in the future to constantly reread this thing and look for Da Vinci-style clues, but I suppose we should probably point out some of the more obvious ones. You go first, Mister Gross.

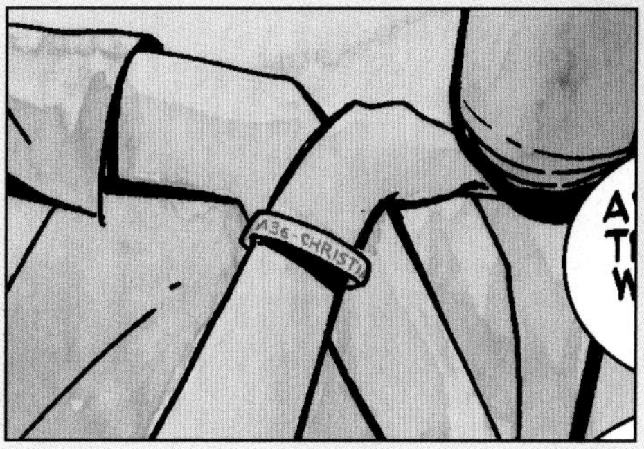
A36-CHRIST

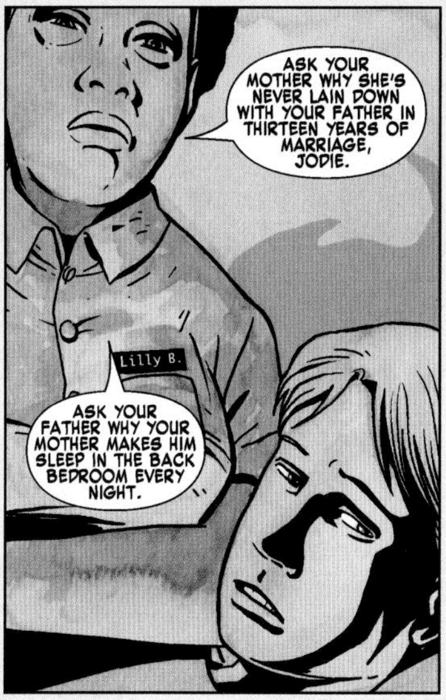
ASK YOUR MOTHER WHY SHE'S NEVER LAIN DOWN WITH YOUR FATHER IN THIRTEEN YEARS OF MARRIAGE, JODIE.
Lilly B.
ASK YOUR FATHER WHY YOUR MOTHER MAKES HIM SLEEP IN THE BACK BEDROOM EVERY NIGHT.

PG: The first clue I put in the first issue is on Jodie's wristband in panel three of page ten—I bet you never saw this one, Mark—it's clear as day zoomed up on the computer but you'd need a magnifying glass to see it in the book. Jodie's band says "A36 CHRIST..." [the first part of his last name Christianson]. I didn't think it would actually show up, but there it is.

MM: God almighty! You're right. How did I miss that?

PG: Because you're high on crack, of course. And the woman visiting Jodie is an emissary of Jodie's true father, and her name is Lilly B.—short for Lilith Beelzebub in my mind—and on the last panel of that same page Jodie has a horned shadow...

MM: The horned shadow appears quite a lot throughout the series, as well as Jodie's shadow quite eerily facing the opposite direction from where it should every time you see it. Counting thirty-three panels into each of the three issues [the series totaled sixty-six pages, by the way] should also give a nice surprise for those of a numerological bent. The most obvious sleight of hand was the names on the characters where we had eleven teenage apostles for Jodie Christianson, and a twelfth eventual believer in the shape of Father doubting Thomas O'Higgins. Maggie was obviously an allegory for Mary Magdalene, and his sexless, TV-watching parents were a 20th century update of the Virgin Mary and her very frustrated-looking husband. All the little details really tickle me when I flick through the book. I love the three telephone poles that appear everywhere in the shape of the three crosses at Golgotha. The *Star Wars* stuff was there, of course, but so were the little unsolved Rubik's Cubes you added to hint that there was a puzzle still to be solved. I remember being too lazy and ill-educated to have the Latin phrase on the blackboard in the first issue translated. For anyone who skipped a classical education, this phrase read "The boy is not what he seems." Who did the eventual translation for us? I can't remember. Was it Mike Carey?

PG: It was Mike. He's the only guy I know educated enough to remember his Latin. He was nice enough to translate your phrase "Things are not what they seem." We went with "things" instead of "boy" because we didn't want to give it totally away if someone actually went through all those blackboard panels and translated them. I liked the *Star Wars* figures on the last page, too—Darth Vader for Jodie and the two stormtroopers for his best friends.

MM: That's brilliant. I'm glad we're doing this "DVD extras" thing because I'm learning as much as anyone.

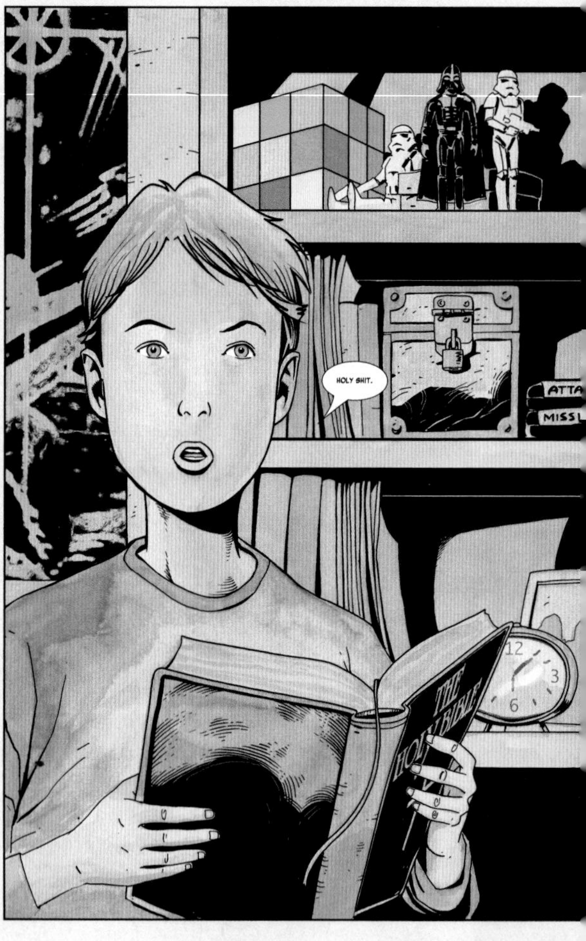
HOLY SHIT.

PG: My pleasure. And the locked box on the second shelf suggests something being kept secret, and on the third shelf the clock is six minutes after six—a recurring repetition of the number six throughout all the issues.

MM: That's great. I honestly didn't catch the two stormtroopers thing. I love these little details. We tried to do this with *Superman: Red Son*, too. We just filled it with clues and lots of secret subplots. My idea was that even if people didn't like the comic, there was at least *something* they could do with the book, having been ripped off to the tune of eighteen bucks. Should we mention that there's part of a message on panel thirty-three of each issue that eventually spells out "Jodie is the Beast?"

PG: Too late. You've already done it. But my burning question for you about the first issue is: why and where did the obscure questions about JFK's cabinet come from? I actually knew the Orville Freeman answer—the guy was the former governor of Minnesota [my home state].

MM: That's my secret hobby. I'm genuinely fascinated by the real world and try to read about it as much as normal people like to get lost in fiction. It's something I noticed a few years ago. I was out for dinner with a whole bunch of writers, and nobody had read the latest bestsellers, but we'd all read the most obscure factual stuff. It's the same with television. I've never watched *The Sopranos* or *Six Feet Under*, or any of those programs people tell me I'd enjoy, because I'm too busy watching news programs. I think it's all to do with balance, and when you're living in the real world with a real job where you wear a tie and have a water cooler, you just need to appease the other side of your brain. You need to get a little lost in fiction. Whereas I work maybe eight to ten hours every day in a fictional world and I'm asleep for at least eight hours, which means I'm usually only spending six hours a day in the world everyone else inhabits. The last thing I want to do in those six hours is get caught up in another fictional reality, and watching people getting blown to bits on the other side of the world, or reading about an amendment to a bill they're trying to pass in Parliament, really does feel like downtime to me because it's so different from what I do all day. It's very relaxing because it's nothing like my job. I was a voracious reader of fiction before I started writing, and read a huge amount of fiction when I'm on holiday, but every writer I know—at least every full-time writer—finds it hard to read fiction when they're working on a project. Is this the same with artists?

PG: I have to confess that the longer I work in comics, the less fiction I read. And I'm a total political junkie—especially before the 2004 election here in the States.

MM: Ah, the one where you waved goodbye to democracy forever. So long, America. It was nice knowing you.

PG: What were we talking about again?

MM: I was just saying that I'm a political geek. I know most obscure facts about this shit and enjoy showing off at every opportunity. Politics in particular really fuels up my imagination and gets me excited about writing. Likewise, religion. As I mentioned earlier, this has never been a negative factor for me. I'm just genuinely interested in the ideas, the mythology, and the social function it has within society. This is something I've never asked you about—which is weird—but do you have any religious background? Did working on the project have any significance for you in terms of how you were raised?

PG: I was raised Catholic, went to Catholic grade school for a few years, and went to a Benedictine liberal arts college. One of my old roommates [and oldest friend] from there is now a Benedictine monk. That said, I think I was born agnostic and I've slid Left ever since. I remember being quite amazed in the second or third grade to realize that my schoolmates believed in God and church—I had always thought it was just an ordeal we had to sit through. But I have all the cultural genetic heritage of a Catholic and I have an appreciation and respect for many of the priests, monks, and nuns I knew in college—and I enjoy liberal, educated Catholics. But I have to say that while working on *Chosen* I had some experiences that really made me aware of fundamental Evangelical Christianity in America, and I found it absolutely chilling and frightening. There was a two week period where I became completely obsessed with the subject and I read everything I could find on it. I'm totally convinced that fundamentalist Christians are as great a threat to the future I'd wish for as any fundamentalist Muslim will ever be.

MM: I'm just very suspicious of anyone who thinks they're right. I mean, I'm a Christian, but I'm also aware that we're around seven percent of the world's population, so that kind of puts things in perspective. It's odd that every single world religion has the notion of respect and tolerance at the heart of their creeds, and yet this is the first thing to be trampled underfoot by the people who profess to be the greatest champions of their faith. Personally, I just can't get my head around the conservatives in America ever clasping Jesus to their bosoms when he's clearly a revolutionary socialist. They love the crying Jesus and the manger and the agonized Jesus on the cross, but both are oddly silent. Neither are espousing the message Jesus came here to preach, and that's universal love and standing up against tyranny. That's the Jesus I'm interested in and—if we ever get around to the sequel—the Jesus I want to write about.

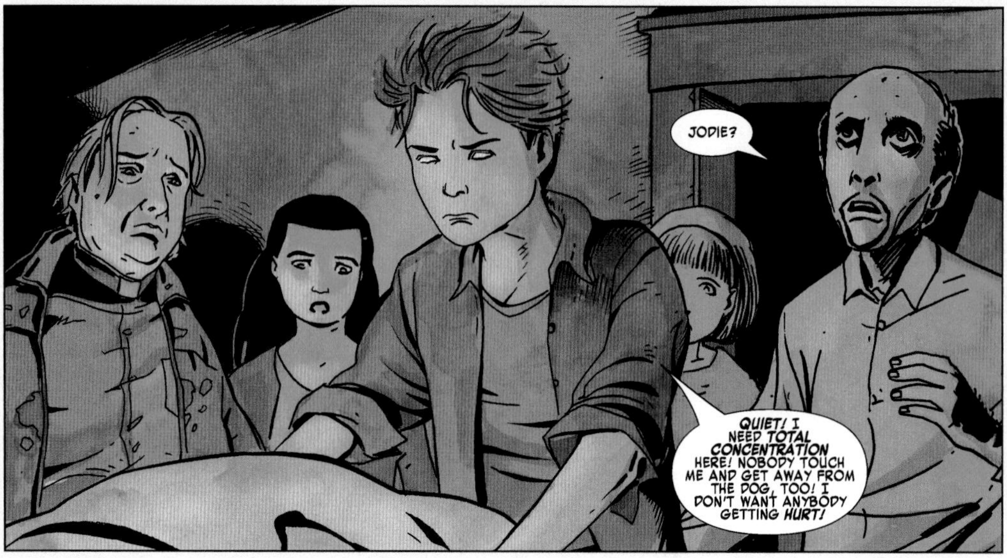
JODIE?
QUIET! I NEED TOTAL CONCENTRATION HERE! NOBODY TOUCH ME AND GET AWAY FROM THE DOG, TOO! I DON'T WANT ANYBODY GETTING HURT!

PG: Speaking of sequel... I'm ready to go anytime...

MM: I originally planned this as a series of books, but then got worried when I saw how well these worked out that we might not match them. But I still have the story of the real modern-day Jesus to tell, and there's so many interesting things going on around us. The Book of Revelation is practically unfolding before our eyes. I don't know how much longer I can stop myself from hammering this all into my computer. It would certainly stop me ranting at people in real life.

PG: And on another religious tangent, I would get a big eye-roll from Jeanne whenever our daughter Alice would ask if Jesus or God are real, and I'd tell her that the stories are important but nobody really knows if they're real. But I realize that for me, stores are my religion—they have the power to transform and reveal, and I'm just as likely to take a powerful lesson from an old comic as I am the Bible—and I don't mean that to denigrate the Bible. I just think that the messages in stories are plenty, and we shouldn't need more than that—it's when people start believing the stories that we run into dodgy territory, and when they start to literally believe the stories, we run into really dangerous territory. I can't help but wonder why it isn't enough for people to take their religion as powerful stories. Am I missing an essential piece of my humanity?

MM: I'm afraid so. Try basing your community's entire belief system around *Action Comics* #500 and see the shambles you're living in before too long. And yet I know what you mean. Superhero comics in particular are essentially just modern-day tellings of the same old myth stories, except God didn't wear Clark Kent's glasses as He moved among mortal men. There's also a brilliant humanity in superhero comics and wonderful life lessons for children. They really were role models in the same lineage as Jesus and Moses... until people like *us* got their hands on them, of course.

PG: And I want to spread some kudos to Jeanne for the great job she did coloring the book.

MM: I must admit my heart froze when Peter first told me he wanted his girlfriend colouring the book. It reminded me of the time I had my next-door neighbour colour a series I did for Fleetway here in the UK, just so he could afford to get his windows double-glazed. My first reaction was that if Peter's bird was colouring it then my sister better get to fucking well letter it. But then the pages started coming in and

I was just blown away. It's really, really beautiful and unique colouring that helped enormously with the tone of the series, and everyone commented on what Jeanne brought to the book. If anything, I think Peter's the hanger-on now.

PG: I think Jeanne's heart froze a bit when I brought up the idea, too—but she has a great eye for color [check out her non-comic work at *jeannemcgee.com*] and I knew how much better this book would look with something a little less traditional going on in the art. It was really gratifying when a number of reviews compared her coloring to Lynn Varley's work [on the **first** *Dark Knight*, I hope]. My favorite "ouch" review was this one on Fanboy Planet:

> "... And the artwork from Gross is absolutely appropriate, with brilliant coloring
> from Jeanne McGee that gives the whole book a slightly ethereal feel."

I'll never hear the end of that one at family holidays.

MM: I can't imagine two artists living together. If Gillian and I had the same kind of job, we'd just kill each other, I think. The only couple I feel should work together every day was Jonathan Hart and his wife in *Hart To Hart*. Together they were much more formidable than when their enemies separated them.

PG: And I just want to say what a pleasure it was working with you on something that you clearly cared so much about. I've really tried in my career to work on projects that have some merit, and for the most part I've been lucky to do that. But this one stood out in its uniqueness and risk-taking, and—dare I say it about the notorious image of a Mark Millar book—its sincerity.

MM: And may I just say how nice it was to be delighted with every page I got back, seeing the book look not only as good as I hoped, but better. Anyway, let's end this now before we make the readers physically sick with all this misty-eyed sentiment. I'd love to do a sequel to this and I'm delighted you're interested.

PG: Let's do it.

MM: It's a date.

AFTERWORD

by Brother Richard Hendrick

"At that time if anyone says to you, 'Look here is the Christ!' or, 'There he is!' do not believe it. For false Christs and false prophets will appear and perform great signs and miracles to deceive even the elect——if that were possible. See, I have told you ahead of time."
Matt 24:23-25

"They will see the Son of Man coming on the clouds of the sky, with power and great glory. And he will send his angels with a loud trumpet call, and they will gather his elect from the four winds, from one end of the heavens to the other."
Matt 24:30-31

I was hugely privileged and taken aback when I got a garbled message from my brother to say that Mark Millar had asked me to write an afterword to this book.

Privileged because I have always loved comics as an art form and as entertainment. Taken aback because, of the three boys in our family, I'm the only one who desn't work in the field. [My brother David is a writer and my brother John runs The 3rd Place comic book store in Temple Bar, Dublin.] But then I read the book and understood. *American Jesus: Chosen* is a very deep and complex book that descends into the roots of mystical theology while being, at the same time, a book nostalgic for lost innocence and the growing awareness of the struggle between Vocation and Choice at the heart of every human being.

Sometimes a beam of light entering through the crack in the curtains can illumine a room in such a way that the ordinary and everyday pass away, and the inner meaning of things is revealed. *Chosen* is such a beam of light. Reading it, I was reminded that Apocalypse, the name of the last book of the Bible [and the one whose events *Chosen* may be seen as a prequel], means "to be revealed," coming from the action of pulling back a curtain so that light may enter a space. It's a good word for the last book of the Bible, and it's even a good word for the work of Millar and Gross. For those who are part of Christian tradition, their book illuminates the last days a little better. For those who are not, it has powerful things to illumine about the fundamental choice at the heart of every human being.

Apocalypse. It's such a beautiful word... sort of just trips off the tongue, and yet no other book of the Bible has caused more discussion, argument and questioning. Whole movements have been founded on interpretations of this book, and almost every year someone claims to have cracked the code or decided upon a date for the advent of the Antichrist and Armageddon. Indeed, in a world increasingly teetering on the brink of war and ecological disaster, it's easy to see the appeal of replacing the uncertainty of a future illuminated by faith alone with the prognosticators' choice of dates for the end... *Chosen* acts instead as a mirror into our uncertainty, holding up our souls to an Apocalyptic light, reminding us to be careful in bartering our faith away for seeming certainties... even the miraculous ones. In the pursuit of wonders we can forget the warnings of Christ Himself in the

Gospels, and time and time again history has proven just how quick we are to believe the lies of those who would mimic, mock and deceive. In the pages of *Chosen* we have a timely reminder that God doesn't barter, but the Devil does, and that we had better look twice at any self-proclaimed messiah.

What we often forget is that the revelation of Apocalypse is a two-way mirror. It doesn't just reveal God to us at the end of time, but reveals us to God [and also to ourselves] now. We are told that each of us is following our own individual story. A story that hinges on a fundamental decision. Will we be for Christ or the Antichrist? There are only two alternatives open to us——follow the Lamb or the beast [who so often tries to look like the Lamb]!

Sitting reading this book for the first time, I was of two minds. As a Catholic priest and Franciscan friar, I was reading with the eyes of faith, interested to see what insights could be gained into the faith tradition I am part of that still confidently insists that "He will come again in glory to judge the living and the dead" and which, through lived day-to-day experience of His presence, knows the reality behind those words. I was also reading as a kid who loved comics then, and loves them now. Aware of my responsibility both to the Church and to the kid in me who loves comics, I was pleasantly surprised at the reverent way the events of *Chosen* are played out, and ultimately challenged by its horrific revelation at the end. It struck me that Millar and Gross have captured some authentic whiff of sulphur, some chink of

celestial light in their pages, where they lull us into a false complacency filled with the calmness of the ordinary things of childhood and suburban growing up, and the extraordinary unfolding of events in their midst. We want it to be true... I even found a part of myself [well schooled in the deceptions of the evil one and in the full knowledge that the second coming will not be as the first, but a glorious one] wishing that Jodie Christianson's self-belief was right! All the more important then was the stomach-churning warning at the end.

We live in a world that, at one and the same time, wants to believe and yet is afraid of faith, that says to be spiritual is fine but to be religious is not, in which gratification should be instantaneous and discipline and effort are laughed at. Perhaps what *Chosen*'s own vocation will be is a reminder to us all that in the midst of light and darkness we must choose, and choose well, the side we are on.

Si Deus nobiscum, quis contra nos? [If God is with us, who can be against us?]

Brother Richard Hendrick OFM Cap.
St. Francis Friary, Blanchardstown
Dublin, Ireland

AFTERWORD
by Brother John Hanson

These are, after all, apocalyptic times. What is left but to add some humor and surprise to the narrative being played out before us? It is difficult to ignore the perception of tha told prophet W. B. Yeats from his poem "The Second Coming": *"The best lack all convictions / while the worst / Are full of passionate intensity."*

To imagine a character emerging from the ordinary setting of middle USA who, after walking away from the moment that, by rights, should have killed him, realizes supernatural gifts are nothing if not amusing... now *that* is clever. Biblical scholars have complained that we know nothing of Jesus' life between the ages of twelve and thirty-three. Jodie's life is on the same sequence, it seems. Apocalpytic tremors seem to be associated with individuals [and whole cultures] who endure extraordinary trauma/stress. Yet, one young, barely pubescent lad who becomes the icon of bewilderment and hope associated with the vague articulation of religious interests is no less strange, alas, than a pretentious leader claiming for himself the very righteousness of God. When sitting in relative comfort, it is easy to ask the question: "Where do the surprising religious movements take us?" When caught in the horror of violent human conflict, or when surrounded by the remains of tragedy or, perhaps, when only given over to extreme personal insecurity, is it not human nature to fish around for a way out?

Given the preference of the modern faithful to emphasize the humanness of Jesus, it becomes possible to then think about his Second Coming in terms of the mundane, the pedestrian... a twelve-year-old exchanging curses, insults, cigarettes, crudely stated [if typically frustrating] dreams of sexual fulfillment... and, of course, intellectual life [lest we forget] with his peers and the "elders." A mere boy who is fated to negotiate his way through the invidious web of neurotic home life, and the banal degradations of the contemporary social matrix of the USA... that prevalent angst of realizing that nothing seems to live up to anyone's expectations except perhaps those of the most diehard pessimists. His naive perception of his growing fate is to realize that the cosmic struggle for the soul of humanity is in his hands... or is it? Wouldn't it be like the Devil to get you to want to gamble rather than show some solidarity with your fellow man? Who needs the common good when the chips are on the table?

Jodie Christianson has the unfortunate task of revealing to us the prevalent distortions of hyperactive religious conviction, and the very honest balancing act between our very best and our very worst. The innocent idealism of youth is always jaded by the corrosive poisons of the real world's games. Jodie at thirty-three is no longer the wonderworker of twelve. Or, the wonderworking is about to become lethal. Jesus awing the elders in the temple has become Mel Gibson's tragic blood victim. Those acting around him do not act so much out of faith as out of a quasi-scientific impulse to be certain. And still he's really a very ordinary kid who seems to be taking on a divine task. Good and evil seem, initially, inextricably woven together. He is every boy who struggles through the apocalypse of adolescence. You and I know that to survive the first nocturnal emission is to seriously consider the role of supernatural activity in the drama of life. Satan can take Jodie to the highest precipice and offer power and control over God, for God's sake. And he may be left with only the troubling awareness that a current of stupidity runs through the human narrative. The shocker for Jodie is when he realizes the "miracle" of walking away from a falling eighteen-wheeler is nothing compared to the viciousness of human sexual hunger that can pass for divine inspiration. One must grow to respect the intentions and the power of the truly stupid. Those folks have imaginations, too. And they can really hurt you. Especially when they claim to have the answers and a mandate from Heaven. The poet is usurped by the commentator. Cynicism is more attractive than compassion. Are we hankering for that ultimate resolution? All too willing to trust the guy with the clearest message? Does anyone wonder if Jesus thinks on the cross that maybe it ain't worth it after all? Man seems intent on doing himself in. Do we find ourselves begging Jesus for some compassionate advice? What was it Pogo said? *"I have seen the enemy..."?*

Brother John Hanson OSB
St. John's Abbey
Collegeville, Minnesota
United States

FROM SCRIPT TO ART
with Peter Gross

When I was asked to send over some pages of script and layouts for this ***American Jesus: Chosen*** collection, I went through the large spiral binder where I store the work stuff from the three issues. The one thing I noticed is that my layouts for ***Chosen*** didn't get reworked too much from my first take at them. Sometimes when I read scripts I literally have no idea what I'm going to draw; there might be something that doesn't flow quite right, or a moment's missing that's essential to telling the story—and the result is pages and pages of different versions of the same scene. But with Mark's script for ***Chosen***, what hits me is how I almost saw it in my head as I read it, and the first pass at the layouts was pretty much what I used for the finished art. Mark wrote exactly what I needed, and not a lot more. As an artist, I like that.

5/ Pull back and end the scene with a wide shot where the Priest puts an arm around this despondent-looking kid, head bowed, as he asks him to make a promise.

PRIEST : Now I want you to put this nonsense out of your head and promise me you'll never mention it to another living soul. Is that clear? Do you and me have a DEAL here?
JODIE : Whatever you say, Father.
CAPTION : Naturally, I was lying through my teeth. Lying like I'd lied to my PARENTS when I promised them I wouldn't talk about this to either them or anybody else.

Page Five

1/ Cut to later in the day and we see the streets in this quiet, suburban sprawl with several young teenagers cycling, walking and running from the left of the panel to the right as all the adults move in the opposite direction. Something interesting is happening somewhere and it's a big secret among the kids.

CAPTION : But we were BOYS, you understand, and this was the most exciting this to happen to anyone in something close to two thousand years.
CAPTION : The truth was I couldn't WAIT to get outside and test the true extent of these spectacular JESUS-POWERS I'd somehow lucked into.

2/ Biggish panel and we cut to a high point in the nearby countryside as Jodie stands here and looks very regal indeed as he dramatically holds the head of a small, Milky-Bar Kid style boy who is kneeling with his head bowed before him. There are maybe a dozen other kids around here, some of which with a job to do. The whole thing seems to be supervised by Maggie (from last issue) and she stands here with a clipboard, ready to boss the others about as they test Jodie's powers.

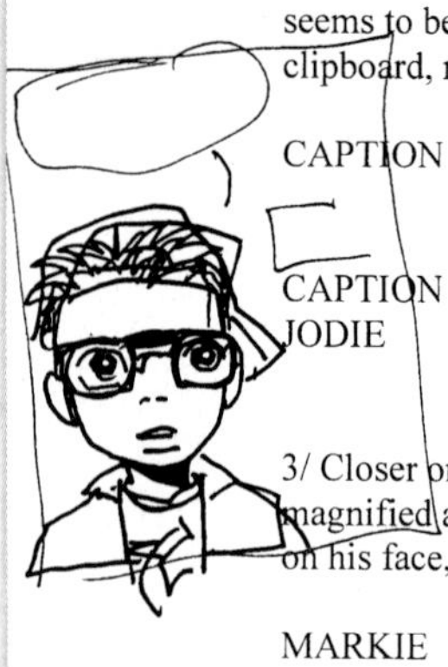

CAPTION : In the absence of the sick, we settled for somebody under the weather. In the absence of the blind, I tried to cure poor Markie Crittenden of that God-awful squint of his.
CAPTION : Poor taste? What are you TALKING about?
JODIE : Now open your eyes, Markie. Open your eyes and let's see if I've made any kind of DIFFERENCE here, huh?

3/ Closer on poor Markie Crittenden as he looks up at us with his big, squinty-eyed, magnified all the larger with his coke-bottle glasses. He has an awkward expression on his face, hoping in some small way that this has worked.

MARKIE : It doesn't FEEL any different, Jodie. Do my eyes LOOK any different to you guys?
OFF-PANEL : Shit.

4/ Lucas snorts, feeling they picked the wrong guy here and we see some bickering going on as little Markie gives him the 'up yours' sign. Jodie looks a little

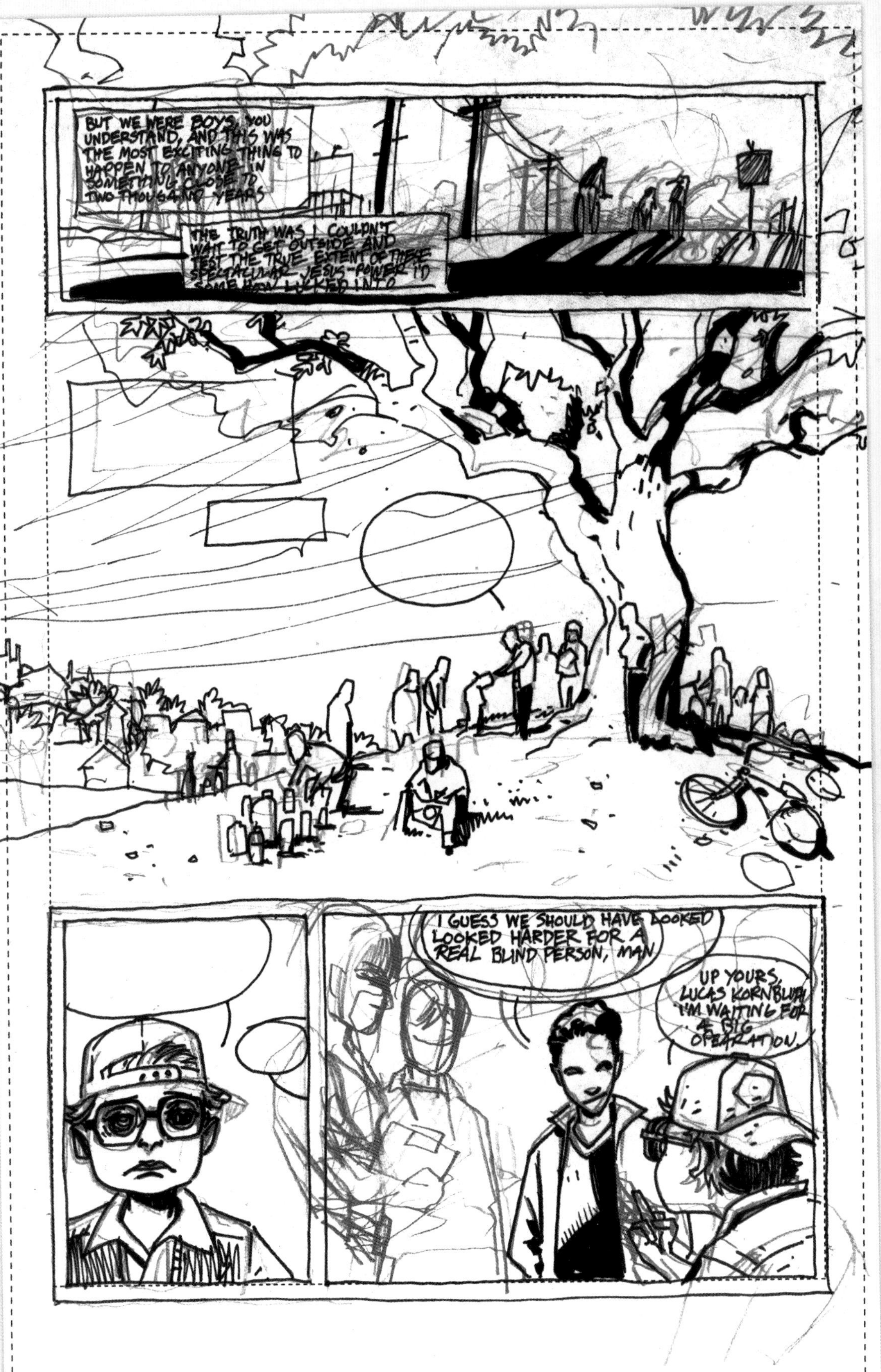
BUT WE WERE BOYS, YOU UNDERSTAND, AND THIS WAS THE MOST EXCITING THING TO HAPPEN TO ANYONE IN SOMETHING CLOSE TO TWO THOUSAND YEARS
THE TRUTH WAS I COULDN'T WAIT TO GET OUTSIDE AND TEST THE TRUE EXTENT OF THESE SPECTACULAR JESUS-POWER I'D SOMEHOW LUCKED INTO
I GUESS WE SHOULD HAVE LOOKED LOOKED HARDER FOR A REAL BLIND PERSON, MAN
UP YOURS, LUCAS KORNBLUH I'M WAITING FOR A BIG OPERATION.

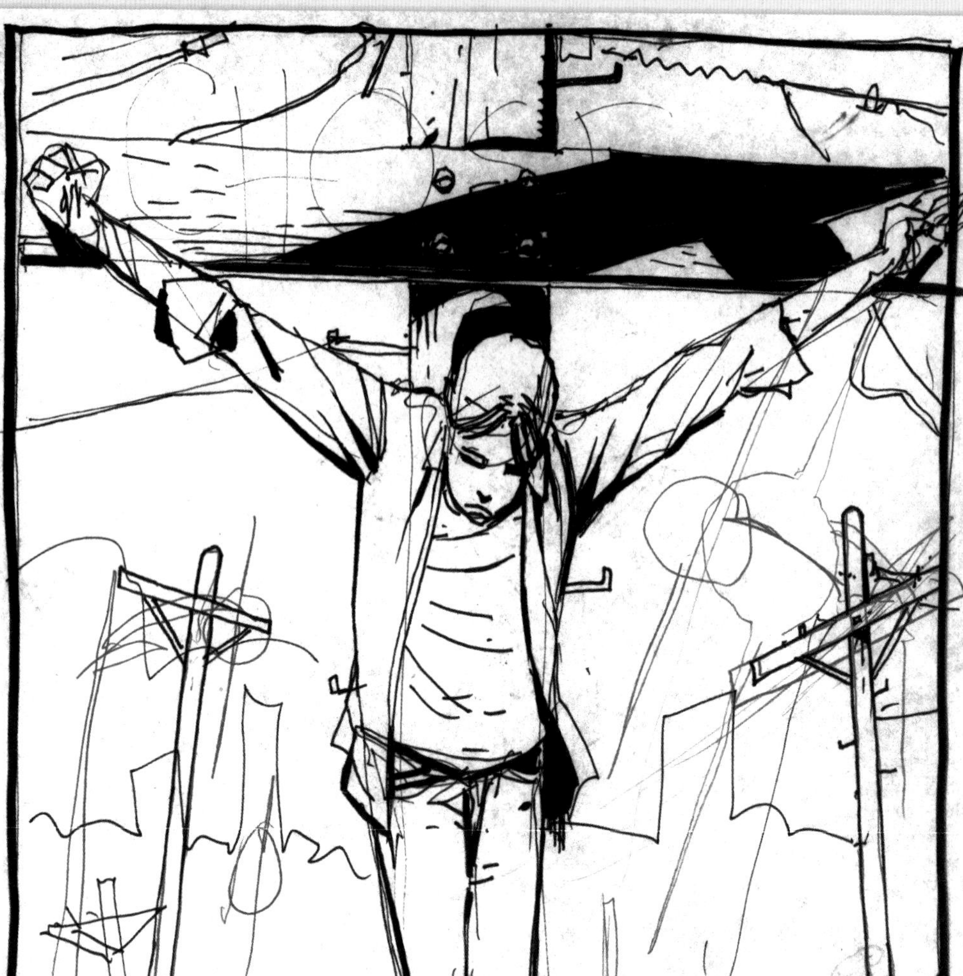

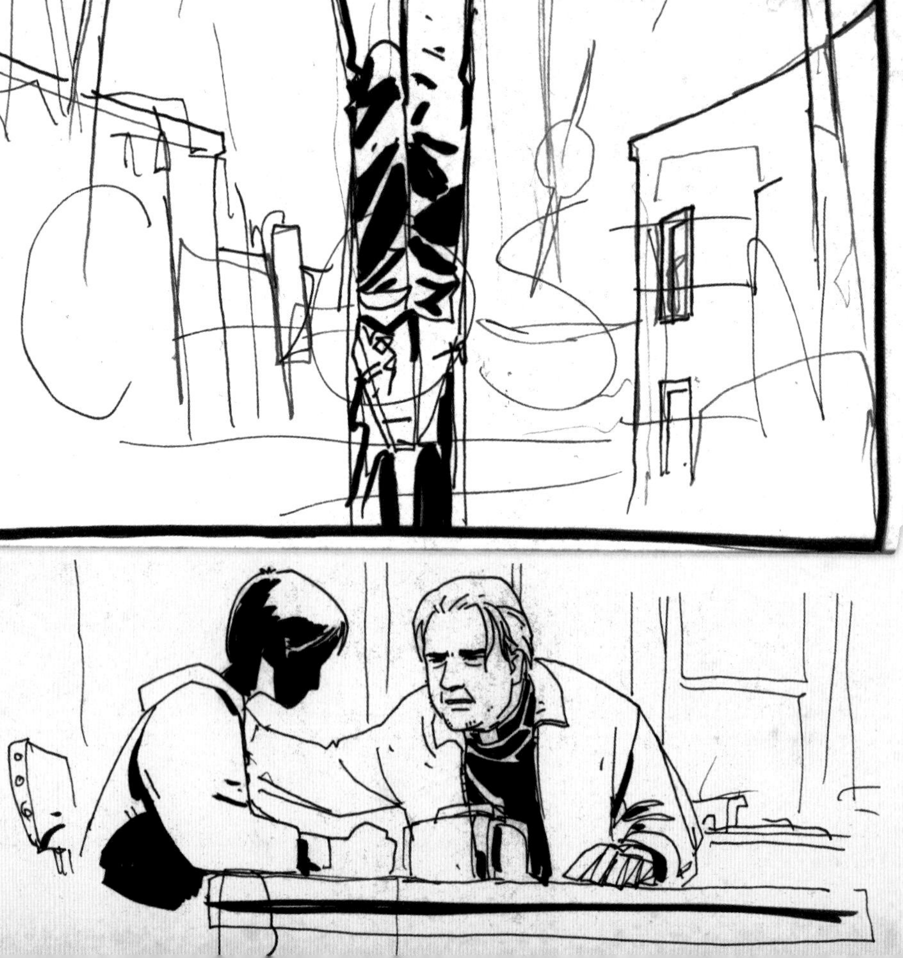

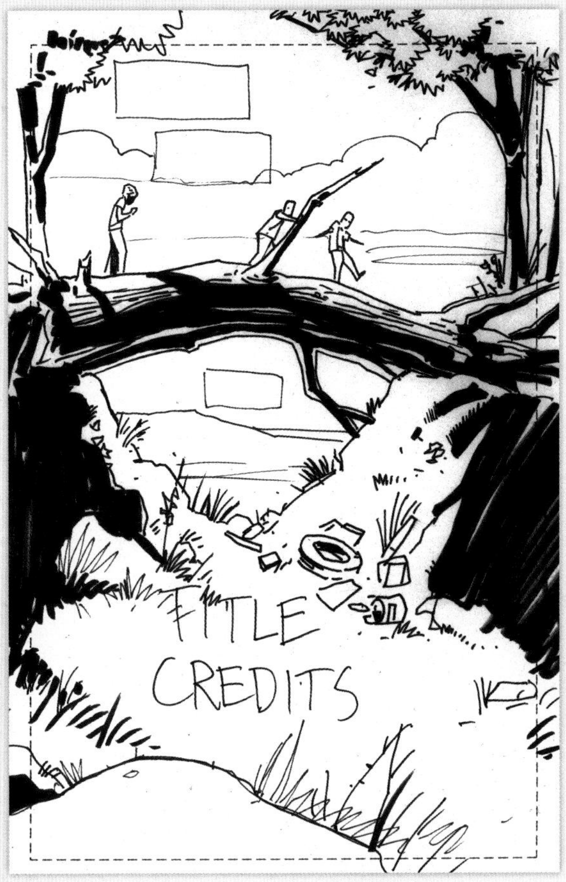
TITLE
CREDITS

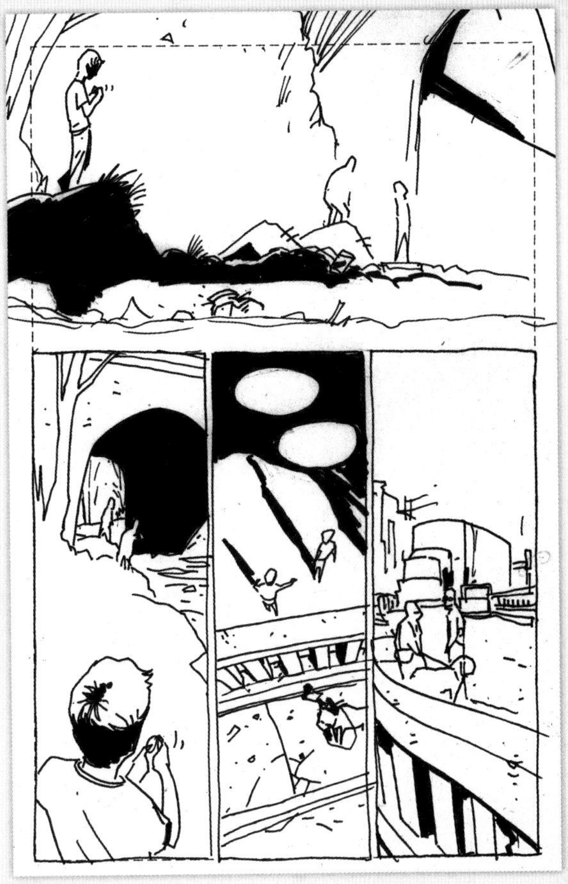

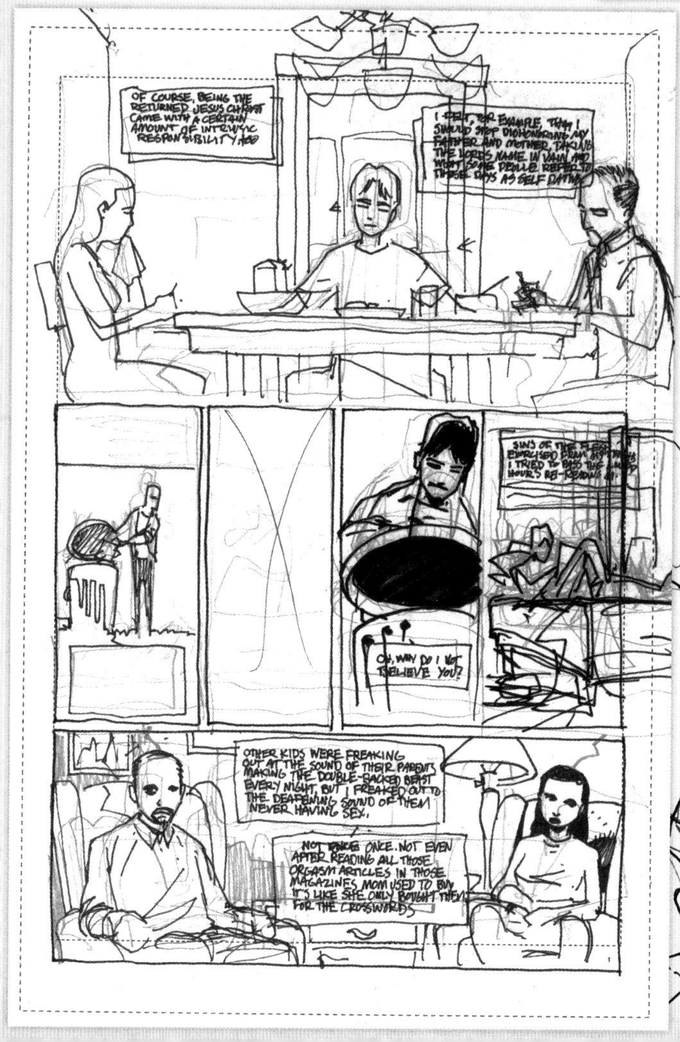
OF COURSE, BEING THE RETURNED JESUS CHRIST CAME WITH A CERTAIN AMOUNT OF INTRINSIC RESPONSIBILITY, AND
I FELT, FOR EXAMPLE, THAT I SHOULD STOP DISHONORING MY FATHER AND MOTHER, TAKING THE LORDS NAME IN VAIN AND WHAT SOME PEOPLE REFER TO THESE DAYS AS SELF
OH, WHY DO I NOT BELIEVE YOU?
OTHER KIDS WERE FREAKING OUT AT THE SOUND OF THEIR PARENTS MAKING THE DOUBLE-BACKED BEAST EVERY NIGHT, BUT I FREAKED OUT TO THE DEAFENING SOUND OF THEM NEVER HAVING SEX.
NOT ONCE. NOT EVEN AFTER READING ALL THOSE ORGASM ARTICLES IN THOSE MAGAZINES MOM USED TO BUY. IT'S LIKE SHE ONLY BOUGHT THEM FOR THE CROSSWORDS

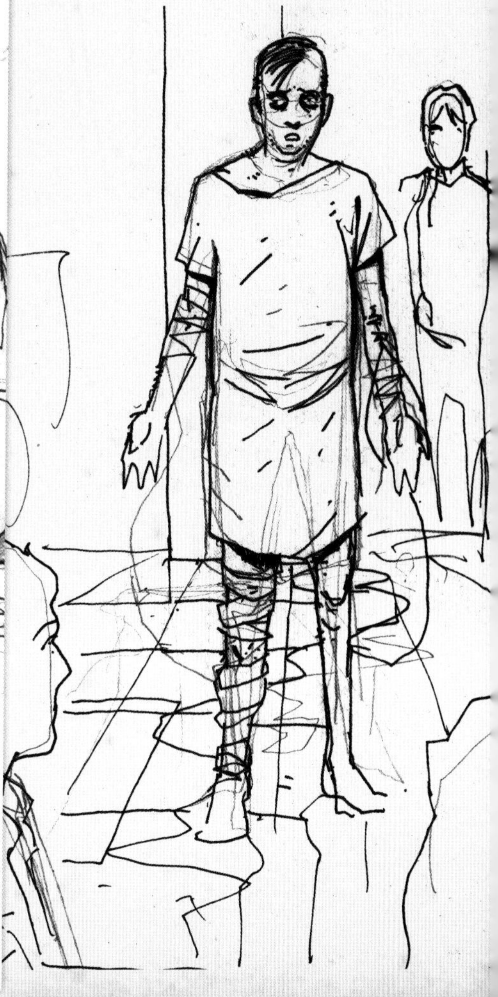

The following scene is one of my favorites in the book. It's a talking head scene——something that's often the bane of us artists because it's panel after panel of two people talking to each other, and little or no action occurs. And to make this one even worse, the two characters are sitting in a car – one of the most annoying scenarios for me anyway. But something about this one appealed to me from the first reading, through the layouts and to the finished art with Jeanne's great muted color that went almost monochromatic for the interior scene.

I thought Father Tom was a great character with a great psychological arc through the series. The poor guy has lost his faith and only regains it at the end——but by unwittingly backing the wrong horse. It's tragic——and I hope we see him again in the sequels.

Mark suggested Philip Seymour Hoffman as the type of actor he was thinking of for Tom, and I started my designs for him with that in mind.

Page Nineteen

1/ Cut to several days later and we see Jodie coming home from school on a bright afternoon, surrounded by all his apostle chums. They're having a laugh and cracking jokes on their way along the road, looking very, very natural as they pass some parked cars. This big Petey Caldwell kid has essentially become his right-hand-man at this point and the two of them clearly get on very well here. We should also always make it look like Maggie and Jodie are going out. They're actually just really close, but nothing physical has happened between them yet.

CAPTION : People were kneeling down and praying outside my house and my class-room, the sick appeared and begged me to cure them and cure them I did with an ever-increasing confidence.

CAPTION : They were selling objects I'd touched, books I'd read and even soil from my garden for its supposed healing properties. My parents were going nuts.

2/ Cut to an image of this scene as reflected in the wing mirror of a parked car. This car belongs to the Priest, although we don't see him from this angle (just looking over his shoulder instead as he checks out the reflection.

CAPTION : At the time I still had no idea why none of these events had made it to the newspapers.

3/ Pull back and see the Priest popping his head out of the car and speaking to the surprised kids. He's obviously been waiting here for Jodie.

PRIEST : Jodie, could I speak to you for a moment, please? ALONE, if you don't mind?

JODIE : Father O'Higgins?

4/ Cut to car interior and we see Jodie climbing in via the other door. The priest is very passive-aggressive here, clearly annoyed but not losing his temper throughout the sequence. Don't forget to have the ever-present dog in the back-seat.

PRIEST : I thought we agreed you were going to stop all this nonsense?
JODIE : What nonsense?
PRIEST : Son, you go around trying to convince people you're the returned Jesus Christ everyone's going to think you're out of your friggin' mind.

5/ Pull back and we see them both sitting in this parked car, the other kids walking on as Jodie has a quiet word with the priest.

JODIE : Really? You see many people in mental hospitals who can turn water into wine? Cure the sick? Heal the blind?

PRIEST : You did NOT heal the blind, Jodie. A little boy with a prescription just thinks he can read a little better without his glasses. You did NOT heal the blind.

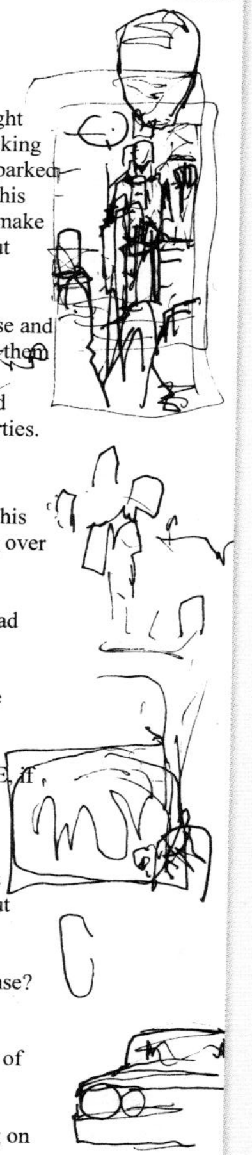

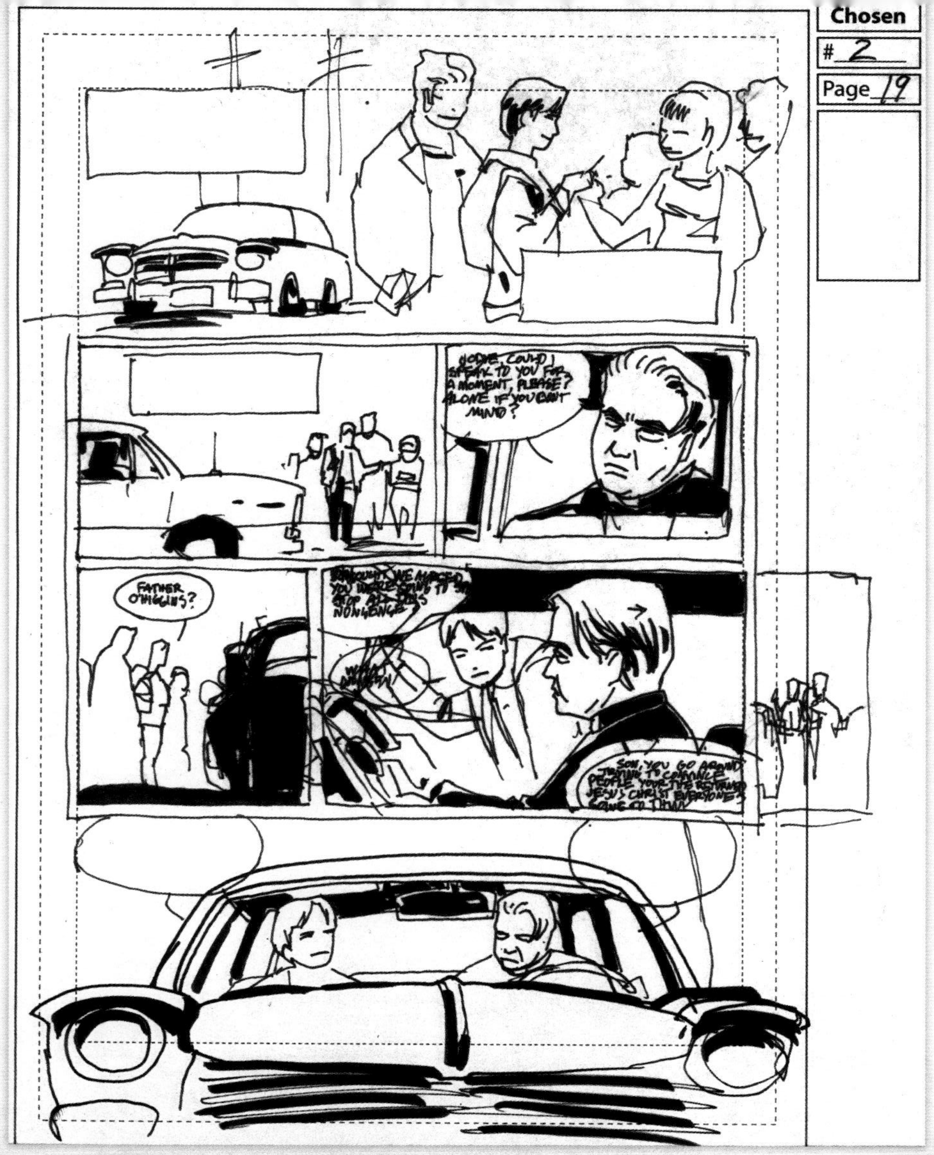
Chosen
2
Page 19
JODIE, COULD I SPEAK TO YOU FOR A MOMENT, PLEASE? ALONE IF YOU DON'T MIND?
FATHER O'HIGGINS?

Page Twenty

1/ Cut back to inside the car and Jodie seems a little cockier than before. He's absolutely convinced of who he is here.

JODIE : Why can't you just accept the simplest explanation of what's happening here, Father?
PRIEST : Because, unlike the rest of this town, I seem to be IMMUNE to mass hysteria.

2/ Closer on Jodie as he narrows his eyes and looks serious.

JODIE : What you mean is you're the one guy in town who doesn't believe in GOD.

3/ The priest is surprised by the kid's frankness.

PRIEST : What?
JODIE : Why do you think nobody even comes to your church anymore? You say the words and do the actions, but you could be mowing the lawn for all you care.
JODIE : You're too busy planning what you're having for dinner or fantasising about that dumpy, old woman who arranges the flowers every Sunday.

4/ Jodie's starting to rant a little, saying a bit more than he really should to the Priest and the guy is becoming visibly irritated. He's very aware of his position in the community and still just simmers at this point.

PRIEST : You watch your mouth, son.
JODIE : When did you stop believing, Father? When that drunk, old Bishop made a pass at you in the seminary?
JODIE : When the cancer took your mother? When that homeless guy stuck a knife in the back of your brother's head?

6/ Switch angles as the narking becomes more intense and the kid just won't let him, the priest's top lip visibly trembling as he tries to contain his rage.

PRIEST (louder) : Shut up!
JODIE : Don't you realize even your brother's MURDER is just part of a great big PLAN?

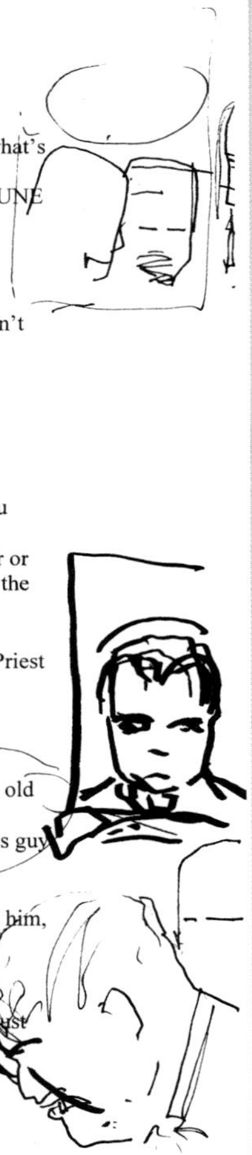

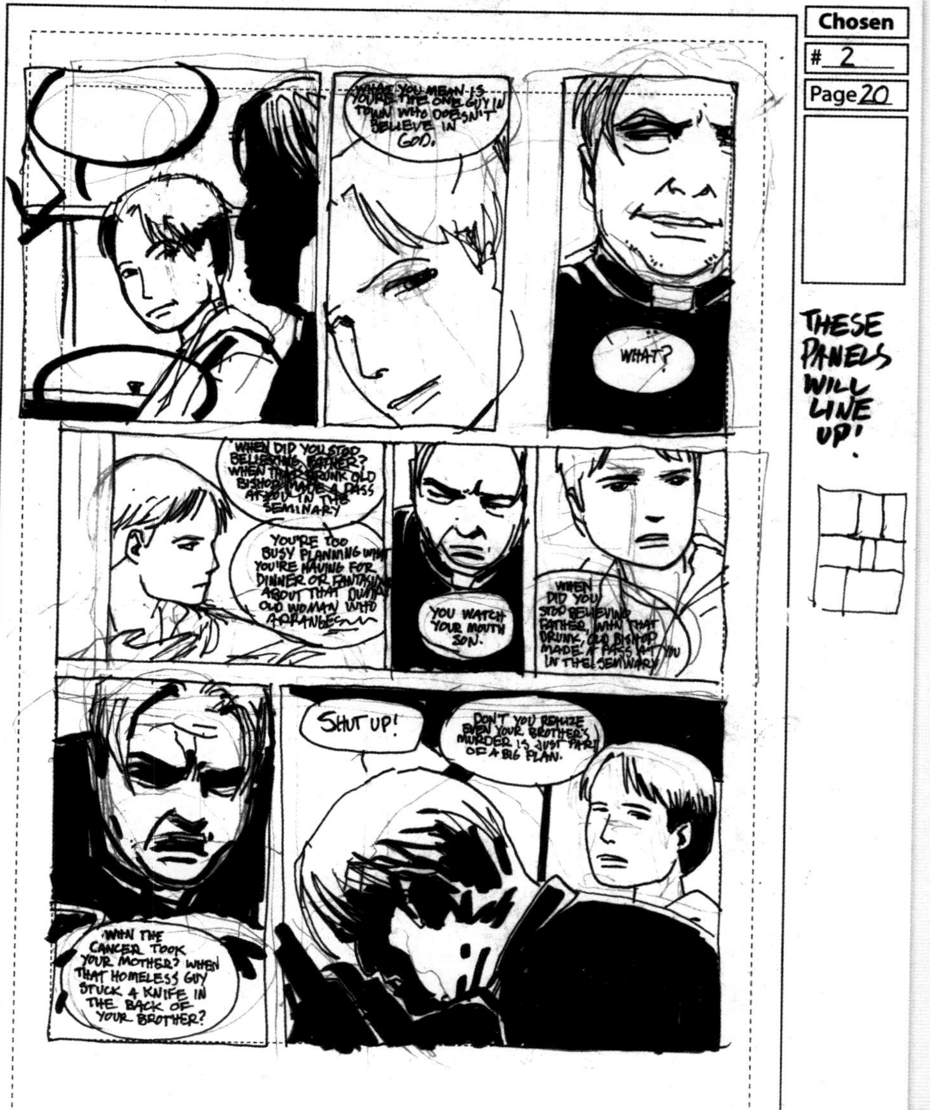
Chosen
2
Page 20
WHAT YOU MEAN IS YOU'RE THE ONE GUY IN TOWN WHO DOESN'T BELIEVE IN GOD.
WHAT?
WHEN DID YOU STOP BELIEVING, FATHER? WHEN THAT DRUNK OLD BISHOP MADE A PASS AT YOU IN THE SEMINARY
YOU'RE TOO BUSY PLANNING WHAT YOU'RE HAVING FOR DINNER OR FANTASIZING ABOUT THAT DUMPY OLD WOMAN WHO ARRANGES
YOU WATCH YOUR MOUTH SON.
WHEN DID YOU STOP BELIEVING FATHER, WHEN THAT DRUNK, OLD BISHOP MADE A PASS AT YOU IN THE SEMINARY
SHUT UP!
DON'T YOU REALIZE EVEN YOUR BROTHER'S MURDER IS JUST PART OF A BIG PLAN.
WHEN THE CANCER TOOK YOUR MOTHER? WHEN THAT HOMELESS GUY STUCK A KNIFE IN THE BACK OF YOUR BROTHER?
THESE PANELS WILL LINE UP!

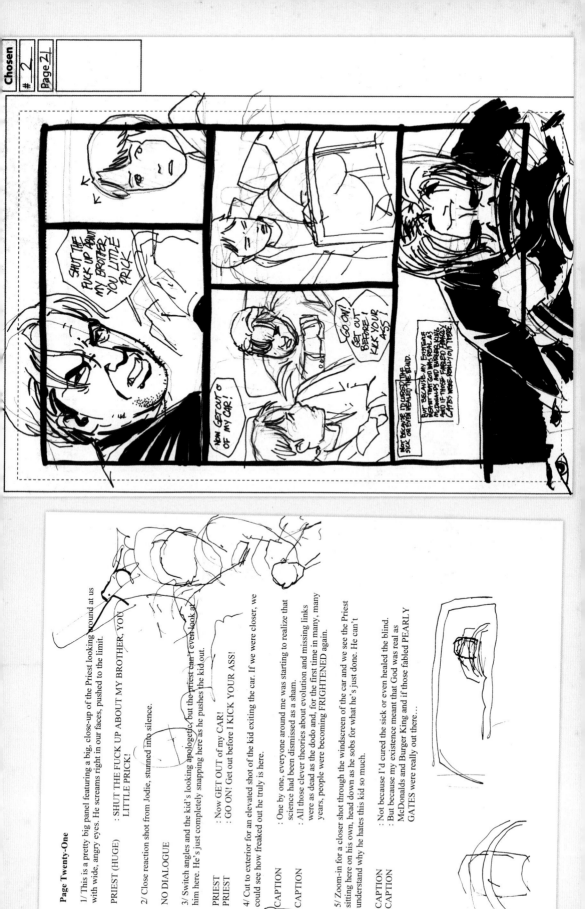

Page Twenty-One

1/ This is a pretty big panel featuring a big, close-up of the Priest looking around at us with wide, angry eyes. He screams right in our faces, pushed to the limit.

PRIEST (HUGE) : SHUT THE FUCK UP ABOUT MY BROTHER, YOU LITTLE PRICK!

2/ Close reaction shot from Jodie, stunned into silence.

NO DIALOGUE

3/ Switch angles and the kid's looking apologetic, but the priest can't even look at him here. He's just completely snapping here as he pushes the kid out.

PRIEST : Now GET OUT of my CAR!
PRIEST : GO ON! Get out before I KICK YOUR ASS!

4/ Cut to exterior for an elevated shot of the kid exiting the car. If we were closer, we could see how freaked out he truly is here.

CAPTION : One by one, everyone around me was starting to realize that science had been dismissed as a sham.
CAPTION : All those clever theories about evolution and missing links were as dead as the dodo and, for the first time in many, many years, people were becoming FRIGHTENED again.

5/ Zoom-in for a closer shot through the windscreen of the car and we see the Priest sitting here on his own, head down as he sobs for what he's just done. He can't understand why he hates this kid so much.

CAPTION : Not because I'd cured the sick or even healed the blind.
CAPTION : But because my existence meant that God was real as McDonalds and Burger King and if those fabled PEARLY GATES were really out there…

Chosen
2
Page 21
SHUT THE FUCK UP ABOUT MY BROTHER, YOU LITTLE PRICK
NOW GET OUT OF MY CAR!
GO ON! GET OUT BEFORE I KICK YOUR ASS!
NOT BECAUSE I'D CURED THE SICK OR EVEN HEALED THE BLIND.
BUT BECAUSE MY EXISTENCE MEANT THAT GOD WAS REAL AS MCDONALDS AND BURGER KING AND IF THOSE FABLED PEARLY GATES WERE REALLY OUT THERE...

MARK MILLAR is the award-winning writer of *Wanted* and *Kick-Ass*, the two highest-selling creator-owned comics this decade. *Wanted* was released as a smash-hit movie in Summer 2008 starring Angelina Jolie and James McAvoy. *Kick-Ass* is scheduled for a 2009 release and stars Nicolas Cage and Christopher Mintz-Plasse. His other works include *The Ultimates*, *Ultimates 2*, *The Fantastic Four*, *Marvel 1985*, *Wolverine*, *The Authority*, *Superman: Red Son* and *Marvel Civil War*. *Civil War* has appeared everywhere from *Rolling Stone* to CNN and is the industry's highest-selling series in over ten years.

He lives in his native Scotland with his wife, his daughter and various pets.

PETER GROSS has been nominated four times for the Eisner award for his work on *Lucifer* and *Books of Magic*. His prolific Vertigo career also includes *Fables*, *Testament* and the upcoming creator owned series *The Unwritten* (May, 2009).

Peter lives in Minnesota with his partner Jeanne [who colored *American Jesus: Chosen*] and their daughter Alice [who did not].